MANUAL/1997–2001
CHURCH OF THE NAZARENE

•

HISTORY
CONSTITUTION
GOVERNMENT
RITUAL

•

NAZARENE PUBLISHING HOUSE
Kansas City, Missouri

Published
by the authority of
the Twenty-fourth General Assembly
held in San Antonio, Texas
June 22-27, 1997

Editing Committee

JOHN BOWLING
MELVIN McCULLOUGH
JESSE C. MIDDENDORF
HAROLD RASER
JACK STONE

ISBN 083-411-6898 (Hard Cover)
ISBN 083-411-6901 (Soft Cover)
ISBN 083-411-691X (Leather Cover)

Printed in the United States of America

To use the thumb index, fan the pages with your right hand until mark appears opposite the chapter head.

FOREWORD

The Church of the Nazarene exists to serve as an instrument for advancing the kingdom of God through the preaching and teaching of the gospel throughout the world. Our well-defined commission is to preserve and propagate Christian holiness as set forth in the Scriptures, through the conversion of sinners, the reclamation of backsliders, and the entire sanctification of believers.

Our objective is a spiritual one, namely, to evangelize as a response to the Great Commission of our Lord to "go and make disciples of all nations" (Matthew 28:19; cf. John 20:21; Mark 16:15). We believe that this aim can be realized through agreed-upon policies and procedures, including doctrinal tenets of faith and time-tested standards of morality and lifestyle.

This 1997 edition of the *Manual* includes a brief historical statement of the church; the church Constitution, which defines our Articles of Faith, our understanding of the church, General Rules for holy living, and principles of organization and government; Special Rules, which address key issues of contemporary society; and policies of church government dealing with the local, district, and general church organization.

The General Assembly is the supreme doctrine-formulating and lawmaking body of the Church of the Nazarene. This *Manual* contains the decisions and judgments of ministerial and lay delegates of the Twenty-fourth General Assembly, which met in San Antonio, Texas, June 22-27, 1997, and is therefore authoritative as a guide for action. Because it is the official statement of the faith and practice of the church and is consistent with the teachings of the Scriptures, we expect our people everywhere to accept the tenets of doctrine and the guides and helps to holy living contained in it. To fail to do so, after formally taking the membership vows of the Church of the Nazarene, injures the witness of the church, violates her conscience, and dissipates the fellowship of the people called Nazarenes.

The government of the Church of the Nazarene is distinctive. In polity it is representative—neither purely episcopal nor wholly congregational. Because the laity and the ministry have equal authority in the deliberative and lawmaking units of the church, there is a desirable and effective balance of power. We see this not only as an opportunity for participation and service in the church but also as an obligation on the part of both laity and ministry.

Commitment and clear purpose are important. But an intelligent and informed people following commonly agreed-upon practices and procedures advance the Kingdom faster and enhance their witness for Christ. Therefore, it is incumbent upon our members to acquaint themselves with this *Manual*—the history of the church and the doctrines and ethical practices of the ideal Nazarene. Adherence to the injunctions of these pages will nurture loyalty and faithfulness both to God and the church and will increase the effectiveness and efficiency of our spiritual efforts.

With the Bible as our supreme Guide, illuminated by the Holy Spirit, and the *Manual* as our official agreed-upon statement of faith, practice, and polity, we look forward to the new quadrennium with joy and unswerving faith in Jesus Christ.

The Board of General Superintendents

JOHN A. KNIGHT
WILLIAM J. PRINCE
JAMES H. DIEHL
PAUL G. CUNNINGHAM
JERRY D. PORTER
JIM L. BOND

CONTENTS

PART V

MINISTRY AND CHRISTIAN SERVICE

PART VI
JUDICIAL ADMINISTRATION

PART VII
BOUNDARIES

PART VIII
RITUAL

PART IX
AUXILIARY CONSTITUTIONS

PART X
FORMS

PART XI
APPENDIX

PART I

Historical Statement

HISTORICAL STATEMENT

Historic Christianity and the Wesleyan-Holiness Heritage

One Holy Faith. The Church of the Nazarene, from its beginnings, has confessed itself to be a branch of the "one, holy, universal, and apostolic" church and has sought to be faithful to it. It confesses as its own the history of the people of God recorded in the Old and New Testaments, and that same history as it has extended from the days of the apostles to our own. As its own people, it embraces the people of God through the ages, those redeemed through Jesus Christ in whatever expression of the one church they may be found. It receives the ecumenical creeds of the first five Christian centuries as expressions of its own faith. While the Church of the Nazarene has responded to its special calling to proclaim the doctrine and experience of entire sanctification, it has taken care to retain and nurture identification with the historic church in its preaching of the Word, its administration of the sacraments, its concern to raise up and maintain a ministry that is truly apostolic in faith and practice, and its inculcating of disciplines for Christlike living and service to others.

The Wesleyan Revival. This Christian faith has been mediated to Nazarenes through historical religious currents and particularly through the Wesleyan revival of the 18th century. In the 1730s the broader Evangelical Revival arose in Britain, directed chiefly by John Wesley, his brother Charles, and George Whitefield, clergymen in the Church of England. Through their instrumentality, many other men and women turned from sin and were empowered for the service of God. This movement was characterized by lay preaching, testimony, discipline, and circles of earnest disciples known as "societies," "classes," and "bands." As a movement of spiritual life, its antecedents included German Pietism, typified by Philip

Jacob Spener; 17th-century English Puritanism; and a spiritual awakening in New England described by the pastor-theologian Jonathan Edwards.

The Wesleyan phase of the great revival was characterized by three theological landmarks: regeneration by grace through faith; Christian perfection, or sanctification, likewise by grace through faith; and the witness of the Spirit to the assurance of grace. Among John Wesley's distinctive contributions was an emphasis on entire sanctification in this life as God's gracious provision for the Christian. British Methodism's early missionary enterprises began disseminating these theological emphases worldwide. In North America, the Methodist Episcopal Church was organized in 1784. Its stated purpose was "to reform the Continent, and to spread scriptural Holiness over these Lands."

The Holiness Movement of the 19th Century. In the 19th century a renewed emphasis on Christian holiness began in the Eastern United States and spread throughout the nation. Timothy Merritt, Methodist clergyman and founding editor of the *Guide to Christian Perfection,* was among the leaders of the Holiness revival. The central figure of the movement was Phoebe Palmer of New York City, leader of the Tuesday Meeting for the Promotion of Holiness, at which Methodist bishops, educators, and other clergy joined the original group of women in seeking holiness. During four decades, Mrs. Palmer promoted the Methodist phase of the Holiness Movement through public speaking, writing, and as editor of the influential *Guide to Holiness.*

The Holiness revival spilled outside the bounds of Methodism. Charles G. Finney and Asa Mahan, both of Oberlin College, led the renewed emphasis on holiness in Presbyterian and Congregationalist circles, as did revivalist William Boardman. Baptist evangelist A. B. Earle was among the leaders of the Holiness Movement within his denomination. Hannah Whitall Smith, a Quaker and popular Holiness revivalist, published *The Christian's Secret of a Happy Life* (1875), a classic text in Christian spirituality.

In 1867 Methodist ministers John A. Wood, John Inskip,

and others began at Vineland, New Jersey, the first of a long series of national camp meetings. They also organized at that time the National Camp Meeting Association for the Promotion of Holiness, commonly known as the National (now the Christian) Holiness Association. Until the early years of the 20th century, this organization sponsored Holiness camp meetings throughout the United States. Local and regional Holiness associations also appeared, and a vital Holiness press published many periodicals and books.

The witness to Christian holiness played roles of varying significance in the founding of the Wesleyan Methodist Church (1843), the Free Methodist Church (1860), and, in England, the Salvation Army (1865). In the 1880s new distinctively Holiness churches sprang into existence, including the Church of God (Anderson, Indiana) and the Church of God (Holiness). Several older religious traditions were also influenced by the Holiness Movement, including certain groups of Mennonites, Brethren, and Friends that adopted the Wesleyan-Holiness view of entire sanctification. The Brethren in Christ Church and the Evangelical Friends Alliance are examples of this blending of spiritual traditions.

Uniting of Holiness Groups

In the 1890s a new wave of independent Holiness entities came into being. These included independent churches, urban missions, rescue homes, and missionary and evangelistic associations. Some of the people involved in these organizations yearned for union into a national Holiness church. Out of that impulse the present-day Church of the Nazarene was born.

The Association of Pentecostal Churches of America. On July 21, 1887, the People's Evangelical Church was organized with 51 members at Providence, Rhode Island, with Fred A. Hillery as pastor. The following year the Mission Church at Lynn, Massachusetts, was organized with C. Howard Davis as pastor. On March 13 and 14, 1890, representatives from these and other independent Holiness congregations met at Rock, Massachusetts, and organized the

Central Evangelical Holiness Association with churches in Rhode Island, New Hampshire, and Massachusetts. In 1892, the Central Evangelical Holiness Association ordained Anna S. Hanscombe, believed to be the first of many women ordained to the Christian ministry in the parent bodies of the Church of the Nazarene.

In January 1894, businessman William Howard Hoople founded a Brooklyn mission, reorganized the following May as Utica Avenue Pentecostal Tabernacle. By the end of the following year, Bedford Avenue Pentecostal Church and Emmanuel Pentecostal Tabernacle were also organized. In December 1895, delegates from these three congregations adopted a constitution, a summary of doctrines, and bylaws, forming the Association of Pentecostal Churches of America.

On November 12, 1896, a joint committee of the Central Evangelical Holiness Association and the Association of Pentecostal Churches of America met in Brooklyn and framed a plan of union, retaining the name of the latter for the united body. Prominent workers in this denomination were Hiram F. Reynolds, H. B. Hosley, C. Howard Davis, William Howard Hoople, and, later, E. E. Angell. Some of these were originally lay preachers who were later ordained as ministers by their congregations. This church was decidedly missionary, and under the leadership of Hiram F. Reynolds, missionary secretary, embarked upon an ambitious program of Christian witness to the Cape Verde Islands, India, and other places. *The Beulah Christian* was published as its official paper.

The Holiness Church of Christ. In July 1894, R. L. Harris organized the New Testament Church of Christ at Milan, Tennessee, shortly before his death. Mary Lee Cagle, widow of R. L. Harris, continued the work and became its most prominent early leader. This church, strictly congregational in polity, spread throughout Arkansas and western Texas, with scattered congregations in Alabama and Missouri. Mary Cagle and a coworker, Mrs. E. J. Sheeks, were ordained in 1899 in the first class of ordinands.

Beginning in 1888, a handful of congregations bearing the

name The Holiness Church were organized in Texas by ministers Thomas and Dennis Rogers, who came from California.

In 1901 the first congregation of the Independent Holiness Church was formed at Van Alstyne, Texas, by Charles B. Jernigan. At an early date, James B. Chapman affiliated with this denomination, which prospered and grew rapidly. In time, the congregations led by Dennis Rogers affiliated with the Independent Holiness Church.

In November 1904, representatives of the New Testament Church of Christ and the Independent Holiness Church met at Rising Star, Texas, where they agreed upon principles of union, adopted a *Manual,* and chose the name Holiness Church of Christ. This union was finalized the following year at a delegated general council held at Pilot Point, Texas. The *Holiness Evangel* was the church's official paper. Its other leading ministers included William E. Fisher, J. D. Scott, and J. T. Upchurch. Among its key lay leaders were Edwin H. Sheeks, R. B. Mitchum, and Mrs. Donie Mitchum.

Several leaders of this church were active in the Holiness Association of Texas, a vital interdenominational body that sponsored a college at Peniel, near Greenville, Texas. The association also sponsored the *Pentecostal Advocate,* the Southwest's leading Holiness paper, which became a Nazarene organ in 1910. E. C. DeJernett, a minister, and C. A. McConnell, a layman, were prominent workers in this organization.

The Church of the Nazarene. In October 1895, Phineas F. Bresee, D.D., and Joseph P. Widney, M.D., with about 100 others, including Alice P. Baldwin, Leslie F. Gay, W. S. and Lucy P. Knott, C. E. McKee, and members of the Bresee and Widney families, organized the Church of the Nazarene at Los Angeles. At the outset they saw this church as the first of a denomination that preached the reality of entire sanctification received through faith in Christ. They held that Christians sanctified by faith should follow Christ's example and preach the gospel to the poor. They felt called especially to this work. They believed that unnecessary elegance and adornment of houses of worship did not represent the spirit of Christ but the spirit of the world, and that their expenditures of time and money should be given to Christlike ministries for the salvation of souls and the relief of the needy. They organized the church accordingly. They adopted general rules, a statement of belief, a polity based on a limited superintendency, procedures for the consecration of deaconesses and the ordination of elders, and a ritual. These were published as a *Manual* beginning in 1898. They published a paper known as *The Nazarene* and then *The Nazarene Messenger.* The Church of the Nazarene spread chiefly along the West Coast, with scattered congregations east of the Rocky Mountains as far as Illinois.

Among the ministers who cast their lot with the new church were H. D. Brown, W. E. Shepard, C. W. Ruth, L. B. Kent, Isaiah Reid, J. B. Creighton, C. E. Cornell, Robert Pierce, and W. C. Wilson. Among the first to be ordained by the new church were Joseph P. Widney himself, Elsie and DeLance Wallace, Lucy P. Knott, and E. A. Girvin.

Phineas F. Bresee's 38 years' experience as a pastor, superintendent, editor, college board member, and camp meeting preacher in Methodism, and his unique personal magnetism, entered into the ecclesiastical statesmanship that he brought to the merging of the several Holiness churches into a national body.

The Year of Uniting: 1907-1908. The Association of Pentecostal Churches of America, the Church of the Nazarene, and the Holiness Church of Christ were brought into association with one another by C. W. Ruth, assistant general superintendent of the Church of the Nazarene, who had extensive friendships throughout the Wesleyan-Holiness Movement. Delegates of the Association of Pentecostal Churches of America and the Church of the Nazarene convened in general assembly at Chicago, from October 10 to 17, 1907. The merging groups agreed upon a church government that balanced the need for a superintendency with the independence of local congregations. Superintendents were to foster and care for churches already established and were to organize and encourage the organizing of churches everywhere, but their authority was not to interfere with the independent actions of a fully organized church. Further, the General Assembly adopted a name for the united body drawn from both organizations: The Pentecostal Church of the Nazarene. Phineas F. Bresee and Hiram F. Reynolds were elected general superintendents. A delegation of observers from the Holiness Church of Christ was present and participated in the assembly work.

During the following year, two other accessions occurred. In April 1908, P. F. Bresee organized a congregation of the Pentecostal Church of the Nazarene at Peniel, Texas, which brought into the church leading figures in the Holiness Association of Texas and paved the way for other members to join. In September, the Pennsylvania Conference of the Holiness Christian Church, after receiving a release from its General Conference, dissolved itself and under the leadership of H. G. Trumbaur united with the Pentecostal Church of the Nazarene.

The second General Assembly of the Pentecostal Church of the Nazarene met in a joint session with the General Council of the Holiness Church of Christ from October 8 to 14, 1908, at Pilot Point, Texas. The year of uniting ended on Tuesday morning, October 13, when R. B. Mitchum moved and C. W. Ruth seconded the proposition: "That the union of the two churches be now consummated." Several spoke favorably on the motion. Phineas Bresee had exerted continual effort toward this proposed outcome. At 10:40 A.M., amid great enthusiasm, the motion to unite was adopted by a unanimous rising vote.

Denominational Change of Name. The General Assembly of 1919, in response to memorials from 35 district assemblies, officially changed the name of the organization to Church of the Nazarene because of new meanings that had become associated with the term "Pentecostal."

Later Accessions

After 1908 various other bodies united with the Church of the Nazarene:

The Pentecostal Mission. In 1898 J. O. McClurkan, a Cumberland Presbyterian evangelist, led in forming the Pentecostal Alliance at Nashville, which brought together Holiness people from Tennessee and adjacent states. This body was very missionary in spirit and sent pastors and teachers to Cuba, Guatemala, Mexico, and India. McClurkan died in 1914. The next year his group, known then as the Pentecostal Mission, united with the Pentecostal Church of the Nazarene.

Pentecostal Church of Scotland. In 1906 George Sharpe, of Parkhead Congregational Church, Glasgow, was evicted from his pulpit for preaching the Wesleyan doctrine of Christian holiness. Eighty members who left with him immediately formed Parkhead Pentecostal Church. Other congregations were organized, and in 1909 the Pentecostal Church of Scotland was formed. That body united with the Pentecostal Church of the Nazarene in November 1915.

Laymen's Holiness Association. The Laymen's Holiness Association was formed under S. A. Danford in 1917 at Jamestown, North Dakota, to serve the cause of Wesleyan-holiness revivalism in the Dakotas, Minnesota, and Montana. This group published a paper, *The Holiness Layman.* J. G. Morrison was elected president in 1919 and led an organization with over 25 other evangelists and workers. In 1922 Morrison, together with most of the workers and more than 1,000 of the members, united with the Church of the Nazarene.

Hephzibah Faith Missionary Association. This missionary body, centered in Tabor, Iowa, organized in 1893 by Elder George Weavers, subsequently sent over 80 workers to more than a half dozen countries. Around 1950 the work at Tabor, the South African mission, and other parts of the organization united with the Church of the Nazarene.

International Holiness Mission. David Thomas, businessman and lay preacher, founded The Holiness Mission in London in 1907. Extensive missionary work developed in southern Africa under the leadership of David Jones, and the church was renamed the International Holiness Mission in 1917. It united with the Church of the Nazarene on October 29, 1952, with 28 churches and more than 1,000 constituents in England under the superintendency of J. B. Maclagan, and work led by 36 missionaries in Africa.

Calvary Holiness Church. In 1934 Maynard James and Jack Ford, who had led itinerant evangelism (or "trekking") in the International Holiness Mission, formed the Calvary Holiness Church. On June 11, 1955, union took place with the Church of the Nazarene, bringing about 22 churches and more than 600 members into the denomination. The accession of the International Holiness Mission and the Calvary Holiness Church came about largely through the vision and efforts of Nazarene District Superintendent George Frame.

Gospel Workers Church of Canada. Organized by Frank Goff in Ontario in 1918, this church arose from an earlier group called the Holiness Workers. It united with the Church of the Nazarene on September 7, 1958, adding five churches and about 200 members to the Canada Central District.

Church of the Nazarene (Nigeria). In the 1940s a Wesleyan-Holiness church was organized in Nigeria under indigenous leadership. It adopted the name Church of the Nazarene, deriving its doctrinal beliefs and name in part from a *Manual* of the international Church of the Nazarene. Under the leadership of Jeremiah U. Ekaidem, it united with the latter on April 3, 1988. A new district with 39 churches and 6,500 members was created.

Toward a Global Church

The Church of the Nazarene had an international dimension from its beginning. By the uniting assembly of 1908, Nazarenes served and witnessed not only in North America but also as missionaries in Mexico, the Cape Verde Islands, India, Japan, and South Africa—living testimony to the impact of the 19th-century missions movement upon the religious bodies that formed the present-day Church of the Nazarene.

Expansion into new areas of the world began in Asia in 1898 by the Association of Pentecostal Churches of America. The Pentecostal Mission was at work in Central America by 1900, in the Caribbean by 1902, and in South America by 1909. In Africa, Nazarenes active there in 1907 were recognized as denominational missionaries at a later date.

Subsequent extension into the Australia-South Pacific area began in 1945 and into continental Europe in 1948. In these instances, the Church of the Nazarene entered by identifying with local ministers who already preached and taught the Wesleyan-Holiness message: A. A. E. Berg of Australia and Alfredo del Rosso of Italy.

In developing a global ministry, the Church of the Nazarene has depended historically on the energies of national workers who have shared with missionaries the tasks of preaching and teaching the word of grace. In 1918 a missionary in India noted that his national associates included three preachers, four teachers, three colporteurs, and five Bible women. By 1936 the ratio of national workers to missionaries throughout the worldwide Church of the Nazarene was greater than five to one.

The world areas where the church has entered reached a total of 116 by 1997. Thousands of ministers and lay workers have indigenized the Church of the Nazarene in their respective cultures, thereby contributing to the mosaic of national identities that form our international communion.

Distinctives of International Ministry. Historically, Nazarene global ministry has centered around evangelism, compassionate ministry, and education. The evangelistic impulse was exemplified in the lives of H. F. Schmelzenbach, L. S. Tracy, Esther Carson Winans, Samuel Krikorian, and others whose names symbolize this dimension of ministry. Around the world, Nazarene churches and districts continue to reflect a revivalistic and evangelistic character.

The international roots of Nazarene compassionate ministry lie in early support for famine relief and orphanage work in India. This impulse was strengthened by the Nazarene Medical Missionary Union, organized in the early

1920s to build Bresee Memorial Hospital in Tamingfu, China. An extensive medical work has developed in Swaziland, and other compassionate ministries have developed around the world.

Education is an aspect of world ministry exemplified early by Hope School for Girls, founded in Calcutta by Mrs. Sukhoda Banarji in 1905 and adopted the following year by the Church of the Nazarene. Outside North America, Nazarenes have established schools for primary education and for specialized ministerial training. There are graduate seminaries in the United States and the Philippines; liberal arts institutions in the United States and Africa; one teacher training college in Swaziland; one junior college in Japan; three nursing schools in Swaziland, Papua New Guinea, and India; and over 40 Bible/theological institutions around the world.

The church has prospered as these components of its mission have developed. In 1997 the Church of the Nazarene had an international membership of 1,216,657, distributed in over 11,900 congregations.

As a result of this historical development, the denomination is poised today with an unfinished agenda of moving from "international presence" to an "international community" of faith. Recognition of this fact led the 1976 General Assembly to authorize a Commission on Internationalization, whose report to the 1980 General Assembly led to the creation of a system of world-region areas. The number and boundaries of the original world regions have since changed. The current ones are: the Africa Region, the Asia-Pacific Region, the Canada Region, the Caribbean Region, the Eurasia Region, the Mexico-Central America Region, the South America Region, and eight regions in the United States.*

---

*A more complete history of the Church of the Nazarene may be found in Timothy L. Smith, *Called unto Holiness, Vol. 1: The Formative Years* (1962); W. T. Purkiser, *Called unto Holiness, Vol. 2: The Second 25 Years* (1983); and J. Fred Parker, *Mission to the World* (1988).

PART II

Church Constitution

ARTICLES OF FAITH

THE CHURCH

ARTICLES OF ORGANIZATION AND GOVERNMENT

AMENDMENTS

PREAMBLE

In order that we may preserve our God-given heritage, the faith once delivered to the saints, especially the doctrine and experience of entire sanctification as a second work of grace, and also that we may cooperate effectually with other branches of the Church of Jesus Christ in advancing God's kingdom, we, the ministers and lay members of the Church of the Nazarene, in accordance with the principles of constitutional legislation established among us, do hereby ordain, adopt, and set forth as the fundamental law or Constitution of the Church of the Nazarene the Articles of Faith, the General Rules, and the Articles of Organization and Government here following, to wit:

ARTICLES OF FAITH

I. The Triune God

1. We believe in one eternally existent, infinite God, Sovereign of the universe; that He only is God, creative and administrative, holy in nature, attributes, and purpose; that He, as God, is Triune in essential being, revealed as Father, Son, and Holy Spirit.

(Genesis 1; Leviticus 19:2; Deuteronomy 6:4-5; Isaiah 5:16; 6:1-7; 40:18-31; Matthew 3:16-17; 28:19-20; John 14:6-27; 1 Corinthians 8:6; 2 Corinthians 13:14; Galatians 4:4-6; Ephesians 2:13-18)[1]

II. Jesus Christ

2. We believe in Jesus Christ, the Second Person of the Triune Godhead; that He was eternally one with the Father; that He became incarnate by the Holy Spirit and was born of the Virgin Mary, so that two whole and perfect natures,

---

1. Scripture references are supportive of the Articles of Faith and were placed here by action of the 1976 General Assembly but are not to be considered as part of the Constitutional text.

that is to say the Godhead and manhood, are thus united in one Person very God and very man, the God-man.

We believe that Jesus Christ died for our sins, and that He truly arose from the dead and took again His body, together with all things appertaining to the perfection of man's nature, wherewith He ascended into heaven and is there engaged in intercession for us.

(Matthew 1:20-25; 16:15-16; Luke 1:26-35; John 1:1-18; Acts 2:22-36; Romans 8:3, 32-34; Galatians 4:4-5; Philippians 2:5-11; Colossians 1:12-22; 1 Timothy 6:14-16; Hebrews 1:1-5; 7:22-28; 9:24-28; 1 John 1:1-3; 4:2-3, 15)

III. The Holy Spirit

3. We believe in the Holy Spirit, the Third Person of the Triune Godhead, that He is ever present and efficiently active in and with the Church of Christ, convincing the world of sin, regenerating those who repent and believe, sanctifying believers, and guiding into all truth as it is in Jesus.

(John 7:39; 14:15-18, 26; 16:7-15; Acts 2:33; 15:8-9; Romans 8:1-27; Galatians 3:1-14; 4:6; Ephesians 3:14-21; 1 Thessalonians 4:7-8; 2 Thessalonians 2:13; 1 Peter 1:2; 1 John 3:24; 4:13)

IV. The Holy Scriptures

4. We believe in the plenary inspiration of the Holy Scriptures, by which we understand the 66 books of the Old and New Testaments, given by divine inspiration, inerrantly revealing the will of God concerning us in all things necessary to our salvation, so that whatever is not contained therein is not to be enjoined as an article of faith.

(Luke 24:44-47; John 10:35; 1 Corinthians 15:3-4; 2 Timothy 3:15-17; 1 Peter 1:10-12; 2 Peter 1:20-21)

V. Sin, Original and Personal

5. We believe that sin came into the world through the disobedience of our first parents, and death by sin. We believe that sin is of two kinds: original sin or depravity, and actual or personal sin.

5.1. We believe that original sin, or depravity, is that corruption of the nature of all the offspring of Adam by reason of which everyone is very far gone from original righteousness or the pure state of our first parents at the time of their creation, is averse to God, is without spiritual life, and inclined to evil, and that continually. We further believe that original sin continues to exist with the new life of the regenerate, until eradicated by the baptism with the Holy Spirit.

5.2. We believe that original sin differs from actual sin in that it constitutes an inherited propensity to actual sin for which no one is accountable until its divinely provided remedy is neglected or rejected.

5.3. We believe that actual or personal sin is a voluntary violation of a known law of God by a morally responsible person. It is therefore not to be confused with involuntary and inescapable shortcomings, infirmities, faults, mistakes, failures, or other deviations from a standard of perfect conduct that are the residual effects of the Fall. However, such innocent effects do not include attitudes or responses contrary to the spirit of Christ, which may properly be called sins of the spirit. We believe that personal sin is primarily and essentially a violation of the law of love; and that in relation to Christ sin may be defined as unbelief.

(Original sin: Genesis 3; 6:5; Job 15:14; Psalm 51:5; Jeremiah 17:9-10; Mark 7:21-23; Romans 1:18-25; 5:12-14; 7:1—8:9; 1 Corinthians 3:1-4; Galatians 5:16-25; 1 John 1:7-8

(Personal sin: Matthew 22:36-40 {with 1 John 3:4}; John 8:34-36; 16:8-9; Romans 3:23; 6:15-23; 8:18-24; 14:23; 1 John 1:9—2:4; 3:7-10)

VI. Atonement

6. We believe that Jesus Christ, by His sufferings, by the shedding of His own blood, and by His meritorious death on the Cross, made a full atonement for all human sin, and that this Atonement is the only ground of salvation, and that it is sufficient for every individual of Adam's race. The Atonement is graciously efficacious for the salvation of the irresponsible and for the children in innocency but is efficacious for the salvation of those who reach the age of responsibility only when they repent and believe.

(Isaiah 53:5-6, 11; Mark 10:45; Luke 24:46-48; John 1:29; 3:14-17; Acts 4:10-12; Romans 3:21-26; 4:17-25; 5:6-21; 1 Corinthians 6:20; 2 Corinthians 5:14-21; Galatians 1:3-4; 3:13-14; Colossians 1:19-23; 1 Timothy 2:3-6; Titus 2:11-14; Hebrews 2:9; 9:11-14; 13:12; 1 Peter 1:18-21; 2:19-25; 1 John 2:1-2)

VII. Free Agency

7. We believe that the human race's creation in Godlikeness included ability to choose between right and wrong, and that thus human beings were made morally responsible; that through the fall of Adam they became depraved so that they cannot now turn and prepare themselves by their own natural strength and works to faith and calling upon God. But we also believe that the grace of God through Jesus Christ is freely bestowed upon all people, enabling all who will to turn from sin to righteousness, believe on Jesus Christ for pardon and cleansing from sin, and follow good works pleasing and acceptable in His sight.

We believe that all persons, though in the possession of the experience of regeneration and entire sanctification, may fall from grace and apostatize and, unless they repent of their sins, be hopelessly and eternally lost.

(Godlikeness and moral responsibility: Genesis 1:26-27; 2:16-17; Deuteronomy 28:1-2; 30:19; Joshua 24:15; Psalm 8:3-5; Isaiah 1:8-10; Jeremiah 31:29-30; Ezekiel 18:1-4; Micah 6:8; Romans 1:19-20; 2:1-16; 14:7-12; Galatians 6:7-8

(Natural inability: Job 14:4; 15:14; Psalms 14:1-4; 51:5; John 3:6*a;* Romans 3:10-12; 5:12-14, 20*a*; 7:14-25

(Free grace and works of faith: Ezekiel 18:25-26; John 1:12-13; 3:6*b;* Acts 5:31; Romans 5:6-8, 18; 6:15-16, 23; 10:6-8; 11:22; 1 Corinthians 2:9-14; 10:1-12; 2 Corinthians 5:18-19; Galatians 5:6; Ephesians 2:8-10; Philippians 2:12-13; Colossians 1:21-23; 2 Timothy 4:10*a;* Titus 2:11-14; Hebrews 2:1-3; 3:12-15; 6:4-6; 10:26-31; James 2:18-22; 2 Peter 1:10-11; 2:20-22)

VIII. Repentance

8. We believe that repentance, which is a sincere and thorough change of the mind in regard to sin, involving a sense of personal guilt and a voluntary turning away from sin, is demanded of all who have by act or purpose become sinners against God. The Spirit of God gives to all who will repent the gracious help of penitence of heart and hope of mercy, that they may believe unto pardon and spiritual life.

(2 Chronicles 7:14; Psalms 32:5-6; 51:1-17; Isaiah 55:6-7; Jeremiah 3:12-14; Ezekiel 18:30-32; 33:14-16; Mark 1:14-15; Luke 3:1-14; 13:1-5; 18:9-14; Acts 2:38; 3:19; 5:31; 17:30-31; 26:16-18; Romans 2:4; 2 Corinthians 7:8-11; 1 Thessalonians 1:9; 2 Peter 3:9)

IX. Justification, Regeneration, and Adoption

9. We believe that justification is the gracious and judicial act of God by which He grants full pardon of all guilt and complete release from the penalty of sins committed, and acceptance as righteous, to all who believe on Jesus Christ and receive Him as Lord and Savior.

10. We believe that regeneration, or the new birth, is that gracious work of God whereby the moral nature of the repentant believer is spiritually quickened and given a distinctively spiritual life, capable of faith, love, and obedience.

11. We believe that adoption is that gracious act of God by which the justified and regenerated believer is constituted a son of God.

12. We believe that justification, regeneration, and adoption are simultaneous in the experience of seekers after God and are obtained upon the condition of faith, preceded by repentance; and that to this work and state of grace the Holy Spirit bears witness.

(Luke 18:14; John 1:12-13; 3:3-8; 5:24; Acts 13:39; Romans 1:17; 3:21-26, 28; 4:5-9, 17-25; 5:1, 16-19; 6:4; 7:6; 8:1, 15-17; 1 Corinthians 1:30; 6:11; 2 Corinthians 5:17-21; Galatians 2:16-21; 3:1-14, 26; 4:4-7; Ephesians 1:6-7; 2:1, 4-5; Philippians 3:3-9; Colossians 2:13; Titus 3:4-7; 1 Peter 1:23; 1 John 1:9; 3:1-2, 9; 4:7; 5:1, 9-13, 18)

X. Entire Sanctification

13. We believe that entire sanctification is that act of God, subsequent to regeneration, by which believers are made free from original sin, or depravity, and brought into a state of entire devotement to God, and the holy obedience of love made perfect.

It is wrought by the baptism with the Holy Spirit, and

comprehends in one experience the cleansing of the heart from sin and the abiding, indwelling presence of the Holy Spirit, empowering the believer for life and service.

Entire sanctification is provided by the blood of Jesus, is wrought instantaneously by faith, preceded by entire consecration; and to this work and state of grace the Holy Spirit bears witness.

This experience is also known by various terms representing its different phases, such as "Christian perfection," "perfect love," "heart purity," "the baptism with the Holy Spirit," "the fullness of the blessing," and "Christian holiness."

14. We believe that there is a marked distinction between a pure heart and a mature character. The former is obtained in an instant, the result of entire sanctification; the latter is the result of growth in grace.

We believe that the grace of entire sanctification includes the impulse to grow in grace. However, this impulse must be consciously nurtured, and careful attention given to the requisites and processes of spiritual development and improvement in Christlikeness of character and personality. Without such purposeful endeavor one's witness may be impaired and the grace itself frustrated and ultimately lost.

(Jeremiah 31:31-34; Ezekiel 36:25-27; Malachi 3:2-3; Matthew 3:11-12; Luke 3:16-17; John 7:37-39; 14:15-23; 17:6-20; Acts 1:5; 2:1-4; 15:8-9; Romans 6:11-13, 19; 8:1-4, 8-14; 12:1-2; 2 Corinthians 6:14—7:1; Galatians 2:20; 5:16-25; Ephesians 3:14-21; 5:17-18, 25-27; Philippians 3:10-15; Colossians 3:1-17; 1 Thessalonians 5:23-24; Hebrews 4:9-11; 10:10-17; 12:1-2; 13:12; 1 John 1:7, 9)

("Christian perfection," "perfect love": Deuteronomy 30:6; Matthew 5:43-48; 22:37-40; Romans 12:9-21; 13:8-10; 1 Corinthians 13; Philippians 3:10-15; Hebrews 6:1; 1 John 4:17-18

("Heart purity": Matthew 5:8; Acts 15:8-9; 1 Peter 1:22; 1 John 3:3

("Baptism with the Holy Spirit": Jeremiah 31:31-34; Ezekiel 36:25-27; Malachi 3:2-3; Matthew 3:11-12; Luke 3:16-17; Acts 1:5; 2:1-4; 15:8-9

("Fullness of the blessing": Romans 15:29

("Christian holiness": Matthew 5:1—7:29; John 15:1-11; Romans 12:1—15:3; 2 Corinthians 7:1; Ephesians 4:17—5:20; Philippians 1:9-11; 3:12-15; Colossians 2:20—3:17; 1 Thessalonians 3:13; 4:7-8; 5:23; 2 Timothy 2:19-22; Hebrews 10:19-25; 12:14; 13:20-21; 1 Peter 1:15-16; 2 Peter 1:1-11; 3:18; Jude 20-21)

XI. The Church

15. We believe in the Church, the community that confesses Jesus Christ as Lord, the covenant people of God made new in Christ, the Body of Christ called together by the Holy Spirit through the Word.

God calls the Church to express its life in the unity and fellowship of the Spirit; in worship through the preaching of the Word, observance of the sacraments, and ministry in His name; by obedience to Christ and mutual accountability.

The mission of the Church in the world is to continue the redemptive work of Christ in the power of the Spirit through holy living, evangelism, discipleship, and service.

The Church is a historical reality, which organizes itself in culturally conditioned forms; exists both as local congregations and as a universal body; sets apart persons called of God for specific ministries. God calls the Church to live under His rule in anticipation of the consummation at the coming of our Lord Jesus Christ.

(Exodus 19:3; Jeremiah 31:33; Matthew 8:11; 10:7; 16:13-19, 24; 18:15-20; 28:19-20; John 17:14-26; 20:21-23; Acts 1:7-8; 2:32-47; 6:1-2; 13:1; 14:23; Romans 2:28-29; 4:16; 10:9-15; 11:13-32; 12:1-8; 15:1-3; 1 Corinthians 3:5-9; 7:17; 11:1, 17-33; 12:3, 12-31; 14:26-40; 2 Corinthians 5:11—6:1; Galatians 5:6, 13-14; 6:1-5, 15; Ephesians 4:1-17; 5:25-27; Philippians 2:1-16; 1 Thessalonians 4:1-12; 1 Timothy 4:13; Hebrews 10:19-25; 1 Peter 1:1-2, 13; 2:4-12, 21; 4:1-2, 10-11; 1 John 4:17; Jude 24; Revelation 5:9-10)

XII. Baptism

16. We believe that Christian baptism, commanded by our Lord, is a sacrament signifying acceptance of the benefits of the atonement of Jesus Christ, to be administered to believers and declarative of their faith in Jesus Christ as their Savior, and full purpose of obedience in holiness and righteousness.

Baptism being a symbol of the new covenant, young children may be baptized, upon request of parents or guardians who shall give assurance for them of necessary Christian training.

Baptism may be administered by sprinkling, pouring, or immersion, according to the choice of the applicant.

(Matthew 3:1-7; 28:16-20; Acts 2:37-41; 8:35-39; 10:44-48; 16:29-34; 19:1-6; Romans 6:3-4; Galatians 3:26-28; Colossians 2:12; 1 Peter 3:18-22)

XIII. The Lord's Supper

17. We believe that the Memorial and Communion Supper instituted by our Lord and Savior Jesus Christ is essentially a New Testament sacrament, declarative of His sacrificial death, through the merits of which believers have life and salvation and promise of all spiritual blessings in Christ. It is distinctively for those who are prepared for reverent appreciation of its significance, and by it they show forth the Lord's death till He come again. It being the Communion feast, only those who have faith in Christ and love for the saints should be called to participate therein.

(Exodus 12:1-14; Matthew 26:26-29; Mark 14:22-25; Luke 22:17-20; John 6:28-58; 1 Corinthians 10:14-21; 11:23-32)

XIV. Divine Healing[2]

18. We believe in the Bible doctrine of divine healing and urge our people to seek to offer the prayer of faith for the healing of the sick. [Providential means and agencies when deemed necessary should not be refused.] *We also believe God heals through the means of medical science.*

(2 Kings 5:1-19; Psalm 103:1-5; Matthew 4:23-24; 9:18-35; John 4:46-54; Acts 5:12-16; 9:32-42; 14:8-15; 1 Corinthians 12:4-11; 2 Corinthians 12:7-10; James 5:13-16)

XV. Second Coming of Christ

19. We believe that the Lord Jesus Christ will come again; that we who are alive at His coming shall not precede them that are asleep in Christ Jesus; but that, if we are abiding in Him, we shall be caught up with the risen saints to meet the Lord in the air, so that we shall ever be with the Lord.

---

2. Constitutional changes adopted by the 1997 General Assembly are in the process of ratification by the district assemblies at the time of printing. Where changes are being made, words in italics are new words and words in brackets [ ] are words being deleted.

(Matthew 25:31-46; John 14:1-3; Acts 1:9-11; Philippians 3:20-21; 1 Thessalonians 4:13-18; Titus 2:11-14; Hebrews 9:26-28; 2 Peter 3:3-15; Revelation 1:7-8; 22:7-20)

XVI. Resurrection, Judgment, and Destiny

20. We believe in the resurrection of the dead, that the bodies both of the just and of the unjust shall be raised to life and united with their spirits—"they that have done good, unto the resurrection of life; and they that have done evil, unto the resurrection of damnation."

21. We believe in future judgment in which every person shall appear before God to be judged according to his or her deeds in this life.

22. We believe that glorious and everlasting life is assured to all who savingly believe in, and obediently follow, Jesus Christ our Lord; and that the finally impenitent shall suffer eternally in hell.

(Genesis 18:25; 1 Samuel 2:10; Psalm 50:6; Isaiah 26:19; Daniel 12:2-3; Matthew 25:31-46; Mark 9:43-48; Luke 16:19-31; 20:27-38; John 3:16-18; 5:25-29; 11:21-27; Acts 17:30-31; Romans 2:1-16; 14:7-12; 1 Corinthians 15:12-58; 2 Corinthians 5:10; 2 Thessalonians 1:5-10; Revelation 20:11-15; 22:1-15)

THE CHURCH

I. The General Church

23. The Church of God is composed of all spiritually regenerate persons, whose names are written in heaven.

II. The Churches Severally

24. The churches severally are to be composed of such regenerate persons as by providential permission, and by the leadings of the Holy Spirit, become associated together for holy fellowship and ministries.

III. The Church of the Nazarene

25. The Church of the Nazarene is composed of those persons who have voluntarily associated themselves together according to the doctrines and polity of said church, and who seek holy Christian fellowship, the conversion of sinners, the entire sanctification of believers, their upbuilding in holiness, and the simplicity and spiritual power manifest in the primitive New Testament Church, together with the preaching of the gospel to every creature.

IV. Agreed Statement of Belief

26. Recognizing that the right and privilege of persons to church membership rest upon the fact of their being regenerate, we would require only such avowals of belief as are essential to Christian experience. We, therefore, deem belief in the following brief statements to be sufficient. We believe:

26.1. In one God—the Father, Son, and Holy Spirit.

26.2. That the Old and New Testament Scriptures, given by plenary inspiration, contain all truth necessary to faith and Christian living.

26.3. That man is born with a fallen nature, and is, therefore, inclined to evil, and that continually.

26.4. That the finally impenitent are hopelessly and eternally lost.

26.5. That the atonement through Jesus Christ is for the whole human race; and that whosoever repents and believes on the Lord Jesus Christ is justified and regenerated and saved from the dominion of sin.

26.6. That believers are to be sanctified wholly, subsequent to regeneration, through faith in the Lord Jesus Christ.

26.7. That the Holy Spirit bears witness to the new birth, and also to the entire sanctification of believers.

26.8. That our Lord will return, the dead will be raised, and the final judgment will take place.

V. The General Rules

27. To be identified with the visible Church is the blessed privilege and sacred duty of all who are saved from their sins and are seeking completeness in Christ Jesus. It is required of all who desire to unite with the Church of the Nazarene, and thus to walk in fellowship with us, that they shall show evidence of salvation from their sins by a godly walk and vital piety; and that they shall be, or earnestly desire to be, cleansed from all indwelling sin. They shall evidence their commitment to God—

27.1. FIRST. By doing that which is enjoined in the Word of God, which is our rule of both faith and practice, including:

(1) Loving God with all the heart, soul, mind, and strength, and one's neighbor as oneself (Exodus 20:3-6; Leviticus 19:17-18; Deuteronomy 5:7-10; 6:4-5; Mark 12:28-31; Romans 13:8-10).

(2) Pressing upon the attention of the unsaved the claims of the gospel, inviting them to the house of the Lord, and trying to compass their salvation (Matthew 28:19-20; Acts 1:8; Romans 1:14-16; 2 Corinthians 5:18-20).

(3) Being courteous to all men (Ephesians 4:32; Titus 3:2; 1 Peter 2:17; 1 John 3:18).

(4) Being helpful to those who are also of the faith, in love forbearing one another (Romans 12:13; Galatians 6:2, 10; Colossians 3:12-14).

(5) Seeking to do good to the bodies and souls of men; feeding the hungry, clothing the naked, visiting the sick

and imprisoned, and ministering to the needy, as opportunity and ability are given (Matthew 25:35-36; 2 Corinthians 9:8-10; Galatians 2:10; James 2:15-16; 1 John 3:17-18).

(6) Contributing to the support of the ministry and the church and its work in tithes and offerings (Malachi 3:10; Luke 6:38; 1 Corinthians 9:14; 16:2; 2 Corinthians 9:6-10; Philippians 4:15-19).

(7) Attending faithfully all the ordinances of God, and the means of grace, including the public worship of God (Hebrews 10:25), the ministry of the Word (Acts 2:42), the sacrament of the Lord's Supper (1 Corinthians 11:23-30); searching the Scriptures and meditating thereon (Acts 17:11; 2 Timothy 2:15; 3:14-16); family and private devotions (Deuteronomy 6:6-7; Matthew 6:6).

27.2. SECOND. By avoiding evil of every kind, including:

(1) Taking the name of God in vain (Exodus 20:7; Leviticus 19:12; James 5:12).

(2) Profaning of the Lord's Day by participation in unnecessary secular activities, thereby indulging in practices that deny its sanctity (Exodus 20:8-11; Isaiah 58:13-14; Mark 2:27-28; Acts 20:7; Revelation 1:10).

(3) Sexual immorality, such as premarital or extramarital relations, perversion in any form, or looseness and impropriety of conduct (Exodus 20:14; Matthew 5:27-32; 1 Corinthians 6:9-11; Galatians 5:19; 1 Thessalonians 4:3-7).

(4) Habits or practices known to be destructive of physical and mental well-being. Christians are to regard themselves as temples of the Holy Spirit (Proverbs 20:1; 23:1-3; 1 Corinthians 6:17-20; 2 Corinthians 7:1; Ephesians 5:18).

(5) Quarreling, returning evil for evil, gossiping, slandering, spreading surmises injurious to the good names of others (2 Corinthians 12:20; Galatians 5:15; Ephesians 4:30-32; James 3:5-18; 1 Peter 3:9-10).

(6) Dishonesty, taking advantage in buying and selling, bearing false witness, and like works of darkness (Leviticus 19:10-11; Romans 12:17; 1 Corinthians 6:7-10).

(7) The indulging of pride in dress or behavior. Our

people are to dress with the Christian simplicity and modesty that become holiness (Proverbs 29:23; 1 Timothy 2:8-10; James 4:6; 1 Peter 3:3-4; 1 John 2:15-17).

(8) Music, literature, and entertainments that dishonor God (1 Corinthians 10:31; 2 Corinthians 6:14-17; James 4:4).

27.3. THIRD. By abiding in hearty fellowship with the church, not inveighing against but wholly committed to its doctrines and usages and actively involved in its continuing witness and outreach (Ephesians 2:18-22; 4:1-3, 11-16; Philippians 2:1-8; 1 Peter 2:9-10).

****

ARTICLES OF ORGANIZATION AND GOVERNMENT

Article I. Form of Government

28. The Church of the Nazarene has a representative form of government.

28.1. We are agreed on the necessity of a superintendency that shall complement and assist the local church in the fulfilling of its mission and objectives. The superintendency shall build morale, provide motivation, supply management and method assistance, and organize and encourage organization of new churches and missions everywhere.

28.2. We are agreed that authority given to superintendents shall not interfere with the independent action of a fully organized church. Each church shall enjoy the right to select its own pastor, subject to such approval as the General Assembly shall find wise to institute. Each church shall also elect delegates to the various assemblies, manage its own finances, and have charge of all other matters pertaining to its local life and work.

Article II. Local Churches

29. The membership of a local church shall consist of all who have been organized as a church by those authorized so to do and who have been publicly received by those having proper authority, after having declared their experience of salvation, their belief in our doctrines, and their willingness to submit to our government. (100-107)

Article III. District Assemblies

30. The General Assembly shall organize the membership of the church into district assemblies, giving such lay and ministerial representation therein as the General Assembly may deem fair and just, and shall determine qualifications of such representatives, provided, however, that all assigned ordained ministers shall be members thereof. The General Assembly shall also fix the boundaries of assembly districts, and define the powers and duties of district assemblies. (200-205.7)

Article IV. The General Assembly

31.1. How Composed. The General Assembly shall be composed of ministerial and lay delegates in equal numbers, elected thereto by district assemblies of the Church of the Nazarene; such ex officio members as the General Assembly shall from time to time direct; and such delegates of districts under the administration of the World Mission and Church Growth departments of the Church of the Nazarene as may be provided for by the General Assembly.

31.2. Election of Delegates. At a district assembly within 16 months of the meeting of the General Assembly or within 24 months in areas where travel visas or other unusual preparations are necessary, an equal number of ministerial and lay delegates to the General Assembly shall be chosen as may be provided by the General Assembly, and provided that the ministerial delegates shall be assigned ordained ministers of the Church of the Nazarene. Each Phase 3 assembly district shall be entitled to at least one ministerial and one lay delegate, and such additional delegates as its membership may warrant on the basis of representation fixed by the General Assembly. Each assembly district shall elect alternate delegates not exceeding the number of its delegates. (203.22, 301-1.1)

31.3. Credentials. The secretary of each district assembly shall furnish certificates of election to the delegates and alternates severally elected to the General Assembly, and shall also send certificates of such elections to the general secretary of the Church of the Nazarene immediately following the adjournment of the district assembly.

31.4. Quorum. When the General Assembly is in session, a majority of the whole number of delegates elected thereto shall constitute a quorum for the transaction of business. If a quorum has once been had, a smaller number may approve the minutes then remaining unapproved, and adjourn.

31.5. General Superintendents. The General Assembly shall elect by ballot from among the elders of the Church of the Nazarene as many general superintendents as it may deem necessary, who shall constitute the Board of General Superintendents. Any vacancy in the office of general superintendent in the interim of General Assemblies shall be filled by a two-thirds vote of the General Board of the Church of the Nazarene. (305.2, 316)

31.6. Presiding Officers. A general superintendent appointed thereto by the Board of General Superintendents shall preside over the daily meetings of the General Assembly. But if no general superintendent be so appointed or be present, the General Assembly shall elect one of its members as temporary presiding officer. (300.1)

31.7. Rules of Order. The General Assembly shall adopt rules of order governing its manner of organization, procedure, committees, and all other matters pertaining to the orderly conduct of its business. It shall be the judge of the election and qualifications of its own members. (300.2)

31.8. General Court of Appeals. The General Assembly shall elect from among members of the Church of the Nazarene a General Court of Appeals and shall define its jurisdiction and powers. (305.7)

31.9. Powers and Restrictions.

(1) The General Assembly shall have power to legislate for the Church of the Nazarene, and to make rules and regulations for all the departments related to or associat-

ed with it in any respect, but not in conflict with this Constitution. (300, 305-5.9)

(2) No local church shall be deprived of the right to call its pastor, subject to such approval as the General Assembly shall find wise to institute. (115)

(3) All local churches, officers, ministers, and laypersons shall always have the right to a fair and orderly trial and the right to make an appeal.

AMENDMENTS

32. The provisions of this Constitution may be repealed or amended when concurred in by a two-thirds vote of all the members of the General Assembly, and when concurred in by not less than two-thirds of all the Phase 3 and Phase 2 district assemblies of the Church of the Nazarene. Either the General Assembly or any Phase 3 or Phase 2 district assembly may take the initiative in the matter of proposing such alterations or amendments. As soon as such alterations or amendments shall have been adopted as herein provided, the result of the vote shall be announced by the Board of General Superintendents, whereupon such alterations or amendments shall have full force and effect.

PART III

Special Rules

THE CHRISTIAN LIFE

MARRIAGE AND DIVORCE AND/OR DISSOLUTION OF MARRIAGE

ABORTION

HUMAN SEXUALITY

CHRISTIAN STEWARDSHIP

CHURCH OFFICERS

RULES OF ORDER

AMENDING SPECIAL RULES

A. The Christian Life

33. The church joyfully proclaims the good news that we may be delivered from all sin to a new life in Christ. By the grace of God we Christians are "to put off [the] old self"—the old patterns of conduct as well as the old carnal mind—and are to "put on the new self"—a new and holy way of life as well as the mind of Christ. (Ephesians 4:17-24)

33.1. The Church of the Nazarene purposes to relate timeless biblical principles to contemporary society in such a way that the doctrines and rules of the church may be known and understood in many lands and within a variety of cultures. We hold that the Ten Commandments, as reaffirmed in the New Testament, constitute the basic Christian ethic and ought to be obeyed in all particulars.

33.2. It is further recognized that there is validity in the concept of the collective Christian conscience as illuminated and guided by the Holy Spirit. The Church of the Nazarene, as an international expression of the Body of Christ, acknowledges its responsibility to seek ways to particularize the Christian life so as to lead to a holiness ethic. The historic ethical standards of the church are expressed in part in the following items. They should be followed carefully and conscientiously as guides and helps to holy living. Those who violate the conscience of the church do so at their own peril and to the hurt of the witness of the church. Culturally conditioned adaptations shall be referred to and approved by the Board of General Superintendents.

33.3. In listing practices to be avoided we recognize that no catalog, however inclusive, can hope to encompass all forms of evil throughout the world. Therefore it is imperative that our people earnestly seek the aid of the Spirit in cultivating a sensitivity to evil that transcends the mere letter of the law; remembering the admonition: "Test everything. Hold on to the good. Avoid every kind of evil." (1 Thessalonians 5:21-22)

33.4. Our leaders and pastors are expected to give strong emphasis in our periodicals and from our pulpits to such fundamental biblical truths as will develop the faculty of discrimination between the evil and the good.

33.5. Education is of the utmost importance for the social and spiritual well-being of society. Public schools have a mandate to educate all. They are limited, however, as to their scope and, in fact, are prohibited by court rulings from teaching the basic tenets of Christianity. Nazarene educational organizations and institutions, such as Sunday Schools, day schools, colleges, and seminaries, are expected to teach children, youth, and adults biblical principles and ethical standards in such a way that our doctrines may be known. This practice may be instead of or in addition to public schools, which often teach secular humanism and fall short of teaching principles of holy living. The education from public sources should be complemented by holiness teaching in the home. Christians should also be encouraged to work in and with public institutions to witness to and influence these institutions for God's kingdom. (Matthew 5:13-14)

34. We hold specifically that the following practices should be avoided:

34.1. Entertainments that are subversive of the Christian ethic. Our people, both as Christian individuals and in Christian family units, should govern themselves by three principles. One is the Christian stewardship of leisure time. A second principle is the recognition of the Christian obligation to apply the highest moral standards of Christian living. Because we are living in a day of great moral confusion in which we face the potential encroachment of the evils of the day into the sacred precincts of our homes through various avenues such as current literature, radio, television, and personal computers, it is essential that the most rigid safeguards be observed to keep our homes from becoming secularized and worldly. The third principle is the obligation to witness against such social evils as violence, sensuality, pornography, profanity, and the occult, as portrayed by and through the commercial entertainment industry in its many forms and to endeavor to bring about the demise of enterprises known to be the purveyors of this kind of entertainment. This would include the avoidance of all types of entertainment ventures and media productions that produce, promote, or feature the violent, the sensual, the pornographic, the profane, or the occultic, or that feature or glamorize the world's philosophy of secularism, sensualism, and materialism and undermine God's standard of holiness of heart and life.

This necessitates the teaching and preaching of these moral standards of Christian living, and that our people be taught to use prayerful discernment in continually choosing the "high road" of holy living. We therefore call upon our leaders and pastors to give strong emphasis in our periodicals and from our pulpits to such fundamental truths as will develop the principle of discrimination between the evil and good to be found in these media.

We suggest that the standard given to John Wesley by his mother, namely, "whatever weakens your reason, impairs the tenderness of your conscience, obscures your sense of God, or takes off the relish of spiritual things, whatever increases the authority of your body over mind, that thing for you is sin," form the basis for this teaching of discrimination. (33.2-33.4, 904.11-4.16)

(Romans 14:7-13; 1 Corinthians 10:31-33; Ephesians 5:1-18; Philippians 4:8-9; 1 Peter 1:13-17; 2 Peter 1:3-11)

34.2. Lotteries and other forms of gambling, whether legal or illegal. The church holds that the final result of these practices is detrimental both to the individual and society.

(Matthew 6:24-34; 2 Thessalonians 3:6-13; 1 Timothy 6:6-11; Hebrews 13:5-6; 1 John 2:15-17)

34.3. Membership in oath-bound secret orders or societies. The quasi-religious nature of such organizations dilutes the Christian's commitment, and their secrecy contravenes the Christian's open witness.

(1 Corinthians 1:26-31; 2 Corinthians 6:14—7:1; Ephesians 5:11-16; James 4:4; 1 John 2:15-17)

34.4. All forms of dancing that detract from spiritual growth and break down proper moral inhibitions and reserve.

(Matthew 22:36-39; Romans 12:1-2; 1 Corinthians 10:31-33; Philippians 1:9-11; Colossians 3:1-17)

34.5. The use of intoxicating liquors as a beverage, or trafficking therein; giving influence to, or voting for, the licensing of places for the sale of the same; using illicit drugs or trafficking therein; using of tobacco in any of its forms, or trafficking therein.

The Holy Scriptures and human experience together justify the condemnation of the use of intoxicating drinks as a beverage. The manufacture and sale of liquors for such purposes is a sin against God and the human race. Total abstinence from all intoxicants should be the Christian rule for the individual, and total prohibition of the traffic in intoxicants the duty of civil government. (903.1, 904.16)

(Proverbs 20:1; 23:29—24:2; Habakkuk 2:5; 1 Corinthians 6:9-12, 19-20; Galatians 5:21; Ephesians 5:18)

(Only unfermented wine and unleavened bread[1] should be used in the sacrament of the Lord's Supper.) (413.10, 427.7-27.8, 428.2, 429.1, 802)

34.6. The unprescribed use of hallucinogenics, stimulants, and depressants, and the misuse and abuse of regularly prescribed medicines. Only on competent medical advice and under medical supervision should such drugs be used.

(Matthew 22:37-39; 27:34; Romans 12:1-2; 1 Corinthians 6:19-20; 9:24-27)

B. Marriage and Divorce and/or Dissolution of Marriage[2]

35. The Christian family, knit together in a common bond through Jesus Christ, is a circle of love, fellowship, and wor-

---

1. In world areas where this may cause special intrafaith difficulties, a district assembly may request the Board of General Superintendents for permission to use common bread.

2. The meaning of divorce in this rule shall include "dissolution of marriage" when it is used as a legal substitute for divorce.

ship to be earnestly cultivated in a society in which family ties are easily dissolved. We urge upon the ministry and congregations of our church such teachings and practices as will strengthen and develop family ties. In particular, we urge upon the ministry the importance of teaching and preaching clearly the biblical plan of the permanence of marriage.

The institution of marriage was ordained by God in the time of man's innocence, and is, according to apostolic authority, "honored by all"; it is the mutual union of one man and one woman for fellowship, helpfulness, and the propagation of the race. Our people should cherish this sacred estate as becomes Christians, and should enter it only after earnest prayer for divine direction, and when assured that the contemplated union is in accordance with scriptural requirements. They should seek earnestly the blessings that God has ordained in connection with the wedded state, namely, holy companionship, parenthood, and mutual love—the elements of home building. The marriage covenant is morally binding so long as both shall live, and breaking of it is a breach of the divine plan of the permanence of marriage.

(Genesis 1:26-28, 31; 2:21-24; Malachi 2:13-16; Matthew 19:3-9; John 2:1-11; Ephesians 5:21—6:4; 1 Thessalonians 4:3-8; Hebrews 13:4)

35.1. In biblical teaching, marriage is the commitment of male and female to each other for life, reflecting Christ's sacrificial love for the Church. As such, marriage is intended to be permanent, and divorce an infraction of the clear teaching of Christ. Such infractions, however, are not beyond the forgiving grace of God when this is sought with repentance, faith, and humility. It is recognized that some have divorce thrust upon them against their will or are compelled to resort to it for legal or physical protection.

(Genesis 2:21-24; Mark 10:2-12; Luke 7:36-50, 16:18; John 7:53—8:11; 1 Corinthians 6:9-11; 7:10-16; Ephesians 5:25-33)

35.2. Ministers of the Church of the Nazarene are instructed to give due care to matters relating to solemnizing marriages. They shall seek, in every manner possible, to convey to their congregations the sacredness of Christian marriage. They shall provide premarital counseling in every instance possible before performing a marriage ceremony including proper spiritual guidance for those who have experienced divorce. They shall only solemnize marriages of persons having the biblical basis for marriage. (107-7.1)

35.3. Members of the Church of the Nazarene are to seek prayerfully a redemptive course of action when involved in marital unhappiness, in full harmony with their vows and the clear teachings of the Scripture, their aim being to save the home and safeguard the good name of both Christ and His Church. Couples having serious marital problems are urged to seek counsel and guidance of their pastor and/or any other appropriate spiritual leaders. Failure to comply with this procedure in good faith and with sincere endeavor to seek a Christian solution, and subsequent obtainment of divorce and remarriage, makes one or both parties subject to possible discipline as prescribed in 504-4.2 and 505-5.12.

35.4. Through ignorance, sin, and human frailties, many in our society fall short of the divine plan. We believe that Christ can redeem these persons even as He did the woman at Samaria's well, and that sin against God's design for marriage does not place one beyond the forgiving grace of the gospel. Where a marriage has been dissolved and remarriage has followed, the marriage partners are enjoined to seek the grace of God and His redemptive help in their marriage relation. Such persons may be received into the membership of the church at such time as they have given evidence of their regeneration and an awareness of their understanding of the sanctity of Christian marriage. (27, 107.1)

C. Abortion

36. The Church of the Nazarene affirms the sanctity of human life as established by God the Creator and believes that such sanctity extends to the child not yet born. Therefore, we oppose induced abortion (surgically or chemically), when used for either personal convenience or population control. We oppose laws that allow abortion. Realizing that there are rare but real medical conditions wherein the mother or the unborn child, or both, could not survive the pregnancy, termination of the pregnancy should only be made after sound medical and Christian counseling.

Responsible opposition to abortion requires our commitment to the initiation and support of programs designed to provide care for mothers and children. The crisis of an unwanted pregnancy calls for the community of believers (represented only by those for whom knowledge of the crisis is appropriate) to provide a context of love, prayer, and counsel. In such instances, support can take the form of counseling centers, homes for expectant mothers, and the creation or utilization of Christian adoption services.

The Church of the Nazarene recognizes that consideration of abortion as a means of ending an unwanted pregnancy often occurs because Christian standards of sexual responsibility have been ignored. Therefore the church calls for persons to practice the ethic of the New Testament as it bears upon human sexuality and to deal with the issue of abortion by placing it within the larger framework of biblical principles that provide guidance for moral decision making.

(Exodus 20:13; 21:12-16; Job 31:15; Psalms 22:9; 139:3-16; Isaiah 44:2, 24; 49:5; Luke 1:23-25, 36-45; Romans 12:1-2; 1 Corinthians 6:16; 7:1 ff.; 1 Thessalonians 4:3-6)

D. Human Sexuality

37. The Church of the Nazarene views human sexuality as one expression of the holiness and beauty that God the Creator intended for His creation. It is one of the ways by which the covenant between a husband and a wife is sealed and expressed. Christians are to understand that in marriage human sexuality can and ought to be sanctified by God. Human sexuality achieves fulfillment only as a sign of comprehensive love and loyalty. Christian husbands and wives should view sexuality as a part of their much larger commitment to one another and to Christ from whom the meaning of life is drawn.

The Christian home should serve as a setting for teaching children the sacred character of human sexuality and for showing them how its meaning is fulfilled in the context of love, fidelity, and patience.

Our ministers and Christian educators should state clearly the Christian understanding of human sexuality, urging Christians to celebrate its rightful excellence, and rigorously to guard against its betrayal and distortion.

Sexuality misses its purpose when treated as an end in itself or when cheapened by using another person to satisfy pornographic and perverted sexual interests. We view all forms of sexual intimacy that occur outside the covenant of heterosexual marriage as sinful distortions of the holiness and beauty God intended for it.

Homosexuality is one means by which human sexuality is perverted. We recognize the depth of the perversion that leads to homosexual acts but affirm the biblical position that such acts are sinful and subject to the wrath of God. We believe the grace of God sufficient to overcome the practice of homosexuality (1 Corinthians 6:9-11). We deplore any action or statement that would seem to imply compatibility between Christian morality and the practice of homosexuality. We urge clear preaching and teaching concerning Bible standards of sexual morality.

(Genesis 1:27; 19:1-25; Leviticus 20:13; Romans 1:26-27; 1 Corinthians 6:9-11; 1 Timothy 1:8-10)

E. Christian Stewardship

38. Meaning of Stewardship. The Scriptures teach that God is the Owner of all persons and all things. We, therefore, are His stewards of both life and possessions. God's ownership and our stewardship ought to be acknowledged, for we shall be held personally accountable to God for the exercise of our stewardship. God, as a God of system and order in all of His ways, has established a system of giving that acknowledges His ownership and human stewardship. To this end all His children should faithfully tithe and present offerings for the support of the gospel. (140)

(Malachi 3:8-12; Matthew 6:24-34; 25:31-46; Mark 10:17-31; Luke 12:13-24; 19:11-27; John 15:1-17; Romans 12:1-13; 1 Corinthians 9:7-14; 2 Corinthians 8:1-15; 9:6-15; 1 Timothy 6:6-19; Hebrews 7:8; James 1:27; 1 John 3:16-18)

38.1. Storehouse Tithing. Storehouse tithing is a scriptural and practical performance of faithfully and regularly placing the tithe into that church to which the member belongs. Therefore, the financing of the church shall be based on the plan of storehouse tithing, and the local Church of the Nazarene shall be regarded by all of its people as the storehouse. All who are a part of the Church of the Nazarene are urged to contribute faithfully one-tenth of all their increase as a minimum financial obligation to the Lord and freewill offerings in addition as God has prospered them for the support of the whole church, local, district, regional, and general.

38.2. Fund-raising and Distribution. In the light of the scriptural teaching concerning the giving of tithes and offerings for the support of the gospel, and for the erection of church buildings, no Nazarene church should engage in any method of fund-raising that would detract from these principles, hinder the gospel message, sully the name of the church, discriminate against the poor, or misdirect the people's energies from promoting the gospel.

In disbursing to meet the requirements of the local, district, regional, and general programs of the Church of the Nazarene, local churches are urged to adopt and practice a financial apportionment plan, and to pay general, regional, and district apportionments monthly. (130, 155, 156-56.2, 413.20)

38.3. Support of the Ministry. "In the same way, the Lord has commanded that those who preach the gospel should receive their living from the gospel" (1 Corinthians 9:14). The church is obligated to support its ministers, who have been called of God, and who, under the direction of the church, have given themselves wholly to the work of the ministry. We urge therefore that the members of the church voluntarily commit themselves to the task of supporting the ministry by gathering money weekly for this holy business and that the pastor's salary be paid regularly every week. (115.4)

38.4. Life Income Gifts and Bequests. It is essential in the exercise of Christian stewardship that careful thought be given as to what shall be done with the residue of one's income and possessions over which the Lord makes the Christian a steward during this life. Civil laws often do not provide for the distribution of an estate in such a way as to glorify God. Each Christian should give attention to the preparation of a last will and testament in a careful and legal manner, and the Church of the Nazarene through its various ministries of missions, evangelism, education, and benevolences—local, district, regional, and general—is recommended for consideration.

F. Church Officers

39. We direct our local churches to elect as church officers only persons who profess the experience of entire sanctification and whose lives bear public witness to the grace of God that calls us to a holy life; who are in harmony with the doctrines, polity, and practices of the Church of the Nazarene; and who support the local church faithfully in attendance and with tithes and offerings. (113.9, 127, 147)

G. Rules of Order

40. Subject to the applicable law, the Articles of Incorporation and the Bylaws of government in the *Manual*, the meetings and proceedings of the members of the Church of the Nazarene, local, district, and general, and the committees of the corporation shall be regulated and controlled according to *Robert's Rules of Order* (latest edition) for parliamentary procedure.

H. Amending Special Rules

41. The provisions of these Special Rules may be repealed or amended when concurred in by a two-thirds vote of the members present and voting of a given General Assembly.

PART IV

Government

THE LOCAL CHURCH

THE DISTRICT ASSEMBLY

THE GENERAL ASSEMBLY

HIGHER EDUCATION

PREAMBLE

The task of the Church of the Nazarene is to make known to all peoples the transforming grace of God through the forgiveness of sins and heart cleansing in Jesus Christ. Our mission first and foremost is to "make disciples," to incorporate believers into fellowship and membership (congregations), and to equip (teach) for ministry all who respond in faith. The ultimate goal of the community of faith is to "present everyone perfect in Christ" (Colossians 1:28) at the last day.

It is in the local church that the saving, perfecting, teaching, and commissioning takes place. The local church, the Body of Christ, is the representation of our faith and mission. These churches are grouped administratively into districts and regions.

The bases of unity in the Church of the Nazarene are those beliefs, polity, definitions, and procedures as articulated in the *Manual of the Church of the Nazarene.*

The core of this unity is declared in the *Articles of Faith* of the *Manual.* We encourage the church in all regions and languages to translate—widely distribute—and teach these beliefs to our constituency. This is the golden strand that is woven into the fabric of all we are and do as Nazarenes.

A visible reflection of this unity is represented by the General Assembly, which is the "supreme doctrine-formulating, lawmaking, and elective authority of the Church of the Nazarene." (300)

A second reflection is the international General Board, which represents the entire church.

A third reflection is the Board of General Superintendents, who may interpret the *Manual,* approve cultural adaptations, and ordain to the ministry.

The government of the Church of the Nazarene is representative, and thus avoids the extremes of episcopacy on the one hand and unlimited congregationalism on the other.

In world regions served by the church where cultural and political differences may necessitate, adaptations of local, district, and regional church government procedures contained in Part IV, Chapters I, II, and III, may be made. Requests for all such adaptations shall be submitted in writing to and approved by the Board of General Superintendents.

CHAPTER I

THE LOCAL CHURCH

A. Organization, Name, Incorporation, Property, Restrictions, Mergers, Disorganization

100. Organization. Local churches may be organized by the district superintendent, or by the general superintendent having jurisdiction, or by an elder authorized by either of them. Official reports of new churches shall be filed in the Evangelism and Church Growth Division office. (29, 107, 208.1, 307.8, 433.12)

100.1. The Multicongregational Church. Organized local churches may enlarge their ministry by establishing Bible classes in various languages using the facilities of these churches. These Bible classes may develop into church-type missions or fully organized churches (100). This may result in more than one congregation existing in the same building, with the approval of the district superintendent. In such multicongregational churches where not all the individual congregations are fully organized churches, the District Advisory Board, with the approval of the district superintendent and the general superintendent in jurisdiction, may grant to such congregations the rights and privileges of an organized local church subject to the following conditions:

1. Such congregations may not be incorporated separate from the organized local church.
2. Such congregations shall not hold title to property separate from the organized local church.

3. Such congregations shall not incur indebtedness without the approval of the district superintendent, the church board of the organized local church, and the District Advisory Board.
4. No such congregation may withdraw as a body from the organized local church or in any way sever its relation thereto except by the express permission of the district superintendent in consultation with the pastor of the local church.

101. Name. The name of a newly organized church shall be determined by the local church in consultation with the district superintendent and with the approval of the District Advisory Board.

101.1. Change of Name. A local Church of the Nazarene may change its name by a majority ballot vote in an annual or special meeting of the church membership. Processes for the change shall be: *(a)* The local church board submits the proposed change to the district superintendent who shall obtain the written approval of the District Advisory Board; *(b)* the local church votes; *(c)* the District Advisory Board reports the change to the district assembly, and the district assembly votes approval of the same.

102. Incorporation. In all places where the statutes will permit, the trustees shall have the local church incorporated, and the said trustees and their successors shall be the trustees of the said corporation. Where not inconsistent with civil law the Articles of Incorporation shall set forth the powers of the corporation and provide that the corporation shall be subject to the government of the Church of the Nazarene, as from time to time authorized and declared in its *Manual* by the General Assembly of said church. All the property of this corporation shall be managed and controlled by the trustees subject to the approval of the local church.

102.1. Where property is purchased and developed by the District Advisory Board for a local church or where a new church is formed, upon the repayment by the local church of the money invested by the District Advisory Board, it is deemed advisable that the District Advisory Board transfer the title to the local church.

102.2. When a local church is incorporated, all property acquired shall be deeded directly to the church in its corporate name when it is possible to do so.

102.3. The pastor and the secretary of the church board shall be the president and secretary of the church, incorporated or not incorporated, and shall execute and sign all conveyances of real estate, mortgages, releases of mortgage, contracts, and other legal documents of the church not otherwise provided for in the *Manual* and subject to the restrictions set forth in 104-4.2.

102.4. The Articles of Incorporation of each local church shall include the following provisions:

1. The corporate name shall include the words "Church of the Nazarene."
2. The bylaws of the corporation shall be the *Manual of the Church of the Nazarene.*
3. The Articles of Incorporation shall not contain any provision that might prevent the local church from qualifying for any tax exemption available to churches in the same area.
4. Upon dissolution, the assets of the corporation shall be distributed to the District Advisory Board.

The Articles of Incorporation may contain additional provisions when appropriate under local law. No provision, however, shall be included that can cause the property of the local church to be diverted from the Church of the Nazarene. (101-1.1, 104.2, 106.1-6.3)

102.5. In multicongregational churches, where more than one organized church shares the same facility, incorporation may take place in partnership where local laws allow.

103. Property. The local church considering the purchase of real estate, the erection of churches or church-related buildings, a major remodeling of either, or leasing real property for any reason, shall submit its proposal to the district superintendent and the District Church Properties Board for their consideration, advice, and approval. No indebtedness, whether involving a mortgage or not, shall be incurred in the purchase of real estate or the erection of buildings or a major remodeling of either, without the written approval of the district superintendent and the District Church Properties Board. (234-35.5)

103.1. In case agreement cannot be reached between the church board and the district superintendent and the District Church Properties Board, the issue may be submitted to the general superintendent having jurisdiction, for a decision. Either the church or the district superintendent may appeal such decision to the Board of General Superintendents for a final decision. All such appeals, rebuttals of appeals, or arguments pertaining thereto, whether to the general superintendent in jurisdiction or the Board of General Superintendents, shall be in writing. A copy of the appeal, rebuttals of appeals, or arguments pertaining thereto by either the church board or the district superintendent shall be sent to the other party involved. The minute record of a church board appeal shall include the appeal resolution, arguments sustaining it, and the record of the vote taken.

104. Restrictions. The local church may not purchase real estate, nor sell, mortgage, exchange, or otherwise dispose of real estate except by two-thirds vote of the members present at an annual meeting, or at a special meeting duly called for that purpose, and except upon the written approval of the district superintendent and the District Church Properties Board. (113.3, 113.6, 113.13, 235.3)

104.1. The real estate of the local church shall not be mortgaged to meet current expenses.

104.2. Trustees and/or a local church may not divert property from the use of the Church of the Nazarene. (113-13.1)

104.3. Withdrawal of Churches. No local church may withdraw as a body from the Church of the Nazarene, or in any way sever its relation thereto, except by provision of the General Assembly, and upon agreed conditions and plans.

105. Mergers. Two or more local churches may be merged upon two-thirds favorable vote by ballot of the members present and voting at specially called meetings of the churches involved, provided: The merger shall be recommended by a majority vote by ballot of all the members of the respective church boards, and the merger shall have been approved in writing by the district superintendent, the District Advisory Board, and the general superintendent in jurisdiction.

The merger shall be finalized in a special meeting of the new congregation for the purpose of electing officers and making pastoral arrangements. The district superintendent, or an elder appointed by the superintendent, shall preside.

The organization thus created shall combine the total membership of the former churches, the membership of all departments of those churches, and may combine part or all of the assets and liabilities of those churches subject to the approval of the district superintendent, the District Advisory Board, and the general superintendent in jurisdiction. The merger will also combine the general, regional, and district apportionments.

Upon the notification by the district superintendent, the general secretary of the Church of the Nazarene is authorized to remove the names of the inactive churches from the roll of churches.

106. Declaring Churches Inactive/Disorganized. Churches may be declared inactive for a period of transition by action of the District Advisory Board.

106.1. A local church may be disorganized by action and formal pronouncement of the Board of General Superintendents. Such action shall be taken only after *(a)* the district superintendent has consulted with the general superintendent in jurisdiction concerning the possibility of discontinuing a local church organization; and *(b)* on recommendation of the district superintendent and the District Advisory Board.

106.2. In case a local church becomes disorganized, any church property that may exist may in no way be diverted to other purposes, but title shall pass to the District

Advisory Board acting as agent for said district where such has been incorporated, or other authorized agents, for the use of the Church of the Nazarene at large, as the district assembly shall direct; and trustees holding property for the disorganized church shall sell or dispose of the same only on the order and under the direction of the District Advisory Board or other appointed agent of the district assembly, with the written approval of the general superintendent in jurisdiction; either conveying said property or delivering the proceeds from the sale thereof as directed by the district assembly or its District Advisory Board.

106.3. No trustee or trustees of a disorganized church may divert property from the use of the Church of the Nazarene. (141-45)

106.4. Only those churches officially disorganized may be dropped from the records of the general secretary.

B. Membership

107. Full Membership. All persons who have been organized into a local church by those authorized so to do, and all who have been publicly received by the pastor, the district superintendent, or the general superintendent, after having declared their experience of salvation, and their belief in the doctrines of the Church of the Nazarene, and their willingness to submit to its government, shall compose the full membership of the local church; however, only church members who have reached their 15th birthday shall be entitled to vote in annual or special church meetings. (29, 35.4, 111, 113.1, 413.3, 417, 427.9, 433.8-33.9)

107.1. When persons desire to unite with the church, the pastor shall explain to them the privileges and responsibilities of membership in the church, the Articles of Faith, the requirements of the General and Special Rules, and the purpose and mission of the Church of the Nazarene. Specific indoctrination and orientation shall be provided to qualify candidates for meaningful church membership.

After consulting with the Evangelism and Church Membership Committee, the minister shall receive acceptable candidates into the membership of the church in a public service, using the approved form for the reception of members (801). (27, 33-39, 110-10.4, 225)

107.2. Members of a Church-Type Mission. Where the organization of a local church has not been effected, a church-type mission shall receive and report church members according to 107 and 107.1 in the annual statistics.

108. Associate Membership. Where a district makes provision, a local church may have associate members who shall have all the privileges of church members, with the exception of voting and holding church office. (203.23)

108.1. Associate members may be received into full membership or dropped at any time, at the discretion of the pastor and Evangelism and Church Membership Committee.

109. Inactive Membership. A local church may designate persons as "inactive members" for the reasons stated in 109.1 and 109.2.

109.1. A member of a local church who has moved to another community and ceases to be active at his or her church of membership should be urged to attend the Church of the Nazarene there and to request a transfer of membership to that church. The pastor of the nearest church should be notified of this change of residence directly or through the Evangelism and Church Growth Division of the General Board. After one year, if a member fails to request a transfer of membership or if that member's address is unknown, the membership may be declared inactive by recommendation of the Evangelism and Church Membership Committee and action of the church board. After such action, the pastor shall write opposite the member's name "Placed on the Inactive Membership Roll by the church board (date)." If this person reestablishes residence in the community where his or her membership was declared inactive, full membership may be granted by recommendation of the Evangelism and Church Membership Committee and action of the church board.

109.2. When a member of a church has been absent from all religious services of the church for six successive months without a reason deemed justifiable by the church board, and attempt has been made to encourage him or her to become active when possible, that person's membership may be declared inactive upon recommendation of the Evangelism and Church Membership Committee and action of the church board. The person shall be informed by a redemptive letter from the pastor within seven days of the action of the church board. After such action of the church board, the pastor shall write opposite the member's name "Placed on the Inactive Membership Roll by the church board (date)." A 120-day waiting period including prayer and supplication shall follow these actions, during which an inactive member may request in writing that the church board return his or her name to the active roll of the church. The request must include a reaffirmation of the vows of membership and renewed participation in the worship activities of the local church. The church board shall respond to the request within 60 days. Full membership may be restored to such a person by recommendation of the Evangelism and Church Membership Committee and action of the church board.

109.3. Inactive members shall be included in the full membership of the local church with active members. Membership shall be reported to the district assembly in separate categories, namely (1) active and (2) inactive members.

109.4. Inactive members shall not be eligible to vote in annual or special church meetings or hold office.

C. Evangelism and Church Membership Committee

110. The church board shall provide an evangelism and church membership committee of not fewer than three persons acting in an advisory capacity to the pastor, who shall be the chairman. Its duties shall be:

110.1. To promote evangelism in the local church and seek to conserve the fruits of evangelism. (107-7.1, 129.25)

110.2. To study and recommend to the church board and departments ways to emphasize evangelism in the whole life of the church.

110.3. To serve as the local committee to implement both general and district denominational programs of evangelism.

110.4. To urge new converts to qualify for church membership by a consistent devotional life, a study of the Bible and the *Manual,* individually and/or in a pastor's membership class, remembering that members received by profession of faith help to conserve the fruits of evangelism. (26-27, 35.4)

110.5. To endeavor to bring new members into total fellowship and service of the church.

110.6. To work with the pastor in developing a continuing program of spiritual guidance for new members.

110.7. To recommend to the church board, upon nomination by the pastor, the evangelists for local campaigns. It is recommended that at least one campaign each year be conducted by a commissioned or registered evangelist.

110.8. No person shall be received into full membership of the local church until the pastor first consults with the Evangelism and Church Membership Committee concerning that person's reception. (107.1)

D. Change of Membership

111. Transfer. The pastor, when requested by a member, may grant a transfer of church membership (see form in 813.4) to any local Church of the Nazarene that may be named, such transfer to be valid for three months only. When the reception of the transfer is acknowledged by the receiving local church, such person's membership in the former local church shall cease. (813.5)

111.1. Commendation. The pastor, when requested by a member, may grant a certificate of commendation (see form in 813.2) to any evangelical church that may be named, after which such person's membership in the local church issuing the certificate shall cease immediately.

E. Termination of Membership

112. Ministers. When a licensed or an ordained minister has united with the church membership or ministry of a church other than the Church of the Nazarene, the pastor of the local church in which the minister is a member shall immediately notify the District Ministerial Credentials Board of the fact. The Ministerial Credentials Board shall investigate and confirm the status of the member of the clergy. If the District Ministerial Credentials Board determines that the member of the clergy will be removed from the roll of ministers, the pastor of the local church will also remove the person's name from the membership roll of the church and shall write opposite the name, "Removed by uniting with another denomination." (427.10, 433.10)

112.1. Laypersons. When a lay member of a local church has accepted membership, license to preach, or ordination from any other religious organizations, or is engaging in independent church or missionary work, his or her membership in the local church shall, because of that fact, immediately cease except in case that person shall secure the annual written approval of the local church board of the church in which said membership is held and the annual written approval of the District Advisory Board of the district in which that church is located.

112.2. Release from Membership. The pastor, when requested by a member, may grant a letter of release (see form in 813.3), thus terminating such person's membership immediately. (111.1)

112.3. After two years from the date when a person's membership was declared inactive, his or her name may be removed from the church roll by action of the church board. After such action of the church board, the pastor shall write opposite the member's name, "Removed by the church board (date)."

112.4. A church board may not remove more than 10 percent of the membership of the local church in any one assembly year without the written approval of the District Advisory Board and the district superintendent. The names of those to be removed and the reason for their removal shall be presented in writing to the Advisory Board by the local church secretary.

F. Church Meetings

113. A meeting of the members of a local church for conference and for the transaction of business shall be known as a church meeting. (104, 113.6, 115, 415)

113.1. Only those persons who have been received into full membership and have reached their 15th birthday shall be entitled to vote in church meetings. (107)

113.2. Business Transactions. Business, including elections, in harmony with the spirit and order of the church, and not otherwise specially provided for, may be transacted at any church meeting.

113.3. Comply with Civil Law. In all cases where the civil law requires a specific course of procedure in calling and conducting church meetings, that course should be strictly followed. (142)

113.4. Presiding Officer. The pastor, who shall be ex officio president of the local church, or the district superintendent, or the general superintendent having jurisdiction, or someone appointed by the district superintendent or the general superintendent, shall preside at annual or special church meetings. (210.1, 307.9, 413.23)

113.5. Secretary. The secretary of the church board shall be the secretary of all church meetings; in his or her absence a secretary pro tempore shall be elected. (134.4)

113.6. Annual Meeting. An annual church meeting shall be held within 90 days prior to the meeting of the district assembly. Public notice of the annual meeting must be given from the pulpit on at least two Sundays before the meeting. This annual meeting may be conducted on more than one day or in more than one service upon approval by the church board.

113.7. Reports. Reports shall be given at the annual church meeting by the pastor (413.15), the Sunday School superintendent (147.6), the president of the Nazarene Youth International (152.3), the president of the Nazarene World Mission Society (154.2), the deaconesses (405), the local ministers (426.1), the stewards (138), the trustees (144), the secretary (134.2), and the treasurer (135.5) of the church board.

113.8. Nominating Committee. A nominating committee shall be used to nominate officers, boards, and district assembly delegates, whose nominations are not provided for elsewhere.

The Nominating Committee shall consist of not fewer than three nor more than seven members of the church, including the pastor, and shall be constituted by whatever method the church board shall propose. The pastor shall be chairman of the committee. All persons nominated by this committee shall affirm that they fulfill the qualifications required of church officers in paragraph 39.

113.9. Elections. At the annual church meeting there shall be an election, by ballot, of the stewards (136), the trustees (141, 142.1), the Sunday School superintendent (147), and the members of the Sunday School Ministries Board (146), to serve for the next church year and until their successors are elected and qualified. All those elected as church officers shall be members of that same local Church of the Nazarene. (39)

113.10. Where laws permit, and in churches where such procedure and the number to be elected are approved by a majority vote of the church members present, the church board may be elected, and then appropriate proportions designated as stewards and trustees, in harmony with 136 and 141. When a church board is elected in this manner, the board shall organize itself into committees to carry out assigned responsibilities. If a church has elected an education committee as part of its board in harmony with 146, that committee will constitute the Education Committee of the church board. (146-46.10)

113.11. Where laws permit, and in churches where such procedure is approved by a majority vote of the church members present at a duly called annual meeting, after receiving the written approval of the district superintendent, a church may elect one-half its church board members for two-year terms, or one-third of its church board members for three-year terms, in either case designating an equal number to be elected annually. When the church board is elected in this manner, the number of stewards and trustees chosen must comply with 136 and 141.

113.12. At the annual church meeting, there shall be an election, by ballot, of lay delegates to the district assembly, on the basis of representation fixed by the General Assembly according to 201-1.2.

113.13. Special church meetings may be called at any time by the pastor, or by the church board after having obtained the consent of the pastor or of the district superintendent or of the general superintendent having jurisdiction. (104)

113.14. Public notice of special church meetings shall always be given from the pulpit in at least two preceding regular services, or in such manner as meets the requirements of civil law. (115-15.1, 121, 136, 139, 142.1, 145)

G. The Church Year

114. The administrative year shall run concurrently with the statistical year of the local church and shall be recognized as the church year.

114.1. The statistical year shall close within 60 days prior to the opening of the district assembly; and the new statistical year shall begin the day following its close. The exact date of the beginning and close of the statistical year within these bounds shall be set by the District Advisory Board. (222.1)

H. Calling of a Pastor

115. An elder or licensed minister (412) may be called to pastor a church by two-thirds favorable vote by ballot of the church members of voting age present and voting at a duly called annual or special meeting of the church, provided that such elder or licensed minister shall have been nominated to the church by the church board, which, after having consulted with the district superintendent, made such nomination by majority vote by ballot of all its members; and provided the nomination shall have been approved by the district superintendent. Any elder or licensed minister with membership in a local church may not be considered for senior pastor of that church without the approval of the District Advisory Board. This call shall be subject to review and continuance as hereinafter provided. (118, 120-22, 129.2, 161.8, 208.8)

115.1. Acceptance of a call to pastoral relations shall be given by the minister not later than 30 days from the date of the church meeting voting the call.

115.2. The church board and the pastor should clearly communicate their goals and expectations to each other in writing.

115.3. As soon as practical after a pastor begins serving, the pastor and the congregation may participate in an installation or bonding service. The objective of the service should be to celebrate unity and direction concerning the will of God. Where practical, the district superintendent shall preside.

115.4. Upon issuing a call, the local church will specify the proposed remuneration. The amount of this remuneration may be determined by the church board, or by vote of the church membership upon the recommendation of the church board. When agreement has been entered into between the church or the church board and the pastor, the payment of the pastor's salary in full shall be considered a moral obligation by the church. If, however, the church becomes unable to continue the payment of the salary agreed upon, such inability and failure shall not be considered a sufficient cause for civil action against the church by the pastor; and in no case shall the church be legally responsible in excess of funds raised during the term of the pastor's actual service, and not otherwise designated.

The local church should also make provision for the pastor's traveling and moving expenses. (38, 129.8-29.9)

115.5. The remuneration of the pastor shall commence on the Monday preceding the first official Sunday of service to the local church.

116. The pastor of a church that has been organized for less than five years, or has less than 35 members voting in the previous annual church meeting, or is receiving regular financial assistance from the district, may be appointed or reappointed by the district superintendent, with the consent of the District Advisory Board. (208.1, 208.4)

117. In case of disagreement between the church board and the district superintendent regarding pastoral arrangements, the church board or the district superintendent may submit the matter to the general superintendent having jurisdiction for his or her decision. From such decision either the church board or the district superintendent may appeal to the Board of General Superintendents. All such appeals, rebuttals of appeals, or arguments pertaining thereto, whether to the general superintendent in jurisdiction or the Board of General Superintendents, shall be in writing. A copy of the appeal, rebuttals of appeals, or arguments pertaining thereto by either the church board or the district superintendent shall be sent to the other party involved. The minute record of a church board appeal shall include the appeal resolution, arguments sustaining it, and the record of the vote taken. If a minister under consideration withdraws his or her name, or if a pastoral candidate is found to be unavailable for consideration, the appeal process should terminate immediately, and the district superintendent and church board shall continue with pastoral arrangements.

118. The call of a pastor who is a licensed minister will terminate at the end of the district assembly if the minister's license is not renewed.

119. No pastor shall terminate the pastorate of a church without giving the church board and the district superintendent written resignation at least 30 days before the termination of the pastorate, and without having this resignation accepted by the church board and approved in writing by the district superintendent. When the resignation has been accepted, termination may be anytime agreed upon within 30 days.

119.1. The pastor who resigns shall, in cooperation with the secretary of the church board, prepare a correct list of the church membership roll with current addresses. This roll must correspond numerically with the last published district minutes showing deletions and additions for the current year.

I. The Pastor/Church Relationship

120. At least every other year, the pastor and the church board shall conduct a self-study to review the expectations, goals, and performance of the church and pastor. At the time of the self-study the written understanding between the church and the pastor should be updated and renewed.

120.1. The district superintendent shall be given reasonable notice and opportunity to participate in each self-study. The pastor shall send the district superintendent a summary of the results of the self-study within 30 days of its completion.

120.2. Pastors and congregations shall seek a clear understanding of each others' expectations and sincerely follow biblical principles to resolve differences in a spirit of reconciliation within the church. Biblical principles for resolving differences in Matthew 18:15-20 and Galatians 6:1-5 include:

1. Seek to resolve differences by discussing them face-to-face.
2. If face-to-face discussion fails to bring resolution, seek the assistance of one or two others in resolving the differences.
3. Bring the differences to the church board only after face-to-face discussion and small-group efforts fail.
4. Christians are obligated to work at resolving differences in a spirit of love, acceptance, and forgiveness.

J. Reviewing the Call of the Pastor

121. The Regular Pastoral Review. The pastoral relationship shall be reviewed by the church board, meeting with the district superintendent, or an ordained minister or layperson appointed by the district superintendent, within 60 days of the second anniversary of pastoral service and every four years thereafter. The district superintendent, or an ordained minister or layperson appointed by the district superintendent, shall be responsible for scheduling and conducting the meeting with the church board. This meeting shall be scheduled in consultation with the pastor. The review meeting shall be conducted in executive session.

A public and/or printed announcement explaining the purpose of this church board meeting shall be conveyed to the congregation the Sunday before the church board and district superintendent meet for the regular pastoral review.

At this review meeting, the question of continuing the pastoral relationship shall be discussed. The objective is to discover consensus without the need of a formal church board vote. If the church board does not vote to present the question of continuing the pastoral relationship to the church membership, the pastoral relationship will continue.

The church board may vote to present to the church membership the question of continuing the pastoral call. The vote by the board will be by ballot and require a majority of all church board members to carry.

If the church board votes to present the question of continuing the pastoral relationship to the church membership, the matter shall be presented at a church meeting duly called for this purpose and held within 30 days following such action. The question shall be presented, "Shall the present pastoral relationship continue?" The vote shall be by ballot and require a two-thirds majority to carry.

If the church membership votes to continue the pastoral relationship, the pastoral relationship shall continue as though such a vote had not been taken; otherwise, the pastoral relationship shall end on a date set by the district superintendent not less than 30 nor more than 180 days following the vote. If the pastor chooses not to proceed with the vote of the congregation, he or she shall submit a resignation. In such case, the pastoral relationship shall end on a date set by the district superintendent not less than 30 nor more than 180 days following the pastor's decision not to proceed with a congregational vote.

121.1. The chairman of the Board of Tellers shall personally inform the pastor of the results of a pastoral vote before any public announcement is made.

122. Special Pastoral Review. In the interim of regular reviews, in case the district superintendent and the church board shall be of the opinion that the question of the continuance of the pastoral relationship should be submitted to the church, the district superintendent and the church board by a two-thirds majority vote of all its members present may order the question submitted for vote at a special church meeting. The question shall be submitted in the following form: "Shall the present pastoral relationship be continued?" This special pastoral review meeting shall be conducted in executive session. (113.13)

If by a two-thirds vote by ballot of the church members of voting age present and voting the church decides to continue its present pastoral relationship, the term of office of the pastor shall continue as though such vote had not been taken.

If, however, the church fails to decide by such vote to continue the present pastoral relationship, the term of office of the pastor shall terminate on a date, set by the district superintendent, not more than 180 days following the vote. (121-21.1)

123. Local Church in Crisis. When in the opinion of the district superintendent and the District Advisory Board, a local church is in crisis—financial, morale, or otherwise—and this crisis seriously affects the stability and future of the church, *(a)* The question of continued pastoral relationship may be submitted to the local congregation by the district superintendent or a member of the District Advisory Board appointed by the district superintendent as if the church board had requested the vote under paragraph 121, or *(b)* the tenure of a pastor and/or church board may be terminated with the approval of the general superintendent in jurisdiction, and by the majority vote of the District Advisory Board. The district superintendent, with approval of the general superintendent in jurisdiction and the District Advisory Board, may appoint members of the church board for any church that has been declared in crisis.

K. The Church Board

127. Membership. Every local church shall have a church board, composed of the pastor, the Sunday School superintendent, the president of the Nazarene Youth International, the president of the Nazarene World Mission Society (or if the president is the pastor's spouse, and chooses not to serve on the board, the vice president may serve), the stewards, and the trustees of the church, and the members of the Sunday School Ministries Board when elected as the Education Committee of the church board by the annual church meeting. There shall be no more than 25 regular members of the church board. Ordained ministers unassigned by the district are not eligible to serve on the local church board. (39, 113.8-13.10, 136, 141, 146, 152, 154.2)

128. Meetings. The church board takes office at the beginning of the church year and shall have regular meetings within the first 15 days of each calendar month and shall meet specially when called by the pastor, the district superintendent, the secretary only with the approval of the pastor, or the district superintendent when there is no pastor. Between the annual church meeting and the beginning of the church year, the newly elected church board may meet for organization purposes, at which time it shall elect a church secretary and a church treasurer as provided hereafter and any other officer that it shall be their duty to elect. (129.20-130)

129. Business. The **business of the church board** shall be:

129.1. To care for the interests of the church and its work, not otherwise provided for, in harmony with the pastor. (157, 415)

129.2. To nominate to the church, after having consulted with the district superintendent, any elder or licensed minister whom it may deem the proper person to become pastor, provided the nomination be approved by the district superintendent. (115, 208.8)

129.3. To cooperate with an incoming pastor in the development of a written statement of goals and expectations. (115.2)

129.4. To conduct at least once every two years, along with the pastor, a self-study for the purpose of developing a clear understanding of expectations, goals, and performance. (120)

129.5. To arrange for pastoral supply, with approval of the district superintendent, until such time as a pastor shall be regularly called by the church. (209, 421)

129.6. To provide for the development and adoption of an annual budget for the church, all auxiliaries, any daycare/preschool/weekday schools projecting income and expenditures.

129.7. To assign a committee of the board responsibilities for: *(a)* monitoring the church budget, *(b)* reporting to the board on the financial conditions and concerns of the church.

129.8. To determine the amount of compensation the pastor shall receive, and to review it at least once a year. (115.4, 121)

129.9. To provide ways and means for the support of the pastor, the pastoral supply, or any other paid workers of the church; to encourage and support through planning and budgeting the lifelong learning commitment of the pastor and staff. (115.4, 143.3)

129.10. In order to encourage the lifelong learning of the pastor in spiritual, emotional, and educational dimensions, the church board may consider supporting a sabbatical/study leave for the pastor during the seventh consecutive year of service in one congregation.

129.11. To determine the financial support and housing allowance an evangelist should receive and notify the person of such minimum support at the time of the call by the church board.

129.12. To give proper attention to the support of the district superintendent and the general superintendents, in accordance with the authorized plans.

129.13. To license, or renew the license of, at its discretion, any person who has been recommended by the pastor for *(a)* local minister, or *(b)* lay minister. (408.3, 426.1, 426.3)

129.14. To recommend, at its discretion, to the district assembly, upon nomination by the pastor, any person who desires to receive a certificate for any of the assigned roles of ministry, including all lay and ministerial candidates aspiring to be recognized for ministries beyond the local church, if such recommendation is required by the *Manual.*

129.15. To recommend, at its discretion, to the district assembly, upon nomination by the pastor, any person who desires the Licensed Minister's Credential or its renewal. (426.5, 427.1)

129.16. To recommend, at its discretion, to the district assembly, upon nomination by the pastor, renewal of deaconess' license in harmony with 405.

129.17. To elect, upon nomination of the Sunday School Ministries Board, with the approval of the pastor, a director of children's ministries and a director of adult ministries. (146.6)

129.18. To approve the NYI president elected by the NYI organization of the local church, as provided in the NYI Constitution.

129.19. To approve the selection of the administrators of Nazarene daycare/preschool/weekday schools. (153, 208.11, 413.18)

129.20. To elect a secretary at the first meeting of the new board, to serve until the close of the church year and until a successor has been elected and qualified. (113.5, 128, 134.1-34.7)

129.21. To elect a treasurer at the first meeting of the new board, to serve until the close of the church year and until a successor has been elected and qualified. (128, 135.1-35.6)

129.22. To cause careful accounting to be kept of all money received and disbursed by the church, including any weekday schools and all auxiliaries, and make report of the same at its regular monthly meetings and to the annual meeting of the church. (135.3)

129.23. To provide a committee, no fewer than two members of which shall count and account for all money received by the church. (143.3)

129.24. To appoint an auditing committee that shall audit, at least annually, the financial records of the treasurer of the church, the Nazarene Youth International, the Sunday School Ministries Board, Nazarene daycare/preschool/weekday schools, and any other financial records of the church.

129.25. To provide an evangelism and church membership committee of no fewer than three persons. (110)

129.26. To function, if advisable, as the Sunday School Ministries Board in churches of no more than 75 members. (146)

129.27. To appoint a trial committee of five in case written charges are pending against a church member. (504)

129.28. To elect, with the written approval of the district superintendent and upon the nomination of the pastor, such paid assistants as assistant pastors, directors of Christian education, directors of youth work, directors of music, and directors of weekday schools. (152, 161, 208.11)

129.29. To elect a local minister or a licensed minister as an unpaid assistant pastor only if approval is given annually in writing by the district superintendent.

129.30. To provide for a long-range planning committee for the church with the pastor as ex officio chairman.

129.31. To adopt and implement a plan to reduce the risk that individuals placed in positions of authority within the church will use the position of trust or authority to engage in misconduct. The plan for each local church must take into consideration its own unique circumstances.

130. The church board, together with the pastor, shall follow plans adopted by the General Assembly and agreed to by the district assembly for raising World Evangelism Fund and District Ministries Fund apportionments made to the local church, and shall raise and regularly pay these apportionments. (317.12, 333.8)

131. The church board shall perform the duties of a

Sunday School Ministries Board in a newly organized church until such board has been regularly elected. (146)

131.1. The church board and pastor of the newly organized church shall decide when a Sunday School superintendent will be elected. (129.26, 146, 147)

132. The church board may remove from the membership roll the name of an inactive church member after a period of two years has elapsed from the date when his or her name was declared inactive. (112.3)

133. The church board may suspend or revoke the license of any locally credentialed person.

134. Church Secretary. The **duties of the secretary** of the church board are:

134.1. To record correctly and preserve faithfully the minutes of all church meetings and meetings of the church board, and do whatever else may pertain to the office. (119.1, 129.20)

134.2. To present to the annual meeting of the church an annual report of the major activities of the local church, including statistics on membership. (113.7)

134.3. To see that official papers, records, and legal documents pertaining to the local church, including deeds, abstracts, insurance policies, loan documents, church membership rolls, historical records, church board minutes, and incorporation papers are held in trust in either fireproof or secure safes on the local church premises, or when feasible, they may be placed in safe deposit facilities in local banks or similar institutions. Access to such shall always be shared with the pastor and church treasurer, and care for such shall be delivered immediately to the church secretary's successor in office.

134.4. To be the secretary of all annual and special church meetings; and to be custodian of the minutes and other papers of such annual and special church meetings. (113.5)

134.5. To certify in writing to the district superintendent the results of the vote from the calling of a pastor and the continuation of the pastoral relationship. Such certification shall be made within one week of the vote.

134.6. To send to the district superintendent a copy of the minutes of all church meetings and meetings of the church board within three days of such meetings when that local church is without a pastor.

134.7. To sign in conjunction with the pastor all conveyances of real estate, mortgages, releases of mortgage, contracts, and other legal documents not otherwise provided for in the *Manual*. (102.3, 103-4.2)

135. Church Treasurer. The **duties of the treasurer** of the church board are:

135.1. To receive all moneys not otherwise provided for, and disburse the same only on order of the church board. (129.22)

135.2. To make monthly remittances of all district funds to the district treasurer, and of all general funds to the general treasurer, except as otherwise provided. (413.17)

135.3. To keep a correct book record of all funds received and disbursed. (129.22)

135.4. To present a detailed monthly financial report for distribution to the church board. (129.22)

135.5. To present an annual financial report to the annual church meeting. (113.7, 129.22)

135.6. To deliver to the church board the complete treasurer's records at such time as the treasurer shall cease to hold the office.

L. The Stewards

136. The stewards of the church shall be no fewer than 3 nor more than 13 in number. They shall be elected by ballot, at the annual or a special church meeting, from among the members of the church, to serve for the next church year and until their successors have been elected and qualified. (39, 113.6, 113.9, 127)

137. The **duties of the stewards** are:

137.1. To serve as a church growth committee, unless otherwise provided for, with the responsibilities of outreach, evangelism, and extension, including sponsoring new churches and missions, with the pastor as ex officio chairman.

137.2. To provide assistance and support for the needy and distressed. A biblical role of lay leaders is that of ministering in areas of practical service (Acts 6:1-3; Romans 12:6-8). Therefore stewards should offer their time and spiritual gifts in acts of service, administration, encouragement, mercy, visitation, and other ministries.

137.3. To serve, at the discretion of the church board, as the Evangelism and Church Membership Committee as outlined in 110-10.8.

137.4. To assist the pastor in organizing the church so that Christian service opportunities are available to all members. Special attention should be given to the development of ministries toward those of other cultural and socioeconomic backgrounds in the immediate and nearby communities.

137.5. To serve as liaisons to community Christian action and service organizations.

137.6. To give assistance to the pastor in public worship and Christian nurture in the local church.

137.7. To provide the elements for the Lord's Supper, and when requested by the pastor, to assist in the distribution of the same. (34.5, 413.11)

138. For faithfulness in the discharge of their duties the stewards shall be amenable to the local church. They shall make a report to the church at the annual church meeting. (113.7)

139. A vacancy in the office of steward may be filled by the local church at a duly called church meeting. (113.13)

M. The Local Stewardship Committee

140. The stewards shall constitute the Stewardship Committee, whose duty it shall be to promote the cause of Christian stewardship in the local church in cooperation with the pastor and the Stewardship Development Ministries office of the Headquarters Financial office (HFO). (38-38.4)

N. The Trustees

141. The trustees of the church shall be no fewer than three nor more than nine in number. They shall be elected from among the members of the local church to serve for the next church year and until their successors have been elected and qualified. (39, 113.9, 127)

142. In all cases where the civil law requires a specific mode of election of church trustees, that mode shall be strictly followed. (113.3)

142.1. Where no particular mode of election is required by civil law the trustees shall be elected by ballot at the annual meeting of the local church or at a special meeting duly called for that purpose. (113.6, 113.9)

143. The **duties of the trustees** are:

143.1. To hold the title to church property and manage it as trustees of the local church, where the local church is not incorporated, or where the civil law requires it, or where for other reasons it is deemed best by the district superintendent or the District Advisory Board, subject to the guidance and the restrictions as set forth in 102-4.3.

143.2. To give guidance to the development of the physical facilities and to financial planning, unless the church board has provided otherwise.

143.3. To give special attention, under the direction of the church board, to raising money for the support of the church and of the pastor, that he or she may be free from secular care and anxiety and may give full-time attention to the work of the ministry. (129.9, 129.23)

144. For faithfulness to their trust, the trustees shall be amenable to the local church. They shall report to the annual church meeting. In the interim of annual church meetings, they shall make reports to the church board of which they are a part. (102, 104.2, 106.2-6.3, 113.7)

145. A vacancy in the office of trustee may be filled by the local church at a duly called church meeting. (113.13)

O. The Sunday School Ministries Board

146. Each local church shall establish a **Sunday School Ministries Board,** or an **Education Committee** as part of the church board, at the annual church meeting, to be responsible for the Christian education ministries of the church. In churches of 75 members or fewer, the responsibilities may be performed by the church board. Members are: ex officio the Sunday School superintendent (147); the pastor; the NWMS president; the NYI president; children's ministries director; adult ministries director; and three to nine persons elected from the church membership at the annual church meeting. All members shall serve until the close of the next church year and until their successors are elected and qualified. When an elected member vacancy occurs, it may be filled at a duly called church meeting. If a church elects an education committee as part of the church board, it shall follow *Manual* requirements for minimum number of stewards and trustees (136, 141). Ex officio personnel shall be members of the committee, though some may not be members of the church board.

The **duties and powers of the Sunday School Ministries Board or Education Committee** are:

146.1. To plan, organize, promote, and conduct the ministry of Christian education for the local church. This is to be done subject to the direct care of the pastor, and the leadership of the Sunday School superintendent, and the direction of the local church board, in keeping with denominational objectives and standards established by the General Board and promoted through the Sunday School Ministries department and offices of adult, NYI, and children's ministries. These include both curriculum and program-oriented ministries for adults and children. The Sunday School, along with the preaching ministry, provides the core of the church's study of Scripture and doctrine. Weekday and annual/special ministries and training, such as Caravan, Vacation Bible Schools, and singles ministries, provide opportunities through which scriptural doctrines are lived out and integrated into the life of the congregation. (413.23)

146.2. To reach the largest number of unchurched people for Christ and the church, bringing them into the fellowship, teaching the Word of God effectively, and encompassing their salvation; teaching the doctrines of the Christian faith and developing Christlike character, attitudes, and habits; helping to establish Christian homes; preparing believers for membership in the church and equipping them for appropriate Christian ministries.

146.3. To determine the curricula of the various ministries, always using Church of the Nazarene materials to form the basis of biblical study and doctrinal interpretation.

146.4. To plan for and organize the total Sunday School ministry of the local church in keeping with the Sunday School Bylaws. (812)

146.5. To nominate to the annual church meeting one or more persons approved by the pastor, for election to the office of Sunday School superintendent. The nominations are to be made in a meeting with the incumbent superintendent not present.

146.6. To nominate to the church board persons approved by the pastor to serve as a director of children's ministries and a director of adult ministries.

146.7. To elect the children's and adult councils from nominations by the directors of children's and adult ministries with approval of the pastor and the Sunday School superintendent.

146.8. To elect all age-group Sunday School supervisors, teachers, and officers who shall be professing Christians, exemplary in life, and in full harmony with the doctrines and polity of the Church of the Nazarene, from nominations by the NYI president and the directors of children's and adult ministries. The nominees shall be approved by the pastor and the Sunday School superintendent.

146.9. To elect a local director of Continuing Lay Training, who shall organize, promote, and supervise regular training opportunities for Sunday School ministries workers and the entire membership of the church. The Sunday School Ministries Board shall have the option of naming the Continuing Lay Training director as an ex officio member to this board.

146.10. To hold regular meetings; and to organize, by electing a secretary and other officers considered necessary, at the beginning of the Sunday School ministries year, which shall be the same as the church year (114). The pastor or the Sunday School superintendent may call special meetings.

147. The Sunday School Superintendent. The annual church meeting shall elect by majority vote by ballot, of those present and voting, from among its full members, a Sunday School superintendent to serve for one year (39), or until his or her successor is elected. The Sunday School Ministries Board, with the pastor's approval, may call for an incumbent Sunday School superintendent to be elected by a "yes" or "no" vote. A vacancy shall be filled by the local church at a duly called church meeting (113.9, 146.5). The Sunday School superintendent, newly elected, shall be a member ex officio of the district assembly (201), the local church board (127), and the Sunday School Ministries Board (146).

The **duties and powers of the Sunday School superintendent** are:

147.1. To have executive supervision of all Sunday School ministries in the local church.

147.2. To administer the Sunday School in keeping with the Sunday School Bylaws. (812)

147.3. To promote programs of growth in enrollment, attendance, and leadership training.

147.4. To preside over the regular meetings of the Sunday School Ministries Board, or the Education Committee of the church board, and to lead the Sunday School Ministries Board in performing its duties.

147.5. To submit an annual budget for Sunday School ministries to the church board.

147.6. To make a monthly report to the church board and to submit a written report to the annual church meeting.

148. Children/Adult Councils and Directors. The work of Sunday School ministries is best organized by age-groups: children, youth, and adults. For each age-group there should be a council responsible to organize and administer the work. Such council is composed of the age-group director and representatives from the Sunday School and other ministries the church provides for that age-group.

The task of the council is to work with the age-group director to plan ministries for that age-group, and to make provisions for the implementation of those plans. All work of the children's and adult councils is subject to approval of its director and the Sunday School Ministries Board.

The **duties of the age-group directors** are:

148.1. To chair the age-group council that he or she directs and to lead the council in organizing, promoting, and coordinating the total Sunday School ministry for persons within that age-group.

148.2. To give leadership to the appropriate age-group of the Sunday School by promoting programs of growth in enrollment and attendance for children, youth, or adults in the local church, in cooperation with the Sunday School Ministries Board.

148.3. To give leadership for additional Sunday, weekday, annual and special ministries, evangelism and fellowship activities for the age-group he or she represents.

148.4. To nominate to the Sunday School Ministries Board the leadership for the various ministries assigned to his or her age-group, including Sunday School supervisors, teachers, and officers, with exception of NYI who will nominate youth Sunday School supervisors, teachers, and officers (39). The nominees shall be approved by the pastor and the Sunday School superintendent.

148.5. To obtain the approval of the Sunday School Ministries Board before using supplemental curriculum.

148.6. To provide leadership training for age-group workers in cooperation with the Sunday School Ministries Board and the director of Continuing Lay Training.

148.7. To submit an annual budget request to the Sunday School Ministries Board and/or church board, and to administer funds in accordance with such budget approval.

148.8. To receive all reports of the various ministries functioning within the age-groups of the local church under his or her direction. A monthly report of Sunday School enrollment, attendance, and ministry activities shall be submitted to the Sunday School superintendent.

148.9. To submit a quarterly calendar of his or her age-group activities to the Sunday School Ministries Board to be coordinated with the total Sunday School ministry of the local church.

149. Children's Ministries Council. The Children's Ministries Council is responsible for planning the total Sunday School ministry for children from birth to age 12 in the local church. The council is composed of at least one Sunday School representative and the directors of any other children's ministry being offered in the local church, such as: children's church, Caravan, Vacation Bible School, Bible quizzing, missions, Cradle Roll Parents, and any others deemed necessary. The council size will vary with the number of ministries being offered to children in the local church as needs are identified and leadership is available.

The **duties of the children's ministries director** are:

149.1. To perform those duties assigned to all age-group directors in 148.1-48.9.

149.2. To work with the NWMS Executive Committee of the local church in appointing a children's mission director. The person appointed becomes a member of both the NWMS and Children's Ministries councils. Nominees for this position shall be approved by the pastor and the Sunday School superintendent.

150. Adult Ministries Council. The Adult Ministries Council shall be responsible for planning the total Sunday School ministry for adults in the local church. The Adult Ministries Council is composed of at least one Sunday School representative and the directors of any other ministry being offered in the local church, such as: marriage and family life, senior adult ministries, single adult ministries, small-group Bible studies, lay ministries, women's ministries, men's ministries, and any others deemed necessary. The council size will vary with the number of ministries being offered to adults in the local church as needs are identified and leadership is available.

The **duties of the adult ministries director** are:

150.1. To perform those duties assigned to all age-group directors in 148.1-48.9.

P. Nazarene Youth International/NYI Council

151. The NYI Council shall be responsible for planning the ministry for youth age 12 through 23 in the local church, including youth Sunday School. All work of the NYI Council pertaining to Sunday School is subject to approval of its director and the Sunday School Ministries Board.

151.1. The NYI Council shall be composed of a president, vice president, secretary, treasurer, at least one elected representative from each functioning age division, and the appointed directors of any other youth ministry in harmony with the NYI Bylaws. All local NYI officers shall be members of the church where they serve. The council shall be responsible to the local church board.

151.2. The Nazarene Youth International may be organized into age divisions in harmony with the NYI Constitution for the local organization. Other ministries of the NYI are subject to the approval of the pastor and church board. (810)

151.3. Only those persons who are members of the local Church of the Nazarene and who have reached their 12th birthday shall be entitled to vote in NYI presidential elections.

152. NYI President. The president of the local Nazarene Youth International (NYI) shall be nominated by a nominating committee, consisting of not less than three nor more than seven members of the local NYI, including the pastor, and appointed by the pastor. This committee shall submit at least two names for the office of president, providing, however, that a president may be reelected by a "yes" or "no" vote when such election is recommended by the pastor. The president shall be elected by majority vote of the NYI members present, who are also members of the Church of the Nazarene and voting by ballot. His or her election shall be subject to the approval of the church board (129.18). The NYI president, newly elected, shall be a member ex officio of the district assembly (201); the church board, to which he or she shall make a monthly report; and the Sunday School Ministries Board. (113.7, 114, 127)

The **duties of the NYI president** are:

152.1. To perform those duties for youth Sunday School as assigned to all age-group directors in 148.1-48.9.

152.2. To work with the NWMS Executive Committee of the local church in appointing a youth mission director. The person appointed becomes a member of both the NWMS and NYI Ministries councils. Nominees for this position shall be approved by the pastor.

152.3. To report monthly to the local church board and the annual meeting of the local church. (113.7, 127, 152)

Q. Nazarene Daycare/K-12 Schools

153. Nazarene daycare/preschool/elementary, junior high, or high schools may be organized by the local church board(s) after receiving the approval of the district superintendent and the District Advisory Board. The director and school board shall be accountable to the local church board(s). (129.19, 208.11-8.12, 222.11, 413.23, 414)

R. The Local Nazarene World Mission Society

154. Upon the authorization of the church board, local organizations of the Nazarene World Mission Society may be formed within any age-group in harmony with the Constitution of such local societies approved by the World Mission Department. (811.1)

154.1. The local Nazarene World Mission Society shall be a constituent part of the local church and subject to the supervision and direction of the pastor and the church board. (414)

154.2. The president of the local society shall be nominated by a committee of three to seven members of the Nazarene World Mission Society appointed by the pastor, who shall serve as chairman. This committee shall submit one or more names for the office of president. The president shall be elected by a majority vote by ballot of the members (excluding associate) present and voting, and this election shall be subject to the approval of the church board. The president shall be a member of the local church whose society is served, a member ex officio of the church board (or in churches where the president is the pastor's spouse, the vice president may serve on the church board), and a member of the district assembly held immediately prior to his or her year of office. The president shall present a report to the annual meeting of the local church. (113.7, 114, 127, 201)

155. All funds raised by the local society for general interests of the Church of the Nazarene shall be applied to the World Evangelism Fund apportionment of the local church with the exception of offerings for Alabaster, World Mission Radio, Memorial Roll, Distinguished Service Award, Medical Plan, and Missionary Christmas Fund.

155.1. The Medical Plan is to be held in trust by the general treasurer for the General Council of the Nazarene World Mission Society, to be used for medical assistance for active and retired missionaries, such assistance to be granted by the World Mission Department according to the established policy. Funds shall be raised by placing of names on the Memorial Roll, the Distinguished Service Award, and offerings.

155.2. After primary consideration has been given to the full payment of the World Evangelism Fund, opportunities may be given to make offerings for the support of world missionary work, such contributions to be known as "specials."

156. Funds for the support of general interests shall be raised in the following manners:

156.1. From gifts and offerings designated for the World Evangelism Fund and general interests.

156.2. From special offerings such as Easter and Thanksgiving.

156.3. No part of the above funds shall be used for local or district expense or charitable purposes.

S. Prohibition of Financial Appeals

157. It shall not be lawful for a local church, its officers, or members, to send appeals to other local churches, their officers, and members, to solicit money or financial assistance for their local church needs or for the interests that they may support. It is provided, however, that such solicitation may be made to local churches and church members located within the bounds of the assembly district in which the solicitor is located, but only on condition that the solicitation be approved in writing by the district superintendent and the District Advisory Board.

158. Members of the Church of the Nazarene who are not authorized by the General Board or one of its departments shall not solicit funds for missionary or kindred activities apart from the World Evangelism Fund, from congregations of local churches, or from members of such churches.

T. Use of the Church Name

159. The name of the Church of the Nazarene, any local church, or any corporation or institution that is a part or in any manner affiliated with the Church of the Nazarene, or any part of any such name, shall not be used by any members of the Church of the Nazarene nor any one or more members thereof, or by any corporation, partnership, association, group, or other entity in connection with any activity (whether of a commercial, social, educational, charitable, or other nature) without the prior written approval of the General Board of the Church of the Nazarene and the Board of General Superintendents, provided, however, that this provision shall not apply to such activities of the Church of the Nazarene as are authorized by its official *Manual*.

U. Church-sponsored Corporation

160. No local church, local church board, district corporation, district board, nor any two or more members of any of them, acting individually or otherwise, shall directly or indirectly form or become members of any corporation, association, partnership, group, or other entity that promotes, sponsors, encourages, or in any manner engages in any activity (whether of a commercial, social, educational, charitable, or other nature) in which members of the Church of the

Nazarene are solicited or in any manner sought as prospective participants, customers, tenants, clients, members, or associates, or in any activity (whether of a commercial, social, educational, charitable, or other nature) that directly or indirectly purports to be sponsored or operated primarily or exclusively by or for the benefit or service of members of the Church of the Nazarene, without the express prior written consent of the district superintendent and the District Advisory Board.

V. Assistants in the Local Church

161. There may be those who feel called to prepare themselves for certain vital lay services in the church, either part-time or full-time. The church recognizes the place of such lay workers, and yet it is basically constituted a voluntary institution, with service to God and others the duty and privilege of all its members according to their abilities. When paid assistants in the local church, or any subsidiary and/or affiliated corporations of the local congregation, whether ministerial or lay, become necessary for greater efficiency, it must be such as will not devitalize the spirit of free service by all its members or tax the church's financial resources including the payment of all financial apportionments. However, a request may be made in writing for review by the district superintendent and District Advisory Board for exceptions in special cases. (129.28)

161.1. All local assistants, paid or unpaid, such as assistant pastors, directors of Christian education, directors of youth work, directors of music, and directors of weekday schools, shall be elected by the church board, having been nominated by the pastor. All nominations must have approval in writing by the district superintendent, who shall respond within 15 days after receipt of the request. (161.4, 208.11)

161.2. The employment of such assistants shall be for no more than one year and may be renewed upon recommendation of the pastor with the written approval of the district superintendent and the favorable vote of the church board.

The senior pastor shall be responsible to conduct an annual review of each staff member. The pastor, in consultation with the church board, may make recommendations for staff development or modifications in job description as indicated by the review. The dismissal of such assistants prior to the end of the employment term must be by recommendation of the pastor, approval of the district superintendent, and the majority vote of the church board. (129.28)

161.3. The duties and services of such assistants are to be determined and supervised by the pastor. A clear, written statement of responsibilities (job description) shall be made available to such assistants within 30 days of the beginning of their responsibility to the local church.

161.4. No paid employee of the church shall be eligible for election to the church board. If a church board member should become a paid employee of the church, he or she shall not remain a member of the church board.

161.5. Upon the resignation or termination of the pastor, the staff members of a local church, or the chief executive officer of any subsidiary and/or affiliated corporations of the local congregation, paid and unpaid, such as assistant pastors, directors of Christian education, directors of youth work, and directors of music, shall submit their resignations effective concurrently with the resignation or termination of the pastor. However, one or more of these associates may remain longer with the written approval of the district superintendent and the local church board, but no longer than the date of the new pastor's assumption of duties. Directors of day schools shall submit their resignations effective at the end of the school year in which the new pastor assumes the duties of the office. The chief executive officer of any subsidiary and/or affiliated corporation shall submit his or her resignation at the end of that contractual period in which the new pastor assumes the duties of the office. The incoming pastor may have the privilege of recommending the employment of staff members previously employed.

161.6. Communication with staff members, the church board, and the congregation regarding the effect of 161.5 on staff members at the time of pastoral change shall be the responsibility of the district superintendent. (208.11)

161.7. The pastor of a congregation having approval to function as a local church according to 100.1 shall not be considered a staff member.

161.8. Any person serving as paid staff would be ineligible to be called as pastor to the church of which he or she is a member without approval of the District Advisory Board. (115)

CHAPTER II

THE DISTRICT ASSEMBLY

A. Bounds and Name

200. The General Assembly shall organize the membership of the church into districts.

The bounds and name of a church assembly district shall be such as shall be declared by the General Assembly, or by the assembly district involved, with the final approval of the general superintendent or superintendents having jurisdiction. (30)

200.1. The Creation of New Districts. New districts in the Church of the Nazarene may be created by:

1. The division of one district into two or more districts
2. The combination of two or more districts out of which a larger number of districts may be created
3. The formation of a new district in an area not encompassed by any existing district, or
4. The merger of two or more districts (30, 200)

200.2. Work in the Church of the Nazarene may lead to the establishment of new districts and district assembly boundaries. Phase 3 districts may emerge as quickly as possible according to the following pattern:

Phase 1. A Phase 1 district shall be designated when opportunity for entry into a new area is presented, within guidelines for strategic development and evangelism. Requests may be made by a regional director, a district through the Regional Advisory Council, or the sponsoring district superintendent and/or District Advisory Board.

A Phase 1 district superintendent in regions related to the World Mission Division shall be recommended by the regional director, in consultation with the division director, to the general superintendent having jurisdiction who shall appoint. The region shall give guidance to the Phase 1 district regarding resources available for development. In other regions, the district superintendent shall be appointed by the general superintendent in jurisdiction after consultation with the district superintendent(s) and Advisory Board(s) of the sponsoring district(s).

Phase 2. A Phase 2 district may be designated when a sufficient number of fully organized churches and ordained elders, and a district infrastructure of adequate maturity exists to recommend such designation.

Such designation will be by the Board of General Superintendents upon recommendation of the general superintendent in jurisdiction after consultation with the division director, regional director, and other individuals and boards involved in the appointment of the district superintendent. A district superintendent will be elected or appointed.

Quantifiable guidelines would be a minimum of 10 organized churches, 500 full members, and 5 ordained elders. A District Advisory Board or national board may request the general superintendent in jurisdiction for an exception to these criteria. A minimum of 50 percent of district administration expense shall be generated by district ministries fund income at the time of designation.

Phase 3. A Phase 3 district may be declared when a sufficient number of fully organized churches, ordained elders, and members exist to warrant such designation. Leadership, infrastructure, budgetary responsibility, and doctrinal integrity must be demonstrated. A Phase 3 district must be able to shoulder these burdens and share the challenges of the Great Commission within the global scope of an international church.

Quantifiable criteria include a minimum of 20 organized churches, 1,000 full members, and 10 ordained elders. A District Advisory Board or national board may request to the general superintendent in jurisdiction for an exception to these criteria.

A Phase 3 district must be 100 percent self-supporting in regard to district administration. The district superintendent shall be elected by the district assembly under provision of the *Manual*.

Phase 3 districts are an integral part of their respective regions. In regions having a regional director, the general superintendent in jurisdiction may enlist the assistance of the regional director to facilitate communication with and supervision of the district.

200.3. Criteria for District Division or District Boundary Changes. A proposal for district development or district boundary changes developed by a regional office, a national board, or a District Advisory Board may be presented to the general superintendent in jurisdiction. Such a plan should take into consideration:

1. That the proposed new districts have population centers that justify the creation of such districts
2. That lines of communication and transportation are available to facilitate the work of the districts
3. That a sufficient number of mature elders and lay leaders are available for the work of the district
4. That the sponsoring districts will have, in every case possible, sufficient district ministries fund income to maintain their Phase 3 district status
5. That the sponsoring districts will have, in every case possible, sufficient membership and organized churches to maintain their Phase 3 district status

200.4. A recommendation to establish a new district shall be submitted to the general superintendent(s) in jurisdiction. The district superintendent(s) and District Advisory Board(s) or national board(s) may approve and refer the matter to the district assembly/assemblies for vote with the approval of the general superintendent(s) in jurisdiction and the Board of General Superintendents.

200.5. If any or all of the district assemblies involved fail to act, or if the actions of the several district assemblies are in disagreement, the recommendation may be submitted to the next General Assembly for action, if requested by a two-thirds majority of the affected District Advisory Boards.

B. Membership and Time of Meeting

201. Membership. The district assembly shall be composed of all assigned elders (429-29.3, 430-30.1, 433.9); all assigned deacons (428-28.4, 433.9); all assigned licensed ministers (427.9); all retired assigned ministers (431-31.1); the district secretary (216.2); the district treasurer (219.2); chairpersons of standing district committees reporting to the district assembly; any lay presidents of Nazarene institutions of higher education, whose local church membership is on the district; the District Sunday School Ministries chairman (242.2); the district age-group ministries directors (children and adult); the District Sunday School Ministries Board; the president of the District Nazarene Youth International (243.2); the president of the District Nazarene World Mission Society (244.2); the newly elected superintendent or vice superintendent of each local Sunday School Ministries Board (147); the newly elected president or vice president of each local Nazarene Youth International (152); the newly elected president or vice president of each local Nazarene World Mission Society (154.2); or an appropriately elected alternate may represent these organizations in the district assembly; those serving in assigned roles of ministry according to 402-23.1; the lay members of the District Advisory Board (221.3); all retired assigned lay career missionaries whose local church membership is on the district; and the lay delegates from each local church in the assembly district. (30, 113.12, 201.1-1.2)

201.1. Local churches in districts of fewer than 5,000 full church members shall be entitled to representation in the district assembly as follows: two lay delegates from each local church of 50 or fewer full church members, and one additional lay delegate for each successive 50 full church members and the final major part of 50 full church members. (30, 113.12, 201)

201.2. Local churches in districts of 5,000 or more full church members shall be entitled to representation in the district assembly as follows: one lay delegate from each local church of 50 or fewer full church members, and one additional lay delegate for each successive 50 full church members and the final major part of 50 full church members. (30, 113.12, 201)

202. Time. The district assembly shall be held annually, at the time appointed by the general superintendent having jurisdiction, and in the place designated by the preceding district assembly or arranged for by the district superintendent.

202.1. Nominating Committee. Prior to the convening of the district assembly, the district superintendent in consultation with the District Advisory Board shall appoint a nominating committee to serve the district assembly; this committee may prepare nominations for the usual committees and offices in advance of the convening of the district assembly. (212.2)

C. Business of the District Assembly

203. The **business of the district assembly** shall be:

203.1. To hear or receive reports from all ordained and licensed ministers serving as pastors or commissioned evangelists; and to consider the character of all elders, deacons, and deaconesses. By vote of the district assembly the record of written reports received by the secretary may be accepted in place of oral reports of all other elders, deacons, deaconesses, and licensed ministers not engaged in active service, and those ministers having district certificates for all roles of ministry in 402-23.1. (418, 427.9, 433.9)

203.2. To license as licensed ministers, after careful examination, persons who have been recommended by church boards or the District Advisory Board and who may be judged to be called to the ministry and to renew such license upon favorable recommendation of the Ministerial Credentials Board. (129.15, 426.5, 427.1, 427.3)

203.3. To renew as licensed deaconesses, after careful examination, persons who have been recommended by church boards and who may be judged to be called to the office of deaconess upon favorable recommendation of the Ministerial Credentials Board. (129.16)

203.4. To elect to the order of elder, or to the order of deacon, persons judged to have fulfilled all the requirements for such orders of ministry upon favorable recommendation of the Ministerial Credentials Board. (428.3, 429.3)

203.5. To recognize the orders of ministry and credentials of persons coming from other denominations who may be judged qualified and desirable for placement in the Church of the Nazarene upon favorable recommendation of the Ministerial Credentials Board. (427.2, 430-30.2)

203.6. To receive, by transfer from other districts, persons having ministerial credentials, members of the clergy, and those having commissions for continuing ministry roles, in harmony with 405-9.1, including interim transfers approved by the District Advisory Board, who may be judged as desirable for membership in the district assembly upon favorable recommendation of the Ministerial Credentials Board. (228.9-28.10, 432-32.2)

203.7. To issue a transfer of members of the clergy, and those having commissions for continuing ministry roles according to 405-9.1, including interim transfers approved by the District Advisory Board, who desire to transfer to another district upon favorable recommendation of the Ministerial Credentials Board. (228.9-28.10, 432-32.1)

203.8. To commission or register for one year those persons deemed qualified for the roles of ministry named and defined in 402-23.1 upon favorable recommendation of the Ministerial Credentials Board.

203.9. To elect, by two-thirds favorable vote, by ballot, an elder to the office of district superintendent, to serve until 30 days following the final adjournment of the second district assembly following his or her election and until a successor is elected or appointed and qualified. The procedure for reelection of a district superintendent shall be by a "yes" or "no" ballot vote. No elder shall be considered eligible for election to this office who has at any time surrendered his or her credentials for disciplinary reasons. No superintendent shall serve beyond 30 days following the district assembly after his or her 70th birthday.

203.10. After a district superintendent of a Phase 2 or Phase 3 district (200.2) has served a district for at least two assembly years, the district assembly may reelect said superintendent for a period of four years subject to the approval of the general superintendent in jurisdiction. The procedure for election to an extended term of office shall be by a two-thirds favorable "yes" or "no" ballot.

203.11. In case the general superintendent and the officers of the district, namely, the District Advisory Board, chairman of the District Sunday School Ministries Board, president of the district NWMS, president of the district NYI, the district secretary, and the district treasurer, shall be of the opinion that the services of the district superintendent should not continue beyond the current year, the general superintendent having jurisdiction and the district officers may order the question submitted for a vote of the district assembly. The question shall be submitted in the following form: "Shall the present district superintendent be continued in office beyond this district assembly?"

If the district assembly, by a two-thirds vote by ballot, decides to continue the district superintendent in office, he or she shall continue to serve as though such vote had not been taken.

If, however, the district assembly fails to decide by such vote to continue the district superintendent in office, his or her term of office shall terminate 30 days following the close of that district assembly. (204.2, 206)

203.12. To elect, by ballot, up to three ordained ministers and up to three laypersons to the District Advisory Board, to serve for a term not to exceed four years, as determined by the district assembly, and until their successors are elected and qualified.

However, when the district exceeds a total membership of 5,000, it may elect one additional ordained minister and one additional layperson for each successive 2,500 members and the final major part of 2,500 members. (221)

203.13. To elect a District Ministerial Credentials Board of not less than 5 nor more than 15 ordained ministers, one of whom shall be the district superintendent, to serve for four years and until their successors are elected and qualified. This board shall meet prior to the district assembly to consider all matters subject to its authority and, insofar as is possible, to complete its work prior to the district assembly. (226-28.10)

203.14. To elect a District Ministerial Studies Board of five or more ordained ministers, to serve for four years and until their successors are elected and qualified. (229)

203.15. To facilitate greater flexibility on districts in the use of the most appropriate persons for specific assignments in preparing candidates for ordination, districts may elect the total number necessary to serve on both the District Ministerial Credentials Board and the District Ministerial Studies Board as a District Board of Ministry.

At the first meeting of this District Board of Ministry, the district superintendent may organize the group into a Ministerial Credentials Board and a Ministerial Studies Board, a Rehabilitation Committee, and any other committees that may be deemed wise. (226, 229)

203.16. To elect a District Church Properties Board in keeping with provisions of 234. (204.1)

203.17. To elect at its discretion either or both of the following: (1) a District Evangelism Board of no less than six members including the district superintendent, (2) a district director of evangelism. The persons elected shall serve until the final adjournment of the next district assembly and until their successors are elected and qualified. (204.1, 212)

203.18. To elect a District Sunday School Ministries Board in harmony with the procedure stated in 239, to serve until their successors are elected and qualified. (204.1, 212)

203.19. To elect a District Home Missions Board, of equal lay and ministerial membership, of no fewer than 6 nor more than 18, not including the district superintendent, who shall be a member ex officio, to serve until the next district assembly and until their successors are elected and qualified; however, the district assembly may order that the

District Advisory Board may constitute the District Home Missions Board. (233)

203.20. To elect a District Assembly Finance Committee of equal lay and ministerial representation to serve the following district assembly until its final adjournment. The district superintendent and district treasurer shall be members ex officio. (237-37.2)

203.21. To elect a District Court of Appeals, consisting of five ordained ministers, including the district superintendent, to serve for a term not to exceed four years and until their successors are elected and qualified. (509)

203.22. To elect, by ballot, at a session within 16 months of the meeting of the General Assembly, or within 24 months in areas where travel visas or other unusual preparations are necessary, all of the lay delegates and all but one of the ministerial delegates, since one shall be the district superintendent. Every Phase 3 district assembly shall be entitled to representation at the General Assembly by an equal number of ministerial and lay delegates. The district superintendent at the time of the General Assembly shall be one of the ministerial delegates, and the remaining ministerial delegates shall be ordained ministers. In case the district superintendent is unable to attend, or in case there has been a vacancy and the new district superintendent has not been appointed, the properly elected alternate shall be seated in the district superintendent's place. The Nominating Committee shall submit ballots containing at least three times the number of delegates eligible from that district, in each category, ministerial and lay. From these nominees, the allowed delegates and alternates shall be elected according to paragraphs 301.1-1.3. Delegates elected are expected to attend faithfully all meetings of the General Assembly from opening to closing unless providentially prevented. (31.1-31.3, 301.1-1.3, 303, 330)

203.23. To establish, at its discretion, a system of associate membership for its local churches, but associate members must not be counted as full members for purposes of representation.

203.24. To provide for the auditing of all district treasurers' books annually, either by an elected District Auditing Committee or by an auditing firm or certified public accountant.

203.25. To present to the General Assembly, through the district secretary, a full official journal for the preceding quadrennium, to be preserved and filed. (205.4-5.5, 217.7)

203.26. To grant a retired relation to a minister upon recommendation of the District Ministerial Credentials Board. Any change in status must be approved by the district assembly, upon recommendation by the District Ministerial Credentials Board. (228.8, 431)

203.27. To consider and care for the entire work of the Church of the Nazarene within the bounds of the assembly district.

203.28. To transact any other business pertaining to the work, not otherwise provided for, in harmony with the spirit and order of the Church of the Nazarene.

204. Other Rules Pertaining to the District Assemblies. The district assembly may authorize, where civil law permits, the District Advisory Board to incorporate. After incorporation as above provided, the District Advisory Board shall have power, on its own resolution, to purchase, own, sell, exchange, mortgage, deed in trust, hypothecate, lease, and convey any property, real and personal, as may be necessary or convenient for the purpose of the corporation. (222.5)

204.1. As far as possible membership of district boards and committees shall be equal between ministers and laypersons unless specifically provided otherwise by the *Manual*.

204.2. The **district superintendents of Phase 1 and Phase 2 districts** shall be chosen in accordance with *Manual* paragraph 200.2. A Phase 2 district may revert to Phase 1 district status until such time as it can meet the requirements for Phase 2 status.

204.3. When the presiding officer of a district assembly deems that it is impossible to continue with the business of the district assembly and therefore adjourns the district assembly, because of uncontrollable physical disaster or local disturbance, the general superintendent in jurisdiction, in consultation with the Board of General Superintendents, shall appoint all district officers not elected prior to the adjournment of the district assembly, to serve for a period of one year.

D. The District Assembly Journal

205. The journal shall be the record of the regular proceedings of the district assembly.

205.1. The journal shall be signed by the presiding officer and the district secretary.

205.2. The journal must be either written or typewritten manuscript, or printed, and substantially bound.

205.3. Separate items of business shall be placed in separate paragraphs.

205.4. The journal should be edited carefully with the view to its examination by the General Assembly. (203.25, 217.7)

205.5. The full official journal for each quadrennium shall be preserved and filed with the district and the General Assembly files. (217.5, 217.7)

205.6. The journal shall be arranged as far as possible according to the table of contents prepared by the general secretary in consultation with the Board of General Superintendents. The table of contents shall be furnished to the district secretary prior to the convening of the district assembly.

205.7. The journal should contain not only the assignment of pastors to local churches but also all regular and special engagements entered into by ministerial and lay members of the district assembly who are engaged in any line of denominational service that would entitle them to consideration if applying for benefits from the Pensions Board having the responsibility for the pensions and benefits program of that district. (115)

E. The District Superintendent

206. The initial term of office for a district superintendent who is elected at a district assembly begins 30 days after the adjournment of the district assembly. It runs for two full assembly years ending 30 days after the adjournment of the assembly that marks the second anniversary of the election. At the time of said assembly the superintendent may be reelected (203.10) or a successor elected or appointed and qualified. The initial term of office for a district superintendent who is appointed by the general superintendent in jurisdiction begins at the time of the appointment, includes the remainder of the church year in which the superintendent was appointed, and extends through the two following church years. The term of office ends 30 days after the adjournment of the assembly that marks the end of the second full assembly year of service. At said assembly the superintendent may be elected (203.10) for another term, or a successor will be elected or appointed and qualified. (203.9-3.11)

207. If for any cause a vacancy shall occur in the interim of sessions of the district assembly, the general superintendents, jointly and severally, may fill the vacancy, upon consultation with a committee composed of the District Advisory Board, the chairman of the District Sunday School Ministries Board, the presidents of the District NWMS and NYI, the district secretary, and the district treasurer. (307.6)

207.1. In the event of temporary incapacitation of an incumbent district superintendent, the general superintendent having jurisdiction, in consultation with the District Advisory Board, may appoint a qualified elder to serve as interim district superintendent. The question of incapacitation shall be determined by the general superintendent in jurisdiction and the District Advisory Board. (307.7)

208. The **duties of a district superintendent** are:

208.1. To organize, recognize, and supervise local churches within the bounds of his or her assembly district, subject to the approval of the general superintendent having jurisdiction. (100, 307.8, 433.12)

208.2. To be available to the local churches in his or her assembly district as needed, and as necessary meet with the church board to consult with reference to spiritual, financial, and pastoral matters, giving such helpful advice and assistance as the superintendent may deem proper.

208.3. To schedule and conduct, with each local church board, the regular pastoral review according to the provisions of 121.

208.4. To have special supervision of all the missions of the Church of the Nazarene within the bounds of his or her assembly district.

208.5. To appoint someone to fill a vacancy, should one occur in the office of district secretary. (216.1)

208.6. To nominate to the District Advisory Board someone to fill a vacancy, should one occur in the office of district treasurer. (219.1)

208.7. To appoint a district chaplaincy director to promote and amplify holiness evangelism through the specialized ministry of chaplaincy. (238)

208.8. To consult with the church board concerning the nomination of an elder or a licensed minister to pastor a local church and to approve or disapprove such nomination. (115, 129.2, 161.8)

208.9. To schedule a special pastoral review (122), within 90 days of the request of a church board for such review, on the continuance of the pastoral relationship.

208.10. To approve or disapprove the granting of license to any member of the Church of the Nazarene who may request local minister's license or renewal of local minister's license from the church board of a local church not having an elder as pastor. (426.1, 426.3)

208.11. To approve or disapprove in writing requests from the pastor and the local church board to employ any paid local assistants (such as assistant pastors; ministers or directors of Christian education, children, youth, adult, music, weekday schools, etc.). The primary criteria for the district superintendent's decisions to approve or disapprove, in concept, the hiring of staff will be the willingness and ability of the church to meet its local, district, and general obligations. It is the senior pastor's responsibility to screen and select pastoral assistants. However, the district superintendent shall have the right to disapprove the nominee. (129.28, 161-61.8)

208.12. To approve or disapprove, with the District Advisory Board, requests from local churches to operate Christian day school programs. (153, 222.11, 414)

208.13. To execute and sign, along with the secretary of the District Advisory Board, all legal documents of the district. (222.5)

208.14. To nominate to the District Advisory Board and to supervise any paid assistants on the district. (246)

208.15. To appoint pastors in keeping with 116.

208.16. The district superintendent may, with the approval of the District Advisory Board, appoint the members of the church board (stewards, trustees), the chairman of the Sunday School Ministries Board, and other church officers (secretary, treasurer) if a church has been organized for less than five years, or has less than 35 voting members, or is receiving regular financial assistance from the district, or has been declared in crisis. (123)

208.17. To cause to be investigated written accusations against a minister in his or her assembly district, according to 505-5.3.

208.18. The district superintendent shall schedule and conduct a self-assessment and review in consultation with the tenured evangelist in accordance with paragraph 407.4.

209. The district superintendent, with the consent of the church board, may appoint a pastoral supply to fill a vacancy in the office of pastor until the next district assembly. Such appointed pastoral supply shall be subject to removal by the district superintendent when his or her services are not satisfactory to the church board and the local church. (129.5, 421, 426.6)

210. The district superintendent is authorized to perform for a local church within the bounds of his or her assembly district all the functions of pastor when that local church is without a pastor or pastoral supply. (412)

210.1. The district superintendent may preside at the annual, or a special meeting of a local church, or appoint a surrogate for such duty. (113.4)

211. If for any reason the general superintendent having jurisdiction fails to be present or to appoint a representative to be present in his or her stead at the district assembly, the district superintendent shall call the district assembly to order and shall preside until other provision may be made by the district assembly. (307.4)

212. The district superintendent may fill vacancies in the District Home Missions Board (203.19), the District Assembly Finance Committee (203.20), the District Auditing Committee (203.24), the District Ministerial Credentials Board (226.1), the District Ministerial Studies Board (229.1), the District Evangelism Board or the district director of evangelism (232), the District Church Properties Board (234), the District Sunday School Ministries Board (239), and the District Court of Appeals (509).

212.1. The district superintendent may appoint all chairmen and secretaries of the district boards and standing committees where such are not provided in the *Manual* or by assembly action.

212.2. The district superintendent, in consultation with the District Advisory Board, shall appoint a nominating committee to prepare nominations for the usual committees and offices in advance of the district assembly. (202.1)

213. The district superintendent shall be ex officio chairman of the District Advisory Council (245), the District Advisory Board (221.2), and the District Ministerial Credentials Board (227.1).

213.1. The district superintendent shall be a member ex officio of the District Sunday School Ministries Board, the District Home Missions Board, the District Church Properties Board, the District Assembly Finance Committee, the council of the District Nazarene Youth International, and the council of the District Nazarene World Mission Society. (203.18-3.20, 234, 239, 810, 811.2)

214. All official acts of the district superintendent shall be subject to review and revision by the district assembly, and subject to appeal. (510.3)

214.1. The district superintendent shall always show due regard for the advice of the general superintendent in jurisdiction and the Board of General Superintendents with regard to pastoral arrangements and other matters relating to the office of the district superintendent.

F. The District Secretary

216. The district secretary, elected by the District Advisory Board, shall serve for a period of one to three years and until his or her successor is elected and qualified. (222.15)

216.1. If the district secretary shall cease to serve, for any cause, in the interim of sessions of the district assembly, the district superintendent shall appoint someone to succeed him or her. (208.5)

216.2. The district secretary shall be a member ex officio of the district assembly. (201)

217. The **duties of the district secretary** are:

217.1. To record correctly and preserve faithfully all minutes of the district assembly.

217.2. To record correctly and preserve all statistics of the district.

217.3. To forward all statistical charts to the general secretary to be audited before their publication in the official journal. (324.6)

217.4. To be custodian of all documents of the district assembly, and turn them over promptly to his or her successor.

217.5. To preserve and file the full official journal for each quadrennium. (205.5)

217.6. To forward sufficient copies of the printed journal of each district assembly to General Headquarters for distribution among the general officers and general boards of the Church of the Nazarene.

217.7. To present to the General Assembly, for the district assembly, the full official journal for the preceding quadrennium to be preserved and filed. (203.25, 205.4-5.5)

217.8. To do whatever else may pertain to his or her office.

217.9. To refer all items of business coming to him or her during the year to the proper assembly committee or standing board.

218. The district secretary may have as many assistants as the district assembly shall elect.

G. The District Treasurer

219. The district treasurer, elected by the District Advisory Board, shall serve until the final adjournment of the next district assembly and until his or her successor is elected and qualified. (222.14)

219.1. If the district treasurer shall cease to serve, for any cause, in the interim of sessions of the district assembly, the District Advisory Board shall elect his or her successor upon nomination by the district superintendent. (208.6)

219.2. The district treasurer shall be a member ex officio of the district assembly. (201)

220. The **duties of the district treasurer** are:

220.1. To receive all such moneys from his or her district as may be designated by the General Assembly, or by the district assembly, or by the District Advisory Board, or as the needs of the Church of the Nazarene may require, and disburse the same according to the direction and policies of the district assembly and/or the District Advisory Board.

220.2. To keep a correct record of all moneys received and disbursed and to render a monthly report to the district superintendent for distribution to the District Advisory Board and an annual report to the district assembly, to which he or she shall be amenable.

H. The District Advisory Board

221. The District Advisory Board shall be composed of the district superintendent ex officio and up to three ordained ministers and up to three laypersons elected by ballot by the district assembly annually or for terms not to exceed four years, to serve until the final adjournment of the next district assembly and until their successors are elected and qualified. However, their terms of service may be staggered by electing a proportion of the board annually.

When a district exceeds a total membership of 5,000, it may elect one additional ordained minister and one additional layperson for each successive 2,500 members or the final major part of 2,500 members. (203.12)

221.1. A vacancy on the District Advisory Board may be filled by the remaining members thereof.

221.2. The district superintendent shall be ex officio chairman of the District Advisory Board.

221.3. The lay members of the District Advisory Board shall be ex officio members of the district assembly, ex officio members of the district Sunday School Ministries convention, ex officio members of the district NWMS convention, and ex officio members of the district NYI convention. (201, 221)

222. The **duties of the District Advisory Board** are:

222.1. To set the date for the beginning and closing of the statistical year in harmony with the provisions of 114.1.

222.2. To give information to and consult with the district superintendent respecting the ministers and local churches of the assembly district. (416)

222.3. To appoint an investigating committee consisting of three or more ordained ministers in case an accusation is filed against a member of the clergy. (505-5.3)

222.4. To select a trial court in case charges are made against a member of the clergy. (505.5-5.6)

222.5. To incorporate, where civil law permits and when authorized by the district assembly. After incorporation, as above provided, the District Advisory Board shall have power, on its own resolution, to purchase, own, sell, exchange, mortgage, deed in trust, hypothecate, lease, and convey any property, real and personal, as may be necessary or convenient for the purpose of the corporation. The district superintendent and the secretary of the District Advisory Board, or other persons authorized by the District Advisory Board, incorporated or not incorporated, shall execute and sign all conveyances on real estate, mortgages, releases of mortgages, contracts, and other legal documents of the District Advisory Board. (204)

222.6. In states where the civil law does not permit such incorporation, then the district assembly may elect the District Advisory Board as district trustee with power, on its own resolution, to purchase, own, sell, exchange, mortgage, deed in trust, hypothecate, lease, and convey any property, real and personal, as may be necessary or convenient for the purpose of carrying on its work in the district. (106.2, 222.5)

222.7. The District Advisory Board, in states where it is possible for local churches to incorporate, shall, with the advice of competent legal counsel, provide pattern incorporation forms adequate for the state or states of its district. This pattern incorporation form shall always include the provisions set forth in 102-2.5.

222.8. To serve in an advisory capacity to the district superintendent in his or her supervision of all the departments, boards, and committees of the district.

222.9. To submit to the Board of General Superintendents any plans proposed for the creation of a district center. Such plans shall require the approval in writing of the Board of General Superintendents before they are put in operation. (319)

222.10. To recommend the renewal of license for the licensed minister serving as pastor. (427.5)

222.11. To approve or disapprove requests from local churches to operate Christian day school programs. At the discretion of the district superintendent and the District Advisory Board, a District Christian Day Schools Committee may be established. Its function shall be to recommend policy, procedures, and philosophy to the District Advisory Board for application in the local church day school, and to help establish, support, and monitor such weekday schools. (153, 208.12, 414)

222.12. To elect or dismiss any paid assistants employed by the district. (246-46.1)

222.13. To protect all district property, real or personal, including all equity therein, from being diverted to any personal or corporate use other than for the Church of the Nazarene. (102.4, 204)

222.14. To elect a district treasurer annually. (219)

222.15. To elect a district secretary, to serve for a period of one to three years and until his or her successor is elected and qualified. (216)

223. The District Advisory Board may issue a transfer of membership to a member of the clergy, a minister of Christian education (409), or a deaconess (405), who desires to transfer to another district assembly, before the meeting of the district assembly in which such person's membership is held. Such transfers may be accepted by the receiving District Advisory Board, granting to those transferred full rights and privileges of membership on the district on which it is received. The receiving district assembly shall have final approval of all such Advisory Board transfer receptions upon favorable recommendation by the Ministerial Credentials Board. (203.6-3.7, 228.9-28.10, 432-32.2)

223.1. The District Advisory Board may, upon request, issue a Certificate of Commendation (813.2) to a member of the district assembly who wishes to unite with another denomination.

224. The District Advisory Board, with the approval of the district superintendent, may suspend a licensed deaconess when it is required for the good of the church, after a conference with the church board of the local church of which the licensed deaconess is a member, and after giving her a fair hearing.

225. In case a licensed or ordained minister presenting credentials from another evangelical denomination shall, during the interim of sessions of the district assembly, make application to unite with the Church of the Nazarene, his or her credentials shall be examined by the District Advisory Board. Only with the favorable recommendation of the District Advisory Board shall such applicant be received into membership in the local church. (417, 427.2, 430)

I. The District Ministerial Credentials Board

226. The District Ministerial Credentials Board shall be composed of not less than 5 nor more than 15 ordained ministers, one of whom shall be the district superintendent. They shall serve for a period of four years and until their successors are elected and qualified. However, their terms of service may be staggered by electing a proportion of the board annually. (203.13)

226.1. A vacancy occurring in the Ministerial Credentials Board in the interim of the district assemblies may be filled by appointment by the district superintendent. (212)

227. Following the election of the Ministerial Credentials Board the district superintendent shall call a meeting of the board for organization as follows:

227.1. The district superintendent shall serve as chairman ex officio of the board; however, upon his or her request the board may elect an acting chairman to serve in such relationship until the close of the next district assembly. (213)

227.2. The board shall elect from its membership a permanent secretary who shall provide a suitable system of records, at the expense of the district assembly, which shall be the property of the district. The secretary shall carefully record all actions of the board and faithfully preserve them along with such other records as shall be relevant to the work of the board and promptly transmit them to his or her successor.

228. The **duties of the Ministerial Credentials Board** are:

228.1. To carefully examine and evaluate all persons who have been properly presented to the district assembly for election to the order of elder, the order of deacon, and for minister's license.

228.2. To carefully examine and evaluate all persons desiring to receive a certificate for any of the assigned roles of ministry, including all lay and ministerial candidates aspiring to be recognized for ministries beyond the local church, and any other special relations provided by the *Manual.*

228.3. To carefully inquire of each candidate and make

any other investigation deemed advisable concerning his or her personal experience of salvation; personal experience of entire sanctification by the baptism with the Holy Spirit; knowledge of the doctrines of the Bible; full acceptance of the doctrines, the General and Special Rules, and the polity of the church; evidence of graces, gifts, intellectual, moral, and spiritual qualifications, and general fitness for the ministry to which the candidate feels called.

228.4. To carefully investigate the conduct of each candidate to seek to identify whether or not the candidate is engaging in or has a pattern of conduct that if continued would be inconsistent with the ministry for which the candidate has applied.

228.5. To review for approval for reappointment any local minister who has been appointed as supply pastor if he or she is to continue such service after the district assembly following the appointment. (426.6)

228.6. To investigate and review the cause of failure of an ordained minister to report to the district assembly for two successive years and make recommendation to the district assembly relative to the continued listing of the name on the published rolls of elders or deacons.

228.7. To investigate reports concerning an ordained minister indicating that he or she has placed his or her church membership with any other church or that he or she has joined with the ministry of another denomination or group or is participating in independent activities without duly authorized permission, and make recommendation to the district assembly relative to his or her retention on the roll of elders or deacons. (112, 433.11)

228.8. To recommend to the district assembly retired relationship for a minister requesting such relation and who, in the judgment of the board, is unable to continue in the active ministerial service because of disability (203.26, 431) or who desires to discontinue active ministerial service because of age.

228.9. To recommend to the district assembly, members of the clergy, and those licensed for continuing ministry roles, for transfer to another district, including interim transfers approved by the District Advisory Board. (203.7, 432-32.2)

228.10. To recommend to the district assembly, persons having ministerial credentials, members of the clergy, and those licensed for continuing ministry roles for reception of transfer from other districts, including interim transfers approved by the District Advisory Board. (203.6, 432-32.2)

J. The District Ministerial Studies Board

229. The District Ministerial Studies Board shall be composed of five or more ordained ministers, elected by the district assembly to serve for a term of four years and until their successors are elected and qualified. However, their terms of service may be staggered by electing a proportion of the board annually. (203.14)

229.1. Vacancies occurring in the District Ministerial Studies Board, in the interim of sessions of the district assembly, may be filled by appointment by the district superintendent. (212)

229.2. The chairman and the secretary of the District Ministerial Studies Board are authorized to enroll a student in the Directed Studies Program, in consultation with the district superintendent. (230.1-30.2, 424.3)

230. Before the close of the district assembly in which the board is elected, the district superintendent or district secretary shall call a meeting of all the members of the board for organization and assignment as follows:

230.1. The board shall elect from among its members a permanent chairman and a permanent secretary, who with the other members shall have the responsibility of examining and advancing candidates through the Minister's Directed Studies Program to the completion of study requirements for ordination. They shall maintain a record of all grades until the candidate is ordained. (230.5, 424.3)

230.2. The chairman shall assign to the other members of the board the responsibility for and supervision of all candidates enrolled in the Directed Studies Program. Such assignment shall continue as long as the candidates remain actively enrolled during the committee member's term of office unless otherwise mutually arranged.

230.3. The chairman shall attend all meetings of the board, unless providentially prevented, and shall oversee the work of the board each year. In case of necessary absence of the chairman, the secretary shall do his or her work pro tempore.

230.4. The secretary shall, at the expense of the district assembly, provide a suitable record book of ministerial studies, which shall be the property of the district assembly, and shall be used according to instructions in the *Sourcebook for Ministerial Development.*

230.5. The other members of the board shall attend faithfully the meetings of the board and shall supervise the candidates assigned to them by (1) fraternal encouragement, counsel, and guidance; (2) tutoring in specific subjects when needed and feasible; (3) administering of or arranging for written examinations in cooperation with the Pastoral Ministries office; and (4) training by example and by conversation concerning the ethics of the clergy with specific attention being given to how a member of the clergy can avoid sexual misconduct. (230.1)

231. The board may establish classes or seminars in order to assist licensed ministers or other candidates in the pursuit of the various courses of study, and establish, subject to approved district funding, central libraries of all books for loan when necessary.

231.1. The board shall cooperate with the district superintendent and the Pastoral Ministries office in seeking ways to encourage, aid, and guide the candidates who are pursuing the courses of study in a Nazarene college/university or seminary.

231.2. The board shall carry out its responsibilities in conformity with the official *Sourcebook for Ministerial Development.*

231.3. The board shall report all relevant data concerning the candidate's educational progress to the District Ministerial Credentials Board in time for that board to process the data before the district assembly. The District Ministerial Studies Board shall recommend to the district assembly placement and advancement in and graduation from the various courses of study. Such placement, advancement, or graduation shall be consistent with guidelines provided by the office of Pastoral Ministries.

231.4. The District Ministerial Studies Board shall be responsible, in cooperation with the regional college/university and the Pastoral Ministries office, and under the general guidance of the district superintendent, for the promotion of continuing education for ordained ministers and other staff ministers on the district. The continuing education shall include education concerning ethics of the clergy with particular attention being given to how a member of the clergy can avoid sexual misconduct.

K. The District Evangelism Board or Director of Evangelism

232. The district assembly may elect either a District Evangelism Board or a district director of evangelism. The persons elected shall serve until the final adjournment of the next district assembly and until their successors are elected and qualified. (203.17)

232.1. In cooperation with the district superintendent, the District Evangelism Board, or the district director of evangelism, shall seek to promote and amplify the necessity of holiness evangelism, by providing training opportunities, by conducting rallies and conferences, by emphasizing the need for local church revivals with God-called evangelists, and by every other available means, to impact the district with the Great Commission of Jesus Christ as a first priority in the functioning of the Body of Christ.

L. The District Home Missions Board

233. The District Home Missions Board shall be composed of equal lay and ministerial membership, of no fewer than 6 nor more than 18, not including the district superintendent, who shall be a member ex officio. Members may be elected by the district assembly to serve for a term of four years and until their successors are elected and qualified; however, the District Advisory Board may constitute the District Home Missions Board. (203.19)

233.1. The District Home Missions Board shall seek by all means—by the diffusion of home missionary information, by the holding of local meetings and district conventions, by the employment of speakers who have the vision and spirit, by careful study of its metropolitan areas, and by any other contributive agency—to stir the people to holy zeal and devotion for and liberality toward the cause of home missions.

233.2. The District Home Missions Board, under direction of the district assembly, and in cooperation with the district superintendent, may have charge of all home mission work conducted by the assembly district within its bounds.

M. The District Church Properties Board

234. The District Church Properties Board shall be composed of the district superintendent ex officio and no fewer than two ministerial and two lay members. Members may be elected by the district assembly to serve for a term of four years or until their successors are elected and qualified. The District Advisory Board may serve as the District Church Properties Board upon favorable vote of the district assembly.

235. The **duties of the District Church Properties Board** are:

235.1. To advance the cause of building local churches and church-related buildings within the bounds of the assembly district, in cooperation with Evangelism and Church Growth Division.

235.2. To verify and conserve the titles to local church property.

235.3. To consider propositions submitted by local churches relating to the purchase of real estate or the erection of church buildings or parsonages, and to advise them concerning the propositions submitted. (103)

235.4. To approve or disapprove, in conjunction with the district superintendent, propositions submitted by local churches relative to church building plans and the incurring of indebtedness in the purchase of real estate or the erection of buildings. The Church Properties Board shall normally approve a request to increase indebtedness subject to the following guidelines:

1. The local church requesting approval to increase indebtedness paid all financial apportionments in full for the two years preceding the request.
2. The amount of total indebtedness will not exceed three times the average of the amount raised for all purposes in each of the preceding three years.
3. The details of the planned remodeling or construction shall have been approved by the Church Properties Board.
4. The amount of indebtedness and the terms of payment will not jeopardize the spiritual life of the church.

The Church Properties Board may approve requests that do not meet these guidelines only with the approval of the district superintendent and the District Advisory Board.

235.5. To do whatever else the district assembly may direct regarding the matter of local church property.

N. The District Assembly Finance Committee

237. The **duties of the District Assembly Finance Committee** are:

237.1. To meet prior to the district assembly and to make recommendation to the district assembly concerning all financial apportionments and the allocation of those apportionments to the local churches.

237.2. To do whatever else the district assembly may direct in areas of district finance. (203.20)

O. The District Chaplaincy Director

238. The district superintendent may appoint a district chaplaincy director. In cooperation with the district superintendent, the district chaplaincy director shall seek to promote and amplify holiness evangelism through the specialized ministry of chaplaincy. The director will promote and support evangelism through industrial, institutional, campus, and military opportunities. The director shall give special attention to Nazarene servicemembers and other military members located on military installations, appointing and assisting host pastors located near these bases to impact servicemembers and their families for Christ, bonding them to our church while they are serving their country. (208.7)

P. The District Sunday School Ministries Board

239. The District Sunday School Ministries Board shall be composed of the district superintendent, the district NWMS president, the district NYI president, and the chairman of the District Sunday School Ministries Board, who comprise an Executive Committee, and at least 3 additional members. The additional members shall be elected by the district assembly or the District Sunday School Ministries Convention to staggered terms of three years and until their successors are elected and qualified. Upon initial organization of the District Sunday School Ministries Board, the 3 additional members are to be elected from 6 nominees, with 1 being elected for a term of three years, 1 for a term of two years, and 1 for a term of one year. However, when the district total membership exceeds 5,000, the number of members nominated and elected may be doubled, and, when possible, at least 4 of the 10 board members should be laypersons. Vacancies occurring in the Sunday School Ministries Board, in the interim of sessions of the district assembly, may be filled by appointment by the district superintendent. (212)

The **duties of the District Sunday School Ministries Board** are:

239.1. To meet within one week following their election and to organize by electing a secretary, treasurer, district directors of adult ministries, children's ministries, and Continuing Lay Training, who then shall become ex officio members of the Sunday School Ministries Board. Other district directors, as deemed necessary, may be nominated by the Executive Committee and elected by the board.

239.2. To give supervision to all Sunday School interests of the district.

239.3. To elect a Children's Ministries Council* whose chairman shall be the district director of children's ministries and whose members shall be the district directors of: boys' and girls' camps, Caravan, Vacation Bible School, Bible quizzing, children's church, Cradle Roll Parents, and any others deemed necessary.

239.4. To elect an Adult Ministries Council* whose chairman shall be the district director of adult ministries and whose members shall be the district directors of: marriage and family life, senior adult ministries, single adult ministries, lay retreat, small-group Bible studies, women's ministries, men's ministries, and any others deemed necessary.

239.5. To arrange for an annual District Sunday School Ministries Convention. (239)

239.6. To determine, in consultation with the district superintendent, whether elections for the District Sunday School Ministries Board members and chairman will be held in the district assembly or in the District Sunday School Ministries Convention.

239.7. To encourage all local Sunday School Ministries chairmen and age-group ministries directors/NYI presidents to be present in the District Sunday School Ministries Convention and take part as opportunity affords.

239.8. To organize the district into zones and appoint zone chairmen who shall assist the board at its direction to carry forward the work of Sunday School ministries on the district.

239.9. To plan and implement district or zone Continuing Lay Training classes.

239.10. To assist the Sunday School Ministries Division

---

*For additional information concerning the duties of Children's and Adult Ministries councils, see the *Sunday School Ministries Handbook.*

of the General Board in securing information relating to district and local Sunday School interests.

239.11. To recommend to the District Assembly Finance Committee the annual District Sunday School Ministries Board budget.

239.12. To be responsible for the district lay retreat. The district director of adult ministries shall be member ex officio of the District Lay Retreat Committee.

239.13. To approve the report of its chairman to be presented to the district assembly.

239.14. To meet as frequently as deemed necessary by the district superintendent or the chairman of the District Sunday School Ministries Board to plan and execute effectively the responsibilities of the board.

242. The District Sunday School Ministries Chairman. The district assembly or the Sunday School Ministries Convention, from two or more nominees submitted by the District Nominating Committee, shall elect a chairman of the District Sunday School Ministries Board to serve for a one- or two-year term. An incumbent chairman may be re-elected by a favorable "yes" or "no" vote when such vote has been recommended by the District Sunday School Ministries Board, with the approval of the district superintendent. A vacancy in the interim of sessions of the district assembly may be filled according to the provisions of 212. (239.6)

The **duties and powers of the District Sunday School Ministries chairman** are:

242.1. To give responsible leadership to the Sunday School on the district by promoting programs of growth in enrollment and attendance, and to coordinate all programs relating to children's and adult ministries, and to work in cooperation with NYI to coordinate youth Sunday School.

242.2. To be an ex officio member of the district assembly and the District Sunday School Ministries Board.

242.3. To report to the General Board Sunday School Ministries Division accurate Sunday School statistics each month and to prepare for the District Sunday School

Ministries Board a written report for the annual assembly journal.

Q. The District Nazarene Youth International

243. The District Nazarene Youth International shall be composed of the local organizations of Nazarene Youth International of the assembly district.

243.1. It shall be governed by the Constitution of the District Nazarene Youth International approved by the General Board. It shall be subject to the district superintendent and the District Advisory Board. (810)

243.2. The president of the District Nazarene Youth International shall be elected by its annual convention to a one- or two-year term and shall serve without salary. When so elected and approved, he or she shall be a member ex officio of the district assembly. (201)*

R. The District Nazarene World Mission Society

244. The District Nazarene World Mission Society shall be composed of the local Nazarene World Mission Societies within the boundaries of the assembly district. The district society shall be auxiliary to the General Nazarene World Mission Society. (811.2-11.3)

244.1. The District Nazarene World Mission Society shall be governed by the Constitution of the District Nazarene World Mission Society approved by the World Mission Department. It shall be subject to the district superintendent, the District Advisory Board, and the district assembly. (811.2)

244.2. The president of the District Nazarene World Mission Society shall serve without salary and shall be a member ex officio of the district assembly. (201)

S. The District Advisory Council

245. The district boards shall form an advisory council over which the district superintendent shall preside; said

---

*For additional information concerning the district NYI president and council, consult the *How to Organize the District NYI Notebook*.

council to meet, if possible, once each six months for counsel and advice as to the best methods of forwarding the work of the assembly district. (213)

T. District Paid Assistants

246. When paid assistants become necessary for the greater efficiency of the district administration, such persons, ministerial or lay, shall be nominated by the district superintendent, after having secured the written approval of the general superintendent in jurisdiction. They shall be elected by the District Advisory Board. The employment of such assistants shall be for no more than one year but may be renewed by recommendation of the district superintendent and the majority vote of the Advisory Board. (208.14)

246.1. Dismissal of such assistants prior to the end of the employment period must be by the recommendation of the district superintendent and the majority vote of the District Advisory Board. (222.12)

246.2. The duties and services of such district assistants are to be determined and supervised by the district superintendent.

246.3. Within 30 days after a new district superintendent assumes administrative duties on the district, the term of service of the paid assistants shall be considered concluded, unless otherwise stipulated by national labor law. (Such clerical assistants as office secretaries shall not be included in the above provisions.)

246.4. Service as a paid district assistant shall not prohibit one from serving in other district elected or appointed offices such as district secretary or district treasurer.

U. Disorganization of a District

247. When it seems clear to the Board of General Superintendents that a district no longer should continue as such, it may, upon their recommendation, be disorganized by a two-thirds favorable vote of the General Board of the Church of the Nazarene and a formal pronouncement thereof. (200)

247.1. In case a district becomes officially disorganized, any church property that shall exist may in no way be diverted to other purposes, but shall pass to the control of the General Board, for the use of the Church of the Nazarene at large, as the General Assembly shall direct; and trustees holding property, or corporations created to hold property, for the disorganized district shall sell or dispose of the same only on the order and under the direction of the appointed agent of the General Board, and turn the funds over to such agent. (106.2, 222.5)

CHAPTER III

THE GENERAL ASSEMBLY

A. Functions and Organization

300. The General Assembly is the supreme doctrine-formulating, lawmaking, and elective authority of the Church of the Nazarene, subject to the provisions of the church Constitution. (31.1-31.9)

300.1. The General Assembly shall be presided over by the general superintendents, jointly and severally. (31.6, 307.2)

300.2. The General Assembly shall elect its other officers and organize itself for the transaction of its business according to its wisdom and pleasure. (31.7)

B. Membership of the General Assembly

301. The General Assembly shall be composed of ministerial and lay delegates in equal numbers from each Phase 3 district, the district superintendent serving as one of the ministerial delegates, the remaining ministerial delegates and all the lay delegates elected thereto by the district assemblies of the Church of the Nazarene; the general superintendents emeriti and retired; the general superintendents; the general secretary; the general treasurer; the editor of the *Herald of Holiness;* the directors of the several divisions, ministries, and services of the General Board; the education commissioner; the regional directors; the General Nazarene World Mission Society president; the General Nazarene Youth International president; the regional college/university presidents (in regions where more than one school exists, one delegate from these schools would be elected by the Regional Advisory Council); presidents of multiregional institutions whose Board of Directors are elected by multiple district representatives; the president of the Nazarene Publishing House; one missionary delegate for every region of 50 or fewer missionaries and two missionary delegates for every region with 51 or more missionaries, elected by the Regional Advisory Council in each region. In the absence of such election the missionary representative shall be elected by the World Mission Department.

301.1. Each Phase 3 district shall be entitled to representation in the General Assembly by: one ordained minister and one layperson for the first 2,000 or fewer full church members, and one additional ordained minister and one additional layperson for the next 1 to 3,500 full members, and for each successive additional 1 to 3,500 full members.[1] The term "ordained minister" shall include elders and deacons.

301.2. Each Phase 2 district shall be entitled to one lay and one ministerial delegate to the General Assembly. The ministerial delegate shall be the district superintendent. An alternate will be elected for each delegate.

301.3. A Phase 1 district shall be entitled to one nonvoting delegate to the General Assembly. The district superintendent shall be the delegate, providing he or she holds his or her membership on the district.[2]

301.4. The right of a ministerial delegate-elect to the General Assembly to represent the district assembly electing him or her shall be vacated in case he or she shall move to a new ministerial assignment on another assembly district, or if the delegate-elect shall leave the active, full-time ministry of the Church of the Nazarene prior to the convening of the General Assembly.

301.5. The right of a lay delegate-elect to the General Assembly to represent the district assembly electing him or her shall be vacated in case he or she shall remove his or her church membership to some local church on another assembly district prior to the convening of the General Assembly.

---

1. 0-2,000; 2,001-5,500; 5,501-9,000; 9,001-12,500; 12,501-16,000; 16,001-19,500; etc.

2. An exception to the rule of transferring Phase 1 districts to nonvoting status will be made for the 25th General Assembly for any Phase 1 district that had voting rights in the 24th General Assembly. They shall retain those voting rights in the 25th General Assembly.

C. The Time and Place of Meeting

302. The General Assembly shall meet in the month of June, every fourth year, at such time and place as shall be determined by a General Assembly Commission composed of the general superintendents and an equal number of persons chosen by the Board of General Superintendents. The general superintendents and said commission shall also have power, in case of an emergency, to change the time and place of the meeting of the General Assembly.

302.1. The General Assembly shall open on Sunday with a full day of devotional and inspirational services. Provision shall be made for the orderly and careful transaction of business, and for such services at the close of the session as it may order. The General Assembly shall fix the time at which its session shall adjourn. (31.4)

D. Special Sessions

303. The Board of General Superintendents, or a majority thereof, by and with the written consent of two-thirds of all the district superintendents, shall have power to call a special session of the General Assembly in case of an emergency, the time and place thereof to be determined by the general superintendents and a commission chosen by the Board of General Superintendents.

303.1. In case of a special session of the General Assembly, the delegates and alternates to the last preceding General Assembly, or their duly elected and qualified successors, shall serve as delegates and alternates to the special session.

E. General Assembly Arrangements Committee

304. The general secretary, the general treasurer, and three persons appointed by the Board of General Superintendents at least one year before the convening of the General Assembly shall constitute the General Assembly Arrangements Committee.

304.1. The General Assembly Arrangements Committee shall have authority to arrange all necessary details regarding offices, exhibits and space, entertainment and meals, and whatever else may be needful to contribute to the comfort, convenience, and efficiency of the General Assembly, and enter into contracts necessary to provide the same.

304.2. The General Assembly Arrangements Committee with the general superintendents shall formulate a program for the General Assembly, including emphases for each of the general interests; a Communion service; and other religious services for the first three days of the General Assembly or until a committee on public worship shall have been appointed; all of which program shall be subject to approval by the General Assembly.

F. Business of the General Assembly

305. The business of the General Assembly, subject to paragraph 31.9 of the church Constitution, shall be:

305.1. To reference, through its Reference Committee, all resolutions, recommendations, and implementing legislation from commissions and special committee reports and other documents to standing or special legislative committees of the assembly, or to regional caucuses for consideration before being presented to the assembly. The Reference Committee may submit legislation affecting only a specific region/regions to the General Assembly delegates of said region(s) meeting in caucus for action. Changes that affect the *Manual* must be acted upon by the entire General Assembly.

305.2. To elect, by a two-thirds vote of its members present and voting, as many general superintendents as it may deem necessary, who shall hold office until the final adjournment of the next General Assembly and until their successors are elected and qualified; provided that the first ballot shall be a “yes” or “no” ballot for the general superintendents then serving, and any vacancies remaining after the first ballot shall be filled by ensuing ballots until the elections are completed. In the event that someone who is ineligible under this provision receives votes on the first ballot, that person’s name shall be deleted from the elective ballot and the report of the first ballot shall include this statement: "One or more names have been deleted due to ineligibility for the office." No elder shall be considered eligible for election to the office of general superintendent who has at any time surrendered his or her credentials for disciplinary reasons. No person shall be elected to the office of general superintendent who has not reached the age of 35 years or who has reached the age of 68 years. (31.5, 306, 435.1-35.4, 900.1)

305.3. To elect a general superintendent to the emeritus honor when deemed advisable, provided the superintendent shall have become disabled or shall have reached 65 years of age, and shall have served as general superintendent for at least two terms, with a term defined as the length of time that is served from one General Assembly to the next. It is thereby understood that election to emeritus relation is of life tenure. (314.1)

305.4. To place in the retired relation a general superintendent who has attained to the age of 68 years, or who, in the judgment of the General Assembly, has become disqualified by physical disability, or by old age, or by any other disqualification that would prevent such a person from caring adequately for the work of the general superintendency; and provided that said superintendent has served in the office of general superintendent for a reasonable term of years. The General Assembly may grant retired relation when a general superintendent who has attained the age of 65 years requests it.

Should a general superintendent who has attained the age of 65 years request retirement in the interim of General Assemblies, the request may be granted by the General Board in regular session upon recommendation of the Board of General Superintendents. (314.1)

305.5. To fix a suitable retirement pension for each retired general superintendent, in accordance with paragraph 314.2.

305.6. To elect a General Board, as provided in 330.1-31.4, to serve until the final adjournment of the next General Assembly and until their successors are elected and qualified. (329, 901.1)

305.7. To elect a General Court of Appeals, consisting of five ordained ministers, to serve until the final adjournment of the next General Assembly and until their successors are elected and qualified. The Board of General Superintendents shall select the chairman and secretary. (31.8, 510, 901.2)

305.8. To elect boards of control for educational institutions serving multiregional areas, to serve until their successors are elected and qualified and in accordance with the following provisions:

a. The boards of control shall be comprised of persons from the respective areas served by the institution.

b. In instances where the institution serves a multiregional area, election of that board shall be conducted in the General Assembly regional caucus(es) composed of delegates from the regions primarily served by the schools.

305.9. To do anything else, in harmony with the Holy Scriptures, that wisdom may dictate for the general welfare of the Church of the Nazarene and the holy cause of Christ, subject to the church Constitution. (31.9)

G. The General Superintendents

306. The general superintendents, elected by the General Assembly, shall serve until the final adjournment of the next General Assembly and until their successors are elected and qualified. (305.2)

306.1. A general superintendent shall hold no other general office in the church while serving as general superintendent. (307.9)

306.2. The general superintendents shall be members ex officio of the General Assembly. (301)

307. The **duties and powers of the general superintendents** are:

307.1. To have general supervision of the Church of the Nazarene, subject to the law and order as adopted by the General Assembly.

307.2. To preside over the General Assembly and over the General Board of the Church of the Nazarene, jointly and severally. (300.1, 333.3)

307.3. To ordain, or appoint others to ordain, in connection with the ordained ministers present, those who have been duly elected to be elders or deacons. (433.5-33.6)

307.4. To preside over each Phase 3 district assembly; or, if hindered from doing so, to make suitable arrangements for such presidency. (202, 211)

307.5. The general superintendent presiding over a district assembly, the district superintendent, and the District Advisory Board, in concurrence with the delegates of local churches, shall appoint pastors over such local churches as have not regularly called pastors. (214.1)

307.6. The general superintendents, jointly and severally, may appoint district superintendents over assembly districts where vacancies occur in the interim of district assembly sessions, upon consultation with a committee composed of the District Advisory Board, the chairman of the District Sunday School Ministries Board, and the presidents of the District NWMS and NYI, the district secretary and the district treasurer. (207)

307.7. In the event of temporary incapacitation of an incumbent district superintendent, the general superintendent having jurisdiction, in consultation with the District Advisory Board, may appoint a qualified elder to serve as interim district superintendent. The question of incapacitation shall be determined by the general superintendent in jurisdiction and the District Advisory Board. (207.1)

307.8. The general superintendent having jurisdiction may, after consulting with the district superintendent, organize local churches or recognize the local churches already organized, wherever there may seem to be need and providential openings. Official reports shall be filed in the Evangelism and Church Growth Division office. Said superintendent may appoint pastors to have charge of such local churches until such time as pastors may be duly elected. (100, 208.1, 433.12)

307.9. The general superintendent having jurisdiction may preside at the annual, or a special meeting of a local church, or appoint a representative to do so. (113.4)

307.10. The general superintendents shall not be members of any of the general boards of the Church of the Nazarene. (306.1)

307.11. All official acts of the general superintendents shall be subject to review and revision by the General Assembly.

307.12. Any official act of a general superintendent may be nullified by a unanimous vote of the remaining members of the Board of General Superintendents.

307.13. The office of any general superintendent may be declared vacant, for cause, by the unanimous vote of the remaining members of the Board of General Superintendents, supported by a majority vote of all the district superintendents of Phase 3 and Phase 2 districts.

H. General Superintendents Emeriti and Retired

314. All general superintendents emeriti and retired general superintendents shall be members ex officio of the General Assembly. (301)

314.1. A general superintendent who has been placed in the retired relation, or voted emeritus honor, shall not be a member of the Board of General Superintendents and shall be relieved of all official responsibility. However, in the event that an active general superintendent should be incapacitated by illness, hospitalization, or other unavoidable emergency necessitating absence from any assignment, the Board of General Superintendents is empowered to call into temporary assignment any retired general superintendent. (305.3-5.5, 900.1)

314.2. The pension for a general superintendent shall be under the provisions of the General Church Pension Plan, a qualified church plan. (305.5)

I. The Board of General Superintendents

315. The general superintendents shall organize as a board and arrange for and assign to the members thereof the particular work over which they shall have special jurisdiction.

316. Vacancy. If a vacancy occurs, by death or otherwise, in the Board of General Superintendents, in the interim of sessions of the General Assembly, the question of calling for an election to fill the vacancy shall be decided by the Board of General Superintendents. Upon receipt of the board's decision, the general secretary shall notify at once all members of the General Board. When an election is called for, the members of the General Board shall elect, by a two-thirds vote of all eligible to vote, an elder of the Church of the Nazarene to fill the vacancy and to perform the duties of the general superintendent until the final adjournment of the next General Assembly. (31.5, 305.2)

316.1. The general secretary shall report the result of the vote to the Board of General Superintendents, which shall announce the same to the Church of the Nazarene through the *Herald of Holiness*.

317. The **duties of the Board of General Superintendents** shall be:

317.1. To provide supervision of the international Church of the Nazarene. The Board of General Superintendents shall provide appropriate attention to leadership, guidance, motivation, and access to all Phase 3 districts.

317.2. To recommend, in consultation with the director of the World Mission Division, and the respective national administrative directors and/or regional directors, changes in the assignment of the geographical areas subject to the approval of the Board of General Superintendents and the General Board.

317.3. To have supervision of all general boards and the departments of the General Board. The policies and plans adopted by the board or department require the approval of the Board of General Superintendents. The Board of General Superintendents shall have the privilege of making to the General Board and to the departments thereof such recommendations as they shall deem advisable. They shall approve or disapprove all nominations made by the World Mission Department to the General Board of the Church of the Nazarene for appointment as missionaries.

317.4. To function as a nominating committee, in conjunction with the General Board Executive Committee, to bring one or more names to the General Board for election of a general secretary and a general treasurer.

317.5. To declare vacant with cause by a two-thirds vote the office of general secretary, general treasurer, *Herald of Holiness* editor, Nazarene Publishing House president, or division director.

317.6. To fill vacancies that may occur in the membership of the General Court of Appeals in the interim of sessions of the General Assembly, and to select the chairman and secretary of the court. (305.7, 511, 901.2)

317.7. To fill vacancies that may occur in any special commission or committee in the interim of General Assemblies or General Board.

317.8. To approve the appointments and elections made by the General Board of the Church of the Nazarene in filling vacancies that may occur in its membership.

317.9. To fill vacancies, upon nomination made by the remaining members thereof, on the corporate board of the Nazarene Publishing House. (336)

317.10. To appoint general superintendents to serve as advisers of all institutions of higher education affiliated with the International Board of Education and to serve as responsible general superintendents for all divisions of the General Board. (901.5)

317.11. To arrange, in conjunction with Pastoral Ministries, Directed Studies for local ministers, licensed ministers, and those serving in ministerial roles, lay or credentialed. (424-25)

317.12. To plan, preserve, and promote the lifeline of our global mission interests, the Board of General Superintendents, with the General Board, is authorized and empowered to apportion the World Evangelism Fund to the several assembly districts. (130, 333.8)

317.13. To approve in writing the restoration of credentials to a former elder or deacon as required. (434.6, 435.2)

318. The Board of General Superintendents shall be the authority for the interpretation of the law and doctrine of the Church of the Nazarene, and the meaning and force of all provisions of the *Manual,* subject to an appeal to the General Assembly.

319. The Board of General Superintendents shall consider and pass upon plans for district centers, which plans shall not be carried out until they have been approved in writing by the Board of General Superintendents. (222.9)

320. The Board of General Superintendents shall have discretionary power in the ordaining of divorced persons to the office of elder or deacon in the Church of the Nazarene. (35.1-35.3, 428.3, 429.3)

321. The Board of General Superintendents may declare vacant with cause the office of a district superintendent of any Phase 2 or Phase 1 district upon recommendation of the general superintendent having jurisdiction and may declare vacant the office of district superintendents in Phase 3 districts upon a two-thirds majority vote of the District Advisory Board, the chairpersons of district Sunday School Ministries, district NYI, district NWMS, the district secretary, and the district treasurer.

322. The Board of General Superintendents shall have authority to do anything else in the service of the Church of the Nazarene, not otherwise provided for, according to the dictates of its wisdom, in harmony with the general church order, and subject to the church Constitution.

J. The General Secretary

323. The general secretary, elected by the General Board as provided by General Board Bylaws, shall serve until the final adjournment of the next General Assembly and until a successor is elected and qualified, or until removed according to 317.5 or General Board Bylaws. (900.2)

323.1. The general secretary shall be a member ex officio of the General Assembly. (301)

323.2. If in the interim of sessions of the General Board a vacancy should occur in the office of the general secretary for any cause, it shall be filled by the General Board, upon nomination as provided in 317.4. (333.23)

323.3. The general secretary shall be amenable to the Board of General Superintendents and the General Board.

324. The **duties of the general secretary** are:

324.1. To record correctly and preserve the journal of the proceedings of the General Assembly and the General Board.

324.2. To record correctly and preserve all general statistics of the Church of the Nazarene.

324.3. To preserve all documents belonging to the General Assembly, and promptly deliver the same to his or her successor.

324.4. To preserve carefully, in permanent form, all decisions rendered by the General Court of Appeals. (513)

324.5. To catalog and preserve all filed, surrendered, removed, and resigned credentials of ministers and deliver them only on proper order made by the district assembly of the assembly district from which they were received. (434-34.1, 434.5)

324.6. To audit assembly district statistical charts for publication. (217.3)

324.7. To do faithfully whatever else may be necessary for the fulfillment of the duties of the office.

325. The general secretary shall be custodian of, and hold in trust, such legal documents as belong to the general church.

325.1. The general secretary is authorized to collect available historic material relating to the rise and development of our denomination, and shall be the custodian of such records and material.

325.2. The general secretary shall keep a register of Historic Sites and Landmarks according to paragraph 902.11.

326. The general secretary, in conjunction with the general superintendents, shall, prior to the opening of the General Assembly, prepare all necessary forms, including *Rules of Order "Manual" Abridgment* for revision, and other things necessary for expediting the work of the General Assembly. The expense incurred shall be provided for out of the General Assembly expense fund.

326.1. The general secretary may have as many assistants for the work as the General Assembly shall elect, or, in the interim of sessions of the General Assembly, the Board of General Superintendents may appoint.

K. The General Treasurer

327. The general treasurer, elected by the General Board as provided by General Board Bylaws, shall serve until the final adjournment of the next General Assembly and until a successor is elected and qualified or until removed according to 317.5 or General Board Bylaws. (900.3)

327.1. The general treasurer shall be a member ex officio of the General Assembly. (301)

327.2. The general treasurer shall be amenable to the responsible general superintendent for the Headquarters Financial office, the Board of General Superintendents, and the General Board.

328. The **duties of the general treasurer** are:

328.1. To have the custody of all funds belonging to the general interests of the Church of the Nazarene.

328.2. To receive, and disburse on order, the funds of the Church Growth Department, Communications Department, Finance Department, Sunday School Ministries Department, World Mission Department, and such other funds as properly belong to the General Board, or to any of its divisions; the general superintendents' fund; the general contingent fund; the General Assembly expense fund; other general benevolent church funds; the funds of the General Nazarene Youth International; and the funds of the General Nazarene World Mission Society. (329.3)

328.3. To give bond for the faithful performance of duties, in a reliable surety company, in a good and sufficient sum, as the General Board may direct.

328.4. To furnish such reports to the boards and divisions, for whose funds he or she may be custodian, as may be required by them.

328.5. To furnish to the General Board an annual report of all finances of the Church of the Nazarene, including investments. (333.13)

328.6. To safeguard annuity funds invested in real estate by proper insurance policies and to provide against the lapsing of such policies.

328.7. To secure monthly reports of receipts and disbursements from all schools, orphanages, rescue homes, and other institutions of the Church of the Nazarene.

L. The General Board

329. The General Board of the Church of the Nazarene, a religious and charitable corporation incorporated under the laws of the state of Missouri at Kansas City, Missouri, U.S.A., shall be composed of members who shall be elected by ballot by the General Assembly from among the persons nominated as provided in 330.1-31.4. To be elected a member of the General Board as a representative of a church region, one must be a resident on that region as well as a member of a local church on that region. (305.6, 332)

329.1. No one shall be eligible for election to the General Board or shall remain a member of the General Board who is an employee of the General Board, or entities including educational institutions controlled by the General Board. Individuals from districts or other entities receiving operating funds from the general church are likewise ineligible.

329.2. The general secretary shall be ex officio secretary of the General Board.

329.3. The general treasurer of the Church of the Nazarene shall be ex officio treasurer of the General Board and also of the divisions thereof. (328.2)

330. Nominations for the General Board shall be made as herein provided:

330.1. After the delegates to the General Assembly have been elected, each Phase 3 district delegation shall meet to select candidates for nomination to the General Board in the following manner. Each Phase 3 district may present names of two ordained ministers and two laypersons. The multicultural composition of the nominating district should be considered in selecting names for nomination. The names of these candidates shall be sent immediately to the office of the general secretary to be placed on ballots for presentation to the General Assembly delegates from each region. (203.22)

330.2. From the list of these candidates, the General Assembly delegates from each region shall nominate to the General Assembly as follows:

Each region of 50,000 or fewer full members shall nominate one ordained minister and one layperson; each region exceeding 50,000 and up to 100,000 full members shall nominate two ordained ministers, one district superintendent and one pastor or evangelist, and two laypersons; and one additional layperson and one additional ordained minister for regions exceeding 100,000 full members, with the following provisions:

1. On those regions whose membership is in excess of 100,000 full members, one ordained minister shall be a pastor or evangelist; another shall be a district superintendent; and the other ordained minister may be in either category.
2. No district shall be entitled to more than two members on the General Board, and no region shall be entitled to more than six members (with the exception of institutional representatives and auxiliary members). Whenever more than two candidates from a district receive a higher number of votes than candidates from other districts on the region, those on another district receiving the next highest number of votes shall be selected as nominees from the region. (305.6, 901.1)
3. In each region the layperson/laypersons, the pastor or evangelist, and/or the district superintendent who receive the highest number of votes in their respective classifications shall be nominated by majority vote to the General Assembly. In the instance of the larger regions where six members are to be elected, the layperson and the ordained minister who receive the next highest number of votes shall be the additional nominees. (902.10)

330.3. The International Board of Education (IBOE) shall nominate to the General Assembly four persons from the educational institutions, two ordained ministers and two laypersons. (329.1)

330.4. The General Council of the Nazarene Youth International shall nominate to the General Assembly two members of the General Council. (339.1)

330.5. The General Council of the Nazarene World Mission Society shall nominate to the General Assembly two members of the General Council. (340.3)

331. Elections to the General Board shall be as herein provided:

331.1. Each nominee presented by the respective regions shall be elected by the General Assembly by a majority "yes" vote by ballot. (902.10)

331.2. From the nominees presented by the International Board of Education, the General Assembly shall elect two, one of whom shall be an ordained minister and one a layperson.

331.3. From the nominees presented by the General Council of the Nazarene Youth International, the General Assembly shall elect one. (339.1, 901.3)

331.4. From the nominees presented by the General Council of the Nazarene World Mission Society, the General Assembly shall elect one. (340.3, 901.4)

332. The members of the General Board shall hold office until the final adjournment of the next General Assembly and until their successors are elected and qualified. In the event that a member of the General Board shall move his or her church membership or residence from the region he or she represents, or if a minister changes from the category of ministerial assignment for which elected, before the second regular meeting of the quadrennium, his or her membership shall be terminated immediately. The vacancy so created shall be filled promptly. (329)

332.1. Vacancies occurring in the membership of the General Board, and also the departments thereof, shall be filled upon nomination by the Board of General Superintendents, who shall present to the general secretary, as soon as feasible, the names of two eligible persons from whom for regional representation the Advisory Boards of the districts of the region on which the vacancy occurred shall elect one by a majority vote by mail, each District Advisory Board being entitled to one vote. For educational representation, the nominees shall be submitted to the General Board to elect one by a majority vote by mail. For representation from NYI, nominees shall be submitted to the General Council to elect one by a majority vote by mail. For representation from NWMS, nominees shall be submitted from the Executive Committee of the General NWMS Council in consultation with the responsible general superintendent, and with the approval of the Board of General Superintendents to the General NWMS Council to elect one by a majority vote by mail.

Duties of the General Board

333. The General Board shall encourage and expect all national, regional, district, and local boards to fulfill the mission of the Church of the Nazarene, which is to propagate Christian holiness in the Wesleyan tradition, and shall facilitate the progress of the global church in each nation and/or region. The General Board shall promote the financial and material affairs of all the departments of the Church of the Nazarene, subject to such instructions as may be given by the General Assembly. It shall coordinate, correlate, and unify the plans and activities of the several constituent departments so that a unified policy may be established by and in all the activities of the Church of the Nazarene. It shall have the power to direct the auditing of the accounts of all divisions and institutions relating to or associated with the Church of the Nazarene, with a view to securing such uniformity of method and completeness of form as shall be most efficient; and it shall be an advisory body in the business and administrative affairs of the several divisions of the General Board and of all the organizations and institutions that are a part of, related to, or associated with this denomination. These divisions, organizations, and institutions shall give due consideration to the advice and recommendations of the General Board.

333.1. The General Board shall have power to buy, own, hold, manage, mortgage, sell and convey and donate, or otherwise acquire, encumber, and dispose of both real and personal property, sold, devised, bequeathed, donated, or otherwise conveyed to it in trust for any lawful purpose, and to execute such trust; to borrow and to loan money in the execution of its lawful purposes.

333.2. The General Board shall fill a vacancy in the Board of General Superintendents in accordance with paragraphs 316 and 305.2.

333.3. The General Board shall meet before or immediately following the final adjournment of the General Assembly and shall organize by electing officers and committees, and members to departments as required by its articles of incorporation and bylaws, to serve for the quadrennium and until their successors are elected and qualified. The general superintendents, jointly and severally, shall preside over the meetings of the General Board.

333.4. Meetings. The General Board shall meet in session at least three times during the quadrennium, at a time specified by the bylaws of the said board, at Kansas City, Missouri; however, the hour, date, and place of the regular meeting may, by resolution unanimously adopted at any regular or special meeting, be changed to suit the best interests of the General Board and its departments.

333.5. Special Meetings of the General Board may be called by the chairman, the president, or the secretary.

333.6. Finance Department. The Finance Department, elected by the General Board, shall have charge of the proper investment of trust funds. The General Board, after first referring to this department all budget requests submitted by the several divisions and offices of the General Headquarters for the ensuing year, shall receive from the department a report of its recommendations concerning each request. This department shall perform any other work assigned to it by the General Board. It shall keep accurate minutes of all its meetings and submit them to the General Board for approval.

333.7. World Evangelism Fund. The World Evangelism Fund shall be the grand total of all division budgets and other funds to be raised by the whole denomination for the support, maintenance, and promotion of its general activities.

From the statements of budget requests submitted by the various divisions and agencies of the church, and from the statements of the general treasurer, the General Board shall determine the amount to be allotted from the World Evangelism Fund to each division and fund. When the World Evangelism Fund with its proposed allotment to each division shall have been agreed upon, it shall be submitted to the Board of General Superintendents for its consideration, suggestions, or amendments before final adoption by the General Board.

333.8. When the total amount of the World Evangelism Fund has been fixed for the next fiscal year by the General Board, the General Board and the Board of General Superintendents are authorized and empowered to apportion the World Evangelism Fund to the several assembly districts on a basis of equity to both the district and general interests affected. (130, 317.12)

333.9. The General Board shall have authority to increase or diminish the amount requested by any division or fund. Items of finance adopted by the General Assembly shall be referred to the General Board, who shall be authorized to adjust proportionately with existing economic conditions the annual allocation of any institution or agency of the church, in keeping with the total financial commitment of the general church.

333.10. The General Board shall approve appropriations from the World Evangelism Fund for the Nazarene Theological Seminary (U.S.A.) and the Nazarene Bible College (U.S.A.) as it may deem advisable in line with the availability of funds.

333.11. The General Board shall annually review and make appropriate adjustments in the salaries and related benefits of the general superintendents in the interim of General Assemblies.

333.12. Reports. The General Board shall, at its regular meeting, receive a detailed report of the activities of the divisions for the past year, including a financial report. Each division shall also submit a proposed expenditures budget for the ensuing year.

333.13. The general treasurer shall annually present to the General Board a detailed financial report of receipts and disbursements of all funds of which he or she has been custodian during the past year, including trust funds and investments, together with a detailed statement of the proposed expenditures for the ensuing year of funds not included in the budgets of divisions of the General Board. The general treasurer shall be responsible to the General Board for the faithful performance of official duties. (328.5)

333.14. The General Board shall meet before or immediately following the final adjournment of the General Assembly and shall elect a general secretary, a general treasurer, and the editor(s) of the *Herald(s) of Holiness* as provided in General Board Bylaws, who shall hold office until the final adjournment of the next General Assembly and until their successors are elected and qualified.

333.15. The General Board shall elect the editor(s) for the *Herald(s) of Holiness* and its equivalent publications, upon nomination by the Communications Department. Such nomination(s) shall have been approved by the Board of General Superintendents.

333.16. The General Board members representing United States regions shall elect a Board of Pensions and Benefits USA, composed of one member representing each United States region, the boundaries of which are described by the *Manual of the Church of the Nazarene,* and one member-at-large. Nominations shall be submitted by the Board of General Superintendents as provided by the Bylaws of the Board of Pensions and Benefits USA. (335)

333.17. The General Board shall elect a Nazarene Publishing House Board following each General Assembly, who shall serve until the adjournment of the next General Assembly and until their successors are elected and qualified. (336)

333.18. The General Board shall elect a Nazarene Publishing House president in the manner prescribed by 333.21 and General Board Bylaws.

333.19. A General Board agenda item affecting only a specific region/nation shall be referred upon approval of the Executive Committee of the General Board and the Board of General Superintendents, to the General Board members of said region/nation meeting in caucus.

333.20. The General Board shall properly relate any commission or committee authorized by the General Assembly or General Board to some division or divisions, or to the board as a whole, and assign its work, responsibility, and budget.

333.21. Division Directors. The General Board shall elect a division director, by ballot, for each of its several divisions, to serve until the final adjournment of the next General Assembly and until their successors are elected and qualified, unless removed from office as provided in paragraph 317.5. They shall be **nominated according to the following procedures:** If there is an incumbent director, the Nominating Committee may recommend either a "yes" or "no" vote, or present multiple nominees. The search for capable candidates for these offices shall be conducted by a search committee as provided by General Board Bylaws. This committee will bring two or more names to the Nominating Committee along with supporting rationale for their recommendation.

The Nominating Committee, composed of the six general superintendents and the Personnel Committee from the respective department, shall submit one or more names to the General Board for election by majority vote.

333.22. Executives' Salaries. The General Board shall establish and document a "performance evaluation" and salary administration program that includes the division director and ministry/service directors and provides for a salary structure that recognizes both levels of responsibility and merit. The General Board shall annually review and approve the salaries of division directors, the Nazarene Publishing House president, and such other officers as may be authorized and elected by the General Board.

333.23. The General Board, during the interim of sessions of the General Assembly and/or General Board, upon nomination as provided in the General Board Bylaws and 317.4, shall fill any vacancy that may occur in the offices listed in 333.14, 333.21, and any other executive offices created by the General Assembly, General Board, or their elected departments.

334. The **retirement** for all officers and any other director listed in 333.14 and 333.21, and any other agency head employed by the General Assembly or its elected commissions, the General Board and its divisions, shall occur at the time of the General Board meeting following their 70th birthday. Where there are vacancies, they shall be filled in accordance with *Manual* procedures.

M. General Church-related Boards

Pension Boards

335. There shall be a Pensions Board, or equivalent authorized body, with fiduciary responsibility for each church-related pension plan. A pension plan may apply at organizational, district, multidistrict, national, regional, or multiregional level as the needs may dictate. (333.16)

335.1. The General Board shall establish and maintain suggested guidelines that are relevant to all pension programs worldwide. The General Board does not guarantee any pension plan from loss or depreciation. The General Board does not guarantee the payment of any money that may be or becomes due to any person from any pension plan, and shall not be liable in the case of the underfunding of any pension plan.

335.2. All pension plans shall submit an annual report to the General Board through Pensions and Benefits International in the form and format requested.

Nazarene Publishing House Board

336. The Nazarene Publishing House, a corporation of Kansas City, Missouri, shall have a Board of Directors composed of nine members: the general secretary, who shall be the secretary ex officio of the corporation; one shall be a General Board member of the Communications Department; one shall be a General Board member of the Sunday School Ministries Department; the president of the Nazarene Publishing House, who shall be the chief executive officer of the House; and five who shall have special professional qualifications, nominated by the Board of General Superintendents and elected by the General Board. They shall hold office until the final adjournment of the next General Assembly and until their successors are elected and qualified. Vacancies therein shall be filled by the remaining members from nominations made by the Board of General Superintendents.

336.1. The Board of Directors shall be concerned with the policy, planning, and business operations and shall serve in accordance with the charter and bylaws approved by the General Board and be accountable to the Board of General Superintendents and the General Board.

336.2. The Nazarene Publishing House Board shall meet annually, or more frequently, as specified in the NPH Bylaws.

336.3. The capital expenditures and annual budget shall be prepared by the president of the Nazarene Publishing House for approval by the Nazarene Publishing House Board before adoption by the General Board.

336.4. The president of the Nazarene Publishing House shall be responsible to the NPH Board of Directors for the efficient operation of the House as the Church of the Nazarene production and merchandising agency.

336.5. The president of the Nazarene Publishing House shall be elected in accordance with 333.21, except that the Nazarene Publishing House Board will select one of their number to serve on the Search Committee when a new president is to be elected, and the Nominating Committee shall be composed of the six general superintendents, three members of the NPH Board who are not members ex officio, and three members of the General Board Executive Committee, one of whom is the chairman of the Communications Department of the General Board. He or she shall be amenable to the responsible general superintendent.

336.6. The president of the Nazarene Publishing House shall be a member of the Headquarters Directors Fellowship and the Planning and Budget Council.

N. The Christian Action Committee

337. Following the General Assembly, the Board of General Superintendents shall appoint a **Christian Action Committee,** one of whom shall be the general secretary, who shall report the committee's work to the General Board.

The **duties of the General Christian Action Committee** are:

337.1. To provide for our people constructive information on such matters as alcohol, tobacco, narcotics, and gambling.

337.2. To emphasize the sanctity of marriage and the sacredness of the Christian home and to point out the problems and evils of divorce. In particular, stress should be laid upon the biblical plan of marriage as a lifelong covenant, to be broken only by death.

337.3. To lend encouragement to our people who are serving in places of leadership in temperance organizations and in similar organizations working for civic righteousness.

337.4. To alert our people regarding the Lord's Day observance, oath-bound secret orders, entertainments that are subversive of the Christian ethic, worldliness of other types, and such related subjects as may need emphasis. (34.1)

337.5. To assist and encourage each district to establish a Christian Action Committee; and to provide each district committee with information and material on current moral issues to be disseminated to each local church for appropriate action.

337.6. To monitor moral issues of national and international importance and to present the scriptural viewpoint to the appropriate organizations for their consideration.

O. Committee on the Interests of the God-Called Evangelist

338. The Committee on the Interests of the God-Called Evangelist shall be composed of the revivalism coordinator, who shall be ex officio chairman of the committee, plus four tenured evangelists and one pastor. The revivalism coordinator shall submit a list of nominees for the committee to the Board of General Superintendents for approval and appointment. The committee or its designee shall personally interview commissioned evangelists who have been recommended by their respective district assemblies for "tenured evangelist" status (407.3). It shall also review the state of itinerant evangelism in the Church of the Nazarene and make recommendations concerning both revivals and evangelists to the appropriate department of the General Board.

P. The General Nazarene Youth International

339. The General Nazarene Youth International shall be composed of all district and local Nazarene Youth International organizations.

It shall be governed by the Constitution of the General Nazarene Youth International approved by the General Board. (810)

339.1. The General Nazarene Youth International shall be represented on the General Board of the Church of the Nazarene by one member elected by the General Assembly from nominations made by the General Council of the General Nazarene Youth International. (330.4, 331.3)

339.2. There shall be a General Quadrennial Convention, which shall meet at a time fixed by the General Council in consultation with the Board of General Superintendents. The General Quadrennial Convention shall be composed of such members as are designated in 810.

339.3. The convention shall elect a general president and a general secretary who shall be members ex officio of the General Council of the General Nazarene Youth International.

339.4. The General Nazarene Youth International shall

be represented at the General Assembly by the general NYI president currently in office.

339.5. The General NYI Council members shall hold office until the conclusion of the subsequent General Assembly when their successors are elected and qualified.

Q. The General Council of the General Nazarene World Mission Society

340. The General Council of the General Nazarene World Mission Society shall be composed of the general president, general director, and the number of members prescribed by the Constitution of the General Nazarene World Mission Society and elected in accordance therewith.

340.1. The General Council shall be governed by the Constitution of the General Nazarene World Mission Society. This organization shall be auxiliary to the World Mission Division. (811.3)

340.2. The general director shall be nominated by the World Mission Division director, in consultation with the responsible general superintendent for the World Mission Division, and shall be approved by a majority vote of the General Council before being submitted to the World Mission Department for approval by a majority vote with the recommendation submitted for election by the Board of General Superintendents. In the event the nomination is not approved, the director of the World Mission Division and the Board of General Superintendents shall submit further nominations until one is approved by majority ballot vote of the General Council. The general director shall be an ex officio member of the General NWMS Council and a member of the staff of the World Mission Division.

340.3. The General Nazarene World Mission Society shall be represented on the General Board by one member elected thereto by the General Assembly from nominations made by the General Council of the General Nazarene World Mission Society. (330.5, 331.4)

340.4. There shall be a Quadrennial Convention held under the direction of the General Council of the General

Nazarene World Mission Society at the same time as, or immediately preceding, the regular meeting of the General Assembly. This convention shall elect the General Council of the General Nazarene World Mission Society in harmony with the Constitution. The convention shall elect a general president, who shall be a member ex officio of the General Council of the General Nazarene World Mission Society. (811.3)

R. National Boards

341. Where deemed necessary, a national board shall be established to facilitate the fulfillment of the church's mission allowing for unified strategies for evangelism, discipleship, church planting, district development, new districts, ministerial preparation, resource development, and ministerial retirement savings plans; by providing for the acquiring, holding, selling, and conveying of property; or by dealing with any other administrative and/or legal business matters relative to the Church of the Nazarene in that nation, for which no other provision is made in the *Manual*. Such a board shall be recognized as a lawful authority of the Church of the Nazarene in that nation.

Where only one district of the Church of the Nazarene is organized in the nation, the duly elected District Advisory Board shall be the national board to conduct business as outlined above.

Where there are two or more organized districts in one nation, the national board shall be composed of the duly appointed or elected district superintendents, as well as one elder and two lay representatives elected by the District Assembly, from the members of the District Advisory Board; or, with the approval of the General Board and the Board of General Superintendents, the membership shall consist of those persons duly elected or appointed as district superintendents and additional representation of ordained ministers and laypersons as agreed upon.

Where there is more than one region in one nation, the duly elected representatives from said regions to the

General Board shall constitute the national board. (330-30.2)

A copy of the articles of organization or incorporation of such board shall be filed immediately with the general secretary. Any business transacted by the national board shall be subject to the approval of the Board of General Superintendents. The minutes of the annual and special meetings of the national board shall be submitted to the general secretary for reading and approval by the General Board.

S. The Region

342. Origin and Purpose. In the growth of the church worldwide, there has developed a grouping of several organized districts into geographical areas identified as regions. A cluster of districts amenable to the general government of the Church of the Nazarene and having a sense of area and cultural identification may be formed into an administrative region by action of the General Board and approval of the Board of General Superintendents.

342.1. Regional Policy. In keeping with the nonsymmetrical approach to organization, the Board of General Superintendents may, when deemed necessary, and in consultation with the Regional Advisory Council, structure administrative regions according to the particular needs, potential problems, existing realities, and diverse cultural and educational backgrounds in their particular geographic areas of the world. In such situations, the Board of General Superintendents shall establish a policy that embraces nonnegotiable commitments including our Articles of Faith, faithful adherence to our Holiness doctrine and lifestyle, and support of our extensive missionary outreach efforts.

342.2. Duties. The **principal duties of the regions** are:

1. To implement the mission of the Church of the Nazarene through the established pioneer areas, districts, and institutions
2. To develop regional awareness, fellowship, and strategies to fulfill the Great Commission, bringing district

and institutional representatives together periodically for planning, prayer, and inspiration

3. To nominate persons to the General Assembly and General Conventions for elections to the General Board
4. In harmony with *Manual* provisions, to establish and maintain such schools and colleges or other institutions as they shall determine
5. To be authorized to recruit and screen missionary candidates from the region in accordance with policy (342.3)
6. To plan Regional Advisory Council meetings and conferences for the region
7. To encourage and develop as fully as possible, national boards who shall coordinate strategies for evangelism, growth, literature, programs, education, and discipleship among the districts and local churches of said nation under the direction of the Regional Advisory Council where applicable (342.3)

342.3. Regional Advisory Council (RAC). A region may have a Regional Advisory Council whose responsibilities will be to assist the regional director in strategy development for the region, to review and recommend approval or disapproval of all national board minutes before forwarding the same to the office of the general secretary, to recruit and screen missionary candidates for recommendation to the World Mission Division and/or for deployment as regional missionaries (*Manual* 342.2, item 5), to receive reports from the regional director, field directors, and ministry coordinators, to elect missionary delegates to the General Assembly in accordance with provisions of the *Manual,* and to elect a principal/rector/president of an International Board of Education institution as a delegate to the General Assembly.

Membership of the RAC shall be in accordance with policies of the region as approved by the World Mission Department and/or the general superintendent in jurisdiction; however, all non ex officio members shall be elected.

If the Regional Advisory Council so chooses, they may

convene a Regional Council constituted to facilitate the work of the region, and to deal with matters pertaining to the respective region under the chairmanship of the general superintendent in jurisdiction, or his or her representative.

342.4. The Regional Director. Where deemed necessary a region may have a director elected by the Board of General Superintendents in consultation with the World Mission Division director, and ratified by the General Board, to work in harmony with the policies and practices of the Church of the Nazarene giving leadership to the districts, churches, and institutions of said region in fulfillment of the mission, strategies, and program of the church.

Each regional director is to be administratively accountable to the World Mission Division, and the General Board, and in jurisdictional matters, accountable to the Board of General Superintendents.

CHAPTER IV

HIGHER EDUCATION

A. Church and College/University

380. The Church of the Nazarene, from its inception, has been committed to higher education. The church provides the college/university with students, administrative and faculty leadership, and financial and spiritual support. The college/university educates the church's youth and many of the church's adults, guides them toward spiritual maturity, enriches the church, and sends out into the world thinking, loving servants of Christ. The church college/university, while not a local congregation, is an integral part of the church; it is an expression of the church.

The Church of the Nazarene believes in the value and the dignity of human life and the need for providing an environment in which people can be redeemed and enriched spiritually, intellectually, and physically, "made holy, useful to the Master and prepared to do any good work" (2 Timothy 2:21). The primary task and traditional expressions of local church activity—evangelism, religious education, compassionate ministries, and services of worship—exemplify the church's love for God and concern for people.

At the local church level, the Christian education of youth and adults at various stages of human development intensifies the effectiveness of the gospel. Congregations may incorporate within their objectives and function weekday educational programs at any or all levels from preschool training through high school. At the general church level, the historic practice of providing institutions for higher education or ministerial preparation will be maintained. Wherever such institutions are operated, they shall function within the philosophical and theological framework of the Church of the Nazarene as established by the General Assembly and expressed through the *Manual*.

380.1. Educational Mission Statement. Education in the Church of the Nazarene, rooted in the biblical and theological commitments of the Wesleyan and Holiness movements and accountable to the stated mission of the denomination, aims to guide those who look to it in accepting, in nurturing, and in expressing in service to the church and world consistent and coherent Christian understandings of social and individual life. Additionally, such institutions of higher education will seek to provide a curriculum, quality of instruction, and evidence of scholastic achievement that will adequately prepare graduates to function effectively in vocations and professions such graduates may choose.

380.2. General Assembly authorization, upon the recommendation of the International Board of Education, is required to establish degree granting institutions.

Authorization for the development or change of status of existing institutions may be granted by the General Board upon recommendation of the International Board of Education.

No local church or combination of churches, or persons representing a local church or group of churches, may establish or sponsor a post-high school level or ministerial preparatory institution on behalf of the church, except upon the recommendation of the International Board of Education.

B. International Higher Education Council

381. There shall be an International Higher Education Council composed of the president, principal, rector, or director (or his or her designated representative) of each International Board of Education institution of the Church of the Nazarene, the regional education coordinators, the education commissioner, the World Mission Division director, and the responsible general superintendent for the International Board of Education.

C. International Board of Education

382. The International Board of Education shall be the general church advocate for educational institutions in the Church of the Nazarene worldwide.

This board shall be composed of 13 members: 8 elected by the General Board, plus 5 members ex officio: the 2 education representatives on the General Board, the World Mission Division director, the Pastoral Ministries director, and the education commissioner (383). A nominating committee composed of the education commissioner, the World Mission Division director, the 2 education representatives on the General Board, and the general superintendents responsible for the International Board of Education and World Mission Division shall present 16 nominees approved by the Board of General Superintendents to the General Board for election of the 8 elected members.

In an effort to insure broad representation throughout the church, the Nominating Committee shall submit nominees as follows: two regional education coordinators, of whom one shall be elected; six laypersons, one from each World Mission region, of whom three shall be elected; four ordained ministers from World Mission regions where no person who is an education coordinator has been nominated, two shall be elected; four "at large" nominees, of whom two shall be elected. No World Mission region shall have more than one elected member on the IBOE until each region has a representative.

Throughout the nominating and election process, attention shall be given to the election of persons with cross-cultural perspective and/or experience as educators.

Nominees shall be paired on the ballot as suggested by the Nominating Committee, which will take into consideration all provisions of *Manual* paragraph 382.

The **functions of the International Board of Education** are:

382.1. To insure that institutions are under the legal control of their respective governing boards whose constitutions and bylaws shall conform to their respective charters or articles of incorporation and that shall be in harmony with the guidelines set by the *Manual of the Church of the Nazarene.*

382.2. To insure that members of governing boards of

Nazarene institutions shall be members of the Church of the Nazarene in good standing. They are to be in full accord with the Articles of Faith, including the doctrine of entire sanctification and the usages of the Church of the Nazarene as set forth in the *Manual* of the church. Insofar as possible, the membership of the higher education boards of control shall have an equal number of ministers and laity.

382.3. To receive such funds as may be contributed to it for educational purposes through gifts, bequests, and donations, and shall annually recommend allocations from these funds to each educational institution in accordance with policy adopted by the General Board. Institutions shall not continue to receive regular support unless their education standards, plan of organization, and financial reports are filed with the International Board of Education.

382.4. To receive and deal appropriately with a yearly report from the education commissioner summarizing the following information from all International Board of Education institutions: (1) annual statistical report, (2) annual audit report, and (3) annual fiscal budgets for the upcoming year.

382.5. To recommend and to provide support and advocacy, although its role is advisory to the institutions, to the Board of General Superintendents and to the General Board.

382.6. To serve the church in matters pertaining to Nazarene educational institutions in order to strengthen the bonds between the institutions and the church at large.

382.7. To submit its business and recommendations to the Board of General Superintendents and the General Board for ratification in the same manner as is the business and recommendations of departments of the General Board.

D. Education Commissioner

383. The administrator of the International Board of Education is the education commissioner, who shall be elected by the General Board from two nominees approved by the Board of General Superintendents and presented by a nominating committee composed of the two education representatives on the General Board, the general superintendents responsible for the International Board of Education and the World Mission Division, the World Mission Division director, and the chair of the International Higher Education Council. (382)

The education commissioner may be reelected as an incumbent by a "yes" or "no" vote of the General Board upon approval of the nominating committee.

The duties of the education commissioner shall be detailed in the General Board Bylaws. (382)

384. All institutional constitutions and bylaws must include an article on dissolution and disposal of assets indicating that the Church of the Nazarene shall receive such assets to be used for educational services for the church.

PART V

Ministry and Christian Service

CALL AND QUALIFICATIONS OF THE MINISTER

CATEGORIES AND ROLES OF MINISTRY

EDUCATION FOR MINISTERS

CREDENTIALS AND MINISTERIAL REGULATIONS

CHAPTER I

CALL AND QUALIFICATIONS OF THE MINISTER[1]

400. The Church of the Nazarene recognizes and insists that all believers have committed to them a dispensation of the gospel that they are to minister to all people.

We also recognize and hold that the Head of the Church calls some men and women to the more official and public work of the ministry. As our Lord called to Him whom He would, and chose and ordained His 12 apostles "that they might be with him and that he might send them out to preach" (Mark 3:14), so He still calls and sends out messengers of the gospel. The church, illuminated by the Holy Spirit, will recognize the Lord's call.

The church also recognizes on the basis of Scripture and experience that God calls individuals to a lifetime of ministry who do not witness to a specific call to preach.

When the church discovers a divine call, the proper steps should be taken for its recognition and endorsement, and all suitable help should be given to open the way for the candidate to enter the ministry.

401. The perpetuity and efficiency of the Church of the Nazarene depend largely upon the spiritual qualifications, the character, and the manner of life of its ministers. (433.14)

401.1. The minister of Christ is to be in all things a pattern to the flock—in punctuality, discretion, diligence, earnestness; "in purity, understanding, patience and kindness;

---

1. The *Manual* Editing Committee, in recognition of the validity of the opening words of paragraph 400, has attempted to use language that reflects this distinctive. However, due to the nature of this section of the *Manual,* the terms "minister" or "the minister" will usually refer to a person holding credentials, whether licensed, ordained, or commissioned.

in the Holy Spirit and in sincere love; in truthful speech and in the power of God; with weapons of righteousness in the right hand and in the left" (2 Corinthians 6:6-7).

401.2. The minister of the gospel in the Church of the Nazarene must have peace with God through our Lord Jesus Christ, and be sanctified wholly by the baptism with the Holy Spirit. The minister must have a deep sense of the fact that souls for whom Christ died are perishing, and that he or she is called of God to proclaim or make known to them the glad tidings of salvation.

401.3. The minister must likewise have a deep sense of the necessity of believers going on to perfection and developing the Christian graces in practical living, that their "love may abound more and more in knowledge and depth of insight" (Philippians 1:9). One who would minister in the Church of the Nazarene must have a strong appreciation of both salvation and Christian ethics.

401.4. The minister must have gifts, as well as graces, for the work. He or she will have a thirst for knowledge, especially of the Word of God, and must have sound judgment, good understanding, and clear views concerning the plan of redemption and salvation as revealed in the Scriptures. Saints will be edified and sinners converted through his or her ministry. Further, the minister of the gospel in the Church of the Nazarene must be an example in prayer.

401.5. The minister should respond to opportunities to mentor future ministers and to nurture the call to ministry of those who have obvious gifts and graces for ministry or who are hearing the call of God to Christian ministry.

CHAPTER II

CATEGORIES AND ROLES OF MINISTRY

402. The Church of the Nazarene recognizes only one order of the preaching ministry, that of the elder. It also recognizes that the member of the clergy may serve the church in various capacities. Christ has called "some to be apostles, some to be prophets, some to be evangelists, and some to be pastors and teachers, to prepare God's people for works of service, so that the body of Christ may be built up" (Ephesians 4:11-12). The church recognizes the following categories of service in which a district assembly may place an elder, deacon, or, as circumstances warrant, a licensed minister: pastor, evangelist, missionary, teacher, administrator, chaplain, and special service. Service within these categories that qualifies as being an "assigned minister" would include that service for which ministerial training and ordination are normally required, or greatly desired. The *Sourcebook for Ministerial Development* shall provide guidelines for each category of ministry that will aid district boards in identifying the qualifications necessary for consideration to be an assigned minister. Only assigned ministers shall be voting members of the district assembly.

402.1. All persons assigned to a particular role shall file a report annually to the assigning district assembly.

402.2. All persons assigned to a particular role may request and obtain annually from the assigning district a certificate of their role of service, signed by the district superintendent and the district secretary.

402.3. All persons assigned to a particular role of ministry, when placed on disability by approved medical authority, may be listed as "assigned disabled."

The roles of ministry are listed in alphabetical order for convenience.

A. The Administrator

403. The elder or a deacon who is an administrator is the one who has been elected by the General Assembly as a general official; or a member of the clergy who has been elected or employed by the General Board to serve in the general church; or an elder who has been elected by the district assembly as district superintendent; or a member of the clergy who has been elected or employed full-time in the service of a district. Such person is an assigned minister.

B. The Chaplain

404. The elder or deacon who is a chaplain is one who feels divinely led to specialized ministry in military, institutional, or industrial chaplaincy. All chaplains must be approved by their district superintendent. Persons applying for full-time U.S.A. military chaplaincy must appear before the Chaplaincy Advisory Council and the Board of General Superintendents. The chaplain who gives full-time to this ministry as his or her primary assignment and who does not sustain a retired relationship with the church or any of its departments or institutions, shall be an assigned minister, and shall report annually to the district assembly and give due regard to the advice and counsel of the district superintendent and the District Advisory Board. The chaplain may receive associate members into the Church of the Nazarene in consultation with an officially organized Church of the Nazarene, administer the sacraments in harmony with *Manual* 427.7-27.8, give pastoral care, comfort the sorrowing, reprove and encourage and seek by all means the conversion of sinners, sanctification of believers, and the upbuilding of the people of God in the most holy faith. (416, 433.9, 433.11)

C. The Deaconess

405. A woman who is a member of the Church of the Nazarene and believes that she is divinely led to engage in ministering to the sick and the needy, comforting the sorrowing, and doing other works of Christian benevolence, and who has given evidence in her life of ability, grace, and usefulness, and who was in the years preceding 1985 licensed or consecrated as a deaconess shall continue in such standing. However, those women called to full-time ministry but not called to preach shall complete the requirements for ordination to the order of deacon. Women desiring a credential for compassionate ministries may pursue the requirements for lay minister. (113.7, 408-8.8)

D. The Educator

406. The educator is a member of the clergy or a layperson serving as an educator.

406.1. When an educator having a ministerial credential has been employed to serve on the administrative staff or faculty of one of the educational institutions of the Church of the Nazarene, the district shall designate such a person as an assigned minister.

E. The Evangelist

407. The elder or licensed minister who is an evangelist is one devoted to traveling and preaching the gospel, and who is authorized by the church to promote revivals and to spread the gospel of Jesus Christ abroad in the land. The Church of the Nazarene recognizes three levels of itinerant evangelism to which a district assembly may assign ministers: registered evangelist, commissioned evangelist, and tenured evangelist. An evangelist who dedicates time to evangelism, outside his or her local church as his or her primary assignment and who does not sustain a retired relationship with the church or any of its departments or institutions, shall be an assigned minister.

407.1. A registered evangelist is an elder, or a licensed minister, who has indicated a desire to pursue evangelism as his or her primary ministry. Such registration shall be for one year. Renewal by subsequent district assemblies shall be granted on both the quality and quantity of work in evangelism in the year prior to the assembly.

407.2. A commissioned evangelist is an elder who has met all the requirements of a registered evangelist for two full years. The commission is for one year and may be renewed by subsequent district assemblies for one who continues to meet the requirements.

407.3. A tenured evangelist is an elder who has met all the requirements of a commissioned evangelist for four full and consecutive years immediately prior to application for tenured evangelist status, and has been recommended by the District Ministerial Credentials Board and approved by the Committee on the Interests of the God-Called Evangelist and the Board of General Superintendents. This role designation shall continue until such time as the evangelist no longer meets the requirements of a commissioned evangelist, or until he or she is granted retired status. (228.2, 431)

407.4. A regular self-assessment and review similar to the pastoral review shall be conducted by the evangelist and district superintendent together at least every four years after the election to the tenured role. The district superintendent shall be responsible for scheduling and conducting the meeting. This meeting shall be scheduled in consultation with the evangelist. Upon completion of the review, a report of the results shall be forwarded to the Committee on the Interests of the God-Called Evangelist to evaluate qualification requirements for continued approval. (208.18)

407.5. An elder or licensed minister who sustains a retired relationship with the church or any of its departments, and who wishes to perform a ministerial function through revivals or evangelistic meetings, may receive certification for "retired evangelism service." Such certification shall be for one year, shall be voted by the district assembly upon recommendation by the district superintendent, and may be renewed by subsequent district assemblies on the basis of actual work in evangelism in the year prior to the assembly.

407.6. An elder or licensed minister desiring to enter the field of evangelism between district assemblies may be recognized by the general office of Evangelism Ministries upon recommendation of the district superintendent. The registration or commission shall be voted by the district assembly upon recommendation by the district superintendent.

407.7. Guidelines and procedures for certification of evangelists' roles will be contained in the *Sourcebook for Ministerial Development.*

F. The Lay Minister

408. All Christians should consider themselves ministers of Christ and seek to know the will of God concerning their appropriate avenues of service. (400 and *Sourcebook for Ministerial Development*)

408.1. Any member of the Church of the Nazarene who feels called to serve as a church planter, bivocational pastor, teacher, lay evangelist, lay song evangelist, stewardship minister, church staff minister, and/or other specialized ministry on behalf of the church, but who does not at the present time feel a special call to become an ordained minister, may pursue a course leading to a certificate of lay ministry.

408.2. The church board, upon the recommendation of the pastor, shall initially examine the lay minister as to personal experience of salvation, effective involvement in church ministries, and knowledge of the work of the church, and satisfy itself as to the lay minister's qualifications for such ministry.

408.3. The local church board may issue to each lay minister candidate a certificate signed by the pastor and the secretary of the church board. The certificate of the lay minister may be renewed annually by the church board upon the recommendation of the pastor, if the lay minister has completed at least two subjects in Level I of the ministerial course of study or the area of the ministry specialty.

408.4. The lay minister shall report annually to the church board.

408.5. For a lay minister serving under district assignment as church planter, supply pastor, bivocational pastor, and/or other specialized ministry, upon completion of the required course of study, a certificate of lay ministry may be issued by the District Advisory Board, signed by the district superintendent and the secretary of the District Advisory Board. The certificate of lay ministry may be renewed annually by the District Advisory Board upon the recommendation of the district superintendent.

408.6. The lay minister serving outside the local church where he or she is a member shall be subject to the appointment and supervision of the district superintendent and the District Advisory Board, and shall report annually to them. When district assignment shall cease, reference shall be made back to the local church in which the lay minister holds membership for renewal and reporting.

408.7. After completion of Level I in the ministerial course of study, a lay minister shall proceed in a specialized concentration of study according to his or her chosen ministry. (See *Sourcebook for Ministerial Development.*) However, the provision for taking the course in Level I of the ministerial course of study, and for grading and recording the same, will be made at the district level.

408.8. A lay minister shall not be eligible to administer the sacraments of baptism and the Lord's Supper, and shall not officiate at marriages.

G. The Minister of Christian Education

409. A member of the clergy employed in a ministerial capacity in a Christian education program of a local church may be assigned as a minister of Christian education.

409.1. A person who was, in the years preceding 1985, licensed or commissioned as a minister of Christian education, shall continue in good standing. However, those persons desiring to begin the pursuit of the role of minister of Christian education may complete the requirements for ordination to the order of deacon as their credential for this ministry.

H. The Minister of Music

410. A member of the Church of the Nazarene who feels called to the ministry of music may be commissioned as a minister of music for one year by the district assembly, provided such person (1) has been recommended for such work by the church board of the local church in which membership is held; (2) gives evidence of grace, gifts, and usefulness; (3) has had at least one year of experience in music ministry; (4) has had not less than one year of vocal study under an accredited teacher and is pursuing the course of study or its equivalent prescribed for ministers of music or has completed the same; (5) is regularly engaged as a minister of music; (6) has been carefully examined, under the direction of the district assembly of the assembly district within the bounds of which the person holds his or her church membership, regarding his or her intellectual and spiritual qualifications, and general fitness for such work. (203.8)

410.1. Only such persons who maintain a full-time employment in this ministry as their primary assignment and vocation and have ministerial credentials shall be considered assigned ministers.

I. The Missionary

411. The missionary is a member of the clergy or a layperson who has been appointed by the General Board to minister for the church through the World Mission Department or through the Church Growth Department. A missionary with an appointment and having a ministerial credential shall be considered an assigned minister.

J. The Pastor

412. A pastor is a minister (115) who, under the call of God and His people, has the oversight of a local church. A pastor in charge of a local church is an assigned minister. (210)

413. The **duties of a pastor** are:

413.1. To preach the Word.

413.2. To equip the saints for the work of the ministry.

413.3. To receive persons as members of the local church according to 107 and 107.1.

413.4. To administer the sacraments in harmony with 427.7-27.8.

413.5. To care for the people by pastoral visitation, particularly the sick and needy.

413.6. To comfort those who mourn.

413.7. To correct, rebuke, and encourage, with great patience and careful instruction.

413.8. To seek, by all means, the conversion of sinners, the entire sanctification of the converted, and the upbuilding of God's people in the most holy faith. (25)

413.9. To have the care of all departments of local church work.

413.10. To appoint the teachers of the Sunday School in harmony with 146.8.

413.11. To administer the sacrament of the Lord's Supper at least once a quarter. A licensed minister who has not complied fully with the provisions of 427.7-27.8 (see also 802) shall arrange for the administration of the sacrament by an ordained minister.

413.12. To read to the congregation the Constitution of the Church of the Nazarene and the Special Rules contained in 1-27, 33-39, both inclusive, within each year (114), or have this section of the *Manual* printed and distributed annually to the members of the church.

413.13. To supervise the preparation of all statistical reports from all departments of the local church, and present promptly all such reports through the district secretary to the district assembly. (114.1)

413.14. To give leadership to the evangelism, education, devotion, and expansion programs of the local church in harmony with the district and general church promotional goals and programs.

413.15. To submit a report to the annual church meeting, including a report on the status of the local church and its departments, and an outline of areas of future needs with recommendations for reference by the church to any of its officers or departments for study and/or implementation in future steps for growth and progress.

413.16. To appoint an investigating committee of three in case of accusation filed against a church member. (501-1.2)

413.17. To see that all World Evangelism Fund moneys raised through the local missionary society are remitted promptly to the general treasurer; and that all District Ministries Fund moneys are remitted promptly to the district treasurer. (135.2)

413.18. To nominate to the church board all persons who are paid employees of the local church, and to have supervision of the same. (161.1-61.3)

413.19. To sign in conjunction with the church secretary all conveyances of real estate, mortgages, releases of mortgages, contracts, and other legal documents not otherwise provided for in the *Manual*. (102.1, 103-4.2)

413.20. To notify the pastor of the nearest church when a member or friend of a local church or any of its departments moves to another locality in the same assembly district where vital association with the previous local church is impractical, giving the member's or friend's address. If the move is to a locality beyond the assembly district, the pastor shall immediately inform the CARE-Line of the Evangelism and Church Growth Division, giving the name and the new address.

413.21. To arrange, together with the church board, according to plans adopted by the General Assembly and agreed to by the district assembly, for the raising of the World Evangelism Fund and District Ministries Fund apportionments made to the local church; and to raise these apportionments. (38.2, 130, 155)

413.22. The pastor may, when requested by a member, grant a transfer of church membership, a certificate of commendation, or a letter of release. (111-11.1, 112.2)

413.23. The pastor shall be, ex officio, president of the local church, chairman of the church board, a member of the board or council of the Sunday School ministries and any weekday Nazarene school organization, the Nazarene Youth International, the Nazarene World Mission Society, and all other subsidiary organizations in connection with the local church. (127, 146, 151.2, 153, 154.1)

413.24. To nurture the call that people feel toward

Christian ministry and to mentor such persons as are called. This shall include guiding them toward appropriate preparation for ministry.

413.25. To fulfill the expectations of God and the Church for a program of lifelong learning.

413.26. To nurture his or her own call through the years of ministry, to maintain a life of personal devotion that enriches his or her own soul, and, if married, to guard the integrity and vitality of that marriage relationship.

414. The pastor shall have the right to a voice in the nomination of all heads of all departments of the local church, and any Nazarene weekday school organization.

415. The pastor shall not contract bills, create financial obligations, count moneys, or disburse funds for the local church unless authorized and directed by majority vote of the church board or by majority vote of a church meeting; such action, if taken, must be approved in writing by the District Advisory Board and shall be duly recorded in the minutes of the church board or of the church meeting. No pastor shall be authorized to sign checks on any church account except upon the approval of the district superintendent. (129.1, 129.22-29.23)

416. The pastor shall always show due regard for the united advice of the district superintendent and the District Advisory Board. (222.2, 433.2)

417. In case a licensed or ordained minister presenting credentials from another denomination shall, during the interim of sessions of the district assembly, make application for membership in a local church, the pastor may not receive such applicant without first having obtained the favorable recommendation of the District Advisory Board. (107, 225)

418. For the exercise of this office the pastor shall be amenable to the district assembly, to which he or she shall report annually and give brief testimony to his or her personal Christian experience. (203.1, 427.9, 433.9)

419. The pastor shall automatically become a member of the church of which he or she is pastor; or, in case of more than one church in his or her charge, of the church of his or her choice. (433.8)

420. Pastoral Service includes the ministry of a pastor, an associate pastor, and/or an assistant pastor, who may specialize in such ways as minister of Christian education, minister of music, minister of visitation, or minister of youth. A member of the clergy called to any of these levels of pastoral service in connection with a church or mission may be considered an assigned minister.

421. Supply Pastors. A district superintendent shall have the power to appoint a supply pastor, who shall serve subject to the following regulations:

1. A supply pastor may be a Nazarene member of the clergy serving in some other assignment, a local minister or a lay minister of the Church of the Nazarene, a minister in process of transfer from another denomination, or a minister who belongs to another denomination.
2. A supply pastor shall be appointed temporarily to fill the pulpit and to provide a spiritual ministry, but shall not have authority to administer the sacraments or to perform marriages unless that authority adheres to him or her on some other basis, and he or she shall not perform the administrative function of the pastor except in the filing of reports, unless authorized to do so by the district superintendent.
3. A supply pastor's church membership shall not be automatically transferred to the church where he or she is serving.
4. A supply pastor shall be granted a certificate of authorization to supply on the form provided, and shall be a nonvoting member of the district assembly unless he or she is a voting member by some other right.
5. A supply pastor may be removed or replaced at any time by the district superintendent.

K. The Song Evangelist

422. A song evangelist is a member of the Church of the Nazarene whose intention is to devote the major portion of his or her time to the ministry of evangelism through music. A song evangelist who has a ministerial credential and who gives full time to evangelism as his or her primary assignment, and who does not sustain a retired relationship with the church or any of its departments or institutions, shall be an assigned minister.

422.1. Guidelines and procedures for certification of song evangelists' roles are contained in the *Sourcebook for Ministerial Development.*

L. Special Service

423. A member of the clergy in active service not otherwise provided for shall be appointed to special service, if such service is approved by the district assembly, and shall be listed by the district as an assigned minister.

423.1. An elder or deacon employed in a ministerial capacity as an officer in a church-related organization serving the church, or approved upon careful evaluation of his or her district assembly to serve with an educational institution, evangelistic, or missionary organization not directly related to the church, may be appointed to special service subject to 433.11.

CHAPTER III

EDUCATION FOR MINISTERS

A. For Ministers

424. Ministerial education is designed to assist in the preparation of God-called ministers whose service is vital to the expansion and extension of the Holiness message into new areas of evangelistic opportunity. We recognize the importance of a clear understanding of our mission based on Christ's commission to His Church in Matthew 28:19-20, to "go and make disciples." Much of the preparation is primarily theological and biblical in character, leading toward ordination in the ministry of the Church of the Nazarene. The District Ministerial Studies Board shall determine the placement and evaluate the progress of each student in his or her program of study.

424.1. Fulfillment of Educational Foundations for Ordained Ministry. A variety of educational institutions and programs are provided around the world by the Church of the Nazarene. The resources of some world areas allow more than one program or track to be developed to provide the educational foundations for ministry. The normal expectation is that each student will take advantage of the most appropriate track of ministerial preparation provided by the Church in his or her area of the world. In some instances the particular circumstances of the student may make the ideal impossible. The Church will utilize as much flexibility in delivery systems as is feasible to make adequate preparation available to every person called by God to ministry in the Church. Tracks of a four-level program of Directed Studies, directed and supervised by the District Ministerial Studies Board, and college/seminary tracks, developed by the educational institutions, may be used. If multiple tracks are developed they should cover the same general subject areas. Licensed ministers shall be graduated from the course of study when they have satisfactorily completed a program of study leading toward ordination by Bible and liberal arts colleges/universities and seminaries, whose ordination programs have been endorsed by the International Course of Study Advisory Committee and recommended by Pastoral Ministries for adoption by the General Board and approval by the Board of General Superintendents.

424.2. Cultural Adaptations for the Educational Foundations for Ordained Ministry. The variety of cultural contexts around the world makes one curriculum unsuited for all world areas. Each region of the world will be responsible for the development of specific curricular requirements for providing the educational foundations for ministry in a way that reflects the resources and the expectations of that world area. Approval of the Course of Study Advisory Committee, the General Board, and the Board of General Superintendents (424.5) will be required before implementing a regionally designed program for providing educational foundations for ministry. Even within world regions there are varieties of cultural expectations and resources. As a result cultural sensitivity and flexibility will characterize regional provisions for the educational foundations for ministry that may include the use of a four-level program of Directed Studies, which shall be directed and supervised by the District Ministerial Studies Board. Cultural adaptations of each region's program for providing educational foundations for ministry will be approved by Pastoral Ministries and the Course of Study Advisory Committee in consultation with the regional educational director.

424.3. General Curriculum Areas for Ministerial Preparation. Though curriculum is often thought of only as academic programs and course content, the concept is much larger. The character of the instructor, the relationship of the students and instructor, the environment, and students' past experiences join with the course content to create the full curriculum. Nevertheless, a curriculum for ministerial preparation will include a minimal set of courses that provide educational foundations for ministry.

Cultural differences and a variety of resources will require differing details in curriculum structures. However, all programs for providing educational foundations for the ordained ministry that seek approval by Pastoral Ministries should give careful attention to content, competency, character, and context. All courses involve all four elements in varying degrees. The purpose of an approved program of study is to contain courses that will help ministers fulfill the mission statement of the Church of the Nazarene as agreed upon by the Board of General Superintendents as follows:

> "The mission of the Church of the Nazarene is to respond to the Great Commission of Christ to 'go and make disciples of all nations'" (Matthew 28:19). "The key objective of the Church of the Nazarene is to advance God's kingdom by the preservation and propagation of Christian holiness as set forth in the Scriptures."
>
> "The critical objectives of the Church of the Nazarene are 'holy Christian fellowship, the conversion of sinners, the entire sanctification of believers, their upbuilding in holiness and the simplicity and spiritual power manifest in the primitive New Testament Church, together with the preaching of the gospel to every creature'" (*Manual*, Paragraph 25).

The program of study is described in the following categories:

- Content—Knowledge of the content of the Old and New Testaments, the theology of the Christian faith, and the history and mission of the Church is essential for ministry. Knowledge of how to interpret Scripture, the doctrine of holiness and our Wesleyan distinctives, and the history and polity of the Church of the Nazarene must be included in these courses.
- Competency—Skills in oral and written communication; management and leadership; finance; and analyt-

ical thinking are also essential for ministry. In addition to general education in these areas, courses providing skills in preaching, pastoral care and counseling, worship, effective evangelism, Christian education and Church administration must be included. Graduation from the course of study requires the partnering of the educational provider and a local church to direct students in ministerial practices and competency development.

- Character—Personal growth in character, ethics, spirituality, and personal and family relationship is vital for the ministry. Courses addressing the areas of Christian ethics, spiritual formation, human development, the person of the minister, and marriage and family dynamics must be included.
- Context—The minister must understand both the historical and contemporary context and interpret the worldview and social environment of the culture where the Church witnesses. Courses that address the concerns of anthropology and sociology, cross-cultural communication, missions, and social studies must be included.

424.4. Preparation for the ordained ministry pursued in non-Nazarene schools or under non-Nazarene auspices shall be evaluated by the District Ministerial Studies Board in conformity with the curricular requirements stated in a *Sourcebook for Ministerial Development* developed by the region/language group.

424.5. All courses, academic requirements, and official administrative regulations shall be in a *Sourcebook for Ministerial Development* developed by the region/language group in cooperation with Pastoral Ministries. This *Sourcebook* and such revisions as become necessary shall be endorsed by the International Course of Study Advisory Committee and approved by Pastoral Ministries, the General Board, and the Board of General Superintendents. The *Sourcebook* shall be in compliance with the *Manual* and with an *International Sourcebook on Developmental Standards for Ordination,* produced by Pastoral Ministries with the International Course of

Study Advisory Committee. The International Course of Study Advisory Committee shall be appointed by the Board of General Superintendents.

424.6. Once a minister has fulfilled the expectations of the educational foundations for ministry he or she will continue a pattern of lifelong learning to enhance the ministry to which God has called him or her. A minimum expectation is 20 contact hours each year (2 accredited Continuing Education Units {CEUs}) or the equivalent determined by the region/language group and stated in their *Sourcebook for Ministerial Development.* All assigned ordained ministers shall report on their progress in a program of lifelong learning as part of their report to the district assembly. An up-to-date report on his or her lifelong learning program will be used in the pastoral review process and in the process of calling a pastor. The *Sourcebook for Ministerial Development* for the region/language group will contain the details of the accrediting and reporting process. At least 20 contact hours or its equivalent is recommended annually. (115, 121)

B. General Guidelines for Preparation for Christian Ministry

425. General guidelines for preparation for Christian ministry are:

425.1. The required courses of study, together with the necessary procedures concerning their completion for those seeking a credential as elder and deacon or certification such as for song evangelist and lay minister, are to be found in the *Sourcebook for Ministerial Development.* Language and cultural adaptations may be made with the approval of Pastoral Ministries. Write to Pastoral Ministries, 6401 The Paseo, Kansas City, MO 64131-1213.

425.2. In regions administratively related to the World Mission Division, all courses of study, as stated in the *Sourcebook for Ministerial Development,* may be adapted to the needs and available literature in those districts with the approval of Pastoral Ministries. (424.3, 424.5)

CHAPTER IV

CREDENTIALS AND MINISTERIAL REGULATIONS

A. The Local Minister

426. A local minister is a lay member of the Church of the Nazarene whom the local church board has licensed for ministry, under the pastor's direction, and as opportunity affords, thus providing for the demonstration, employment, and development of ministerial gifts and usefulness. He or she is entering into a process of lifelong learning.

426.1. Any member of the Church of the Nazarene who feels called of God to preach or to pursue lifetime ministry through the church may be licensed as a local minister for one year by the church board of a local church having an elder as pastor, upon the pastor's recommendation; or by the church board of a local church not having an elder as pastor, if the granting of license is recommended by the pastor and approved by the district superintendent. The candidate must first be examined as to his or her personal experience of salvation, knowledge of the doctrines of the Bible, and the order of the church; he or she must also demonstrate that the call is evidenced by grace, gifts, and usefulness. A local minister shall make a report to the local church at its annual church meetings. (113.7, 129.13, 208.10)

426.2. The church board shall issue to each local minister a license signed by the pastor and the secretary of the church board. Where a church is supplied by a person who does not have a district license, that person may be issued a local minister's license, or the renewal of license, by the District Advisory Board upon the recommendation of the district superintendent. (208.10, 222.10)

426.3. The license of a local minister may be renewed by the church board of a local church having an elder as pastor, upon the recommendation of the pastor; or by the church board of a local church not having an elder as pastor, provided that the renewal of license is recommended by the pastor and approved by the district superintendent. (129.13, 208.10)

426.4. Local ministers shall pursue the course of study for ministers under the direction of the District Ministerial Studies Board. Local license cannot be renewed after two years without the written approval of the district superintendent if the local minister has not completed at least two subjects in the course of study.

426.5. A local minister, having served in that relation for at least one full year, and having passed the necessary studies, may be recommended by the church board to the district assembly for minister's license; but, if not received, he or she shall sustain his or her former relation. (129.13, 424, 427.1)

426.6. A local minister who has been appointed as supply pastor must be approved by the Ministerial Credentials Board if he or she continues this service after the district assembly following the appointment. (209, 228.4)

426.7. A local minister shall not be eligible to administer the sacraments of baptism and the Lord's Supper, and shall not officiate at marriages. (427.7-27.8)

B. The Licensed Minister

427. A licensed minister is one whose ministerial calling and gifts have been formally recognized by the district assembly through the granting of a ministerial license, authorizing the minister for, and appointing him or her to, a larger sphere of service and to greater rights and responsibilities than those pertaining to a local minister, as a step toward ordination as an elder or a deacon. The district ministerial license shall include a statement indicating whether the minister is preparing for ordination as an elder or a deacon. (427.7, 427.8)

427.1. When there are members of the Church of the

Nazarene who acknowledge a call to a lifetime of ministry, they may be licensed as ministers by the district assembly provided they (1) have held a local minister's license for one full year; (2) have passed the complete first-year course of study for ministers, or if enrolled in a Nazarene college/university or seminary, have completed one-fourth of the units prescribed in the college/university or college/university-seminary program, or one-third of the Bible college ministerial curriculum. Exceptions to this requirement may be made by the District Ministerial Credentials Board provided the candidate is pastoring an organized church and is registered in a system of approved studies, and provided the candidate annually fulfills the minimum amount of studies required by the *Manual* for the renewal of a license, and provided the district superintendent approves the exception; (3) have been recommended for such work by the church board of the local church of which they are members, to which recommendation shall be attached the Application for Minister's License carefully filled in; (4) have given evidence of grace, gifts, and usefulness; (5) have been carefully examined, under the direction of the district assembly of the district within the bounds of which they hold their church membership, regarding their spiritual, intellectual, and other fitness for such work; (6) have promised to pursue immediately the course of study prescribed for licensed ministers and candidates for ordination; (7) have had any disqualification, which may have been imposed by a district assembly, removed by an explanation in writing by the district superintendent and the District Advisory Board of the district where the disqualification was imposed; and provided further that their marriage relationship does not render them ineligible for a district license or ordination; and (8) in case of a previous divorce and remarriage, the recommendation of the District Ministerial Credentials Board along with supporting documents will be given to the Board of General Superintendents, which may remove this as a barrier to pursuing a license or ordination. (35.1-35.3, 129.15, 205.7, 426.5)

427.2. Licensed ministers from other evangelical denominations, desiring to unite with the Church of the Nazarene, may be licensed as ministers by the district assembly, provided they present the credentials issued to them by the denomination in which they formerly held their membership; and further provided that they (1) have passed a course of study equivalent at least to the course of study prescribed by the Church of the Nazarene for local ministers; (2) have been recommended by the church board of the local Church of the Nazarene of which they are members; (3) have given evidence of grace, gifts, and usefulness; (4) have been carefully examined under the direction of the district assembly regarding their spiritual, intellectual, and other fitness for such work; and (5) have promised to pursue immediately the course of study prescribed for licensed ministers and candidates for ordination. (203.5)

427.3. A minister's license shall terminate with the close of the next district assembly. It may be renewed by vote of the district assembly, provided (1) that the candidate for renewal shall file with the district assembly the Application for Minister's License carefully filled in; and provided (2) that the candidate shall have completed at least two subjects in the year's course of study required, not including subjects in the reading course; and provided (3) that the candidate has been recommended for the renewal of license by the church board of the local church of which he or she is a member, upon the nomination of the pastor. In case, however, he or she shall not have passed the course of study required, the license may be renewed by the district assembly only upon submission of a written explanation for this failure. Such explanation shall be satisfactory to the District Ministerial Credentials Board and approved by the general superintendent presiding. The district assembly may, for cause and at its discretion, vote against the renewal of a minister's license.

Licensed ministers who have graduated from the course of study and have been placed in retired relation by the district assembly shall, with the recommendation of the District Advisory Board, have their license renewed without the filing of an Application for Minister's License. (203.2)

427.4. To qualify for ordination, candidates must achieve graduation from the course of study within 10 years from the granting of the first district license. Any exception, due to unusual circumstances, must be recommended to the district assembly, including a specified time limit, by the Ministerial Credentials Board and be subject to the approval of the general superintendent in jurisdiction.

A licensed minister who is disqualified from ordination for failure to complete the course of study within the prescribed time limit may be granted renewal of minister's license upon recommendation of the District Advisory Board and the Ministerial Credentials Board.

427.5. In the case of licensed ministers who are serving as pastors, the recommendation for the renewal of minister's license shall be made by the District Advisory Board rather than by the local church board. (222.10)

427.6. The general superintendent having jurisdiction shall issue to each licensed minister a minister's license, bearing the signature of the general superintendent in jurisdiction, the district superintendent, and the district secretary.

427.7. Licensed ministers preparing for the order of elder shall be vested with authority to preach the Word; and, provided they pass annually the required studies of the course of study and are acting as pastors, or are involved in a full-time active ministry recognized by the district on which their membership is held, they shall also be vested with authority to administer the sacraments of baptism and the Lord's Supper in their own congregations, and to officiate at marriages where the laws of the state do not prohibit. (34.5, 35.2, 413, 413.4, 413.11, 800, 802, 803)

427.8. Licensed ministers preparing for the order of deacon shall be vested with authority to use their gifts and graces in various associate ministries in servant ministry to the Body of Christ; and, provided they pass annually the required studies of the course of study and are involved in a full-time active ministry recognized by the district on which their membership is held, they shall also be vested with authority to administer the sacraments and, on occasion, to conduct worship and to preach. (34.5, 409-10, 413.4, 413.11, 420, 428-28.2, 800, 802)

427.9. All licensed ministers shall hold their ministerial membership in the district assembly of the district wherein their church membership is held, and shall report to this body annually. (201, 203.1, 418)

427.10. In case a licensed minister has united with the church membership or ministry of another denomination, his or her church membership and ministerial membership in the Church of the Nazarene shall, because of that fact, immediately cease, and the district assembly shall cause to be entered into its minute record the following statement: "Removed from the membership and ministry of the Church of the Nazarene by uniting with another denomination." (107, 112)

C. The Deacon

428. A deacon is a minister whose call of God to Christian ministry, gifts, and usefulness have been demonstrated and enhanced by proper training and experience, who has been separated to the service of Christ by a vote of a district assembly and by the solemn act of ordination, and who has been invested to perform certain functions of Christian ministry.

428.1. The deacon does not witness to a specific call to preach. The church recognizes, on the basis of Scripture and experience, that God calls individuals to lifetime ministry who do not witness to such a specific call, and believes that individuals so called to such ministries should be recognized and confirmed by the church and should meet requirements, and be granted responsibilities, established by the church. This is a permanent order of ministry.

428.2. The deacon must meet the requirements of the order for education, exhibit the appropriate gifts and graces, and be recognized and confirmed by the church. The deacon shall be vested with the authority to administer the sacraments and on occasion to conduct worship and to preach. It is understood that the Lord and the church may use this person's gifts and graces in various associate ministries. As a symbol of the servant ministry of the Body of Christ, the deacon may also use his or her gifts in roles outside the institutional church.

428.3. One who is called of God to this ministry, and who has fulfilled all the requirements of the church for the same, who has successfully completed the full course of study prescribed for licensed ministers and candidates for ordination as deacon, who has been a district licensed minister for two years and recommended for renewal of district license by the church board of the local church in which he or she holds membership or by the District Advisory Board, and has been carefully considered and favorably reported by the Ministerial Credentials Board to the district assembly, may be elected to the order of deacon by two-thirds vote of the district assembly; provided he or she has been an assigned minister not less than two consecutive years; and provided further that any disqualification that may have been imposed by a district assembly has been removed in writing by the district superintendent and District Advisory Board of said district; and provided further that his or her marriage relationship does not render him or her ineligible for ordination. (35.1-35.3)

428.4. If in the pursuance of his or her ministry, the ordained deacon feels called to the preaching ministry, he or she may be ordained elder upon completion of the requirements for that credential and the return of the deacon credential.

D. The Elder

429. An elder is a minister whose call of God to preach, gifts, and usefulness have been demonstrated and enhanced by proper training and experience, and who has been separated to the service of Christ through His church by the vote of a district assembly and by the solemn act of ordination, and thus has been fully invested to perform all functions of the Christian ministry.

429.1. We recognize but one order of preaching ministry—that of elder. This is a permanent order in the church. The elder is to rule well in the church, to preach the Word, to administer the sacraments of baptism and the Lord's Supper, and to solemnize matrimony, all in the name of, and in subjection to, Jesus Christ, the great Head of the Church. (34.5, 35.2, 412-13.3, 413.11, 433.12)

429.2. The church expects that one called to this official ministry should be a steward of the Word and give full energy through a lifetime to its proclamation.

429.3. One who is called of God to this ministry, and who has fulfilled all the requirements of the church for the same, who has successfully completed the full course of study prescribed for licensed ministers and candidates for ordination as elder, who has been a district licensed minister for two years and recommended for renewal of district license by the church board of the local church in which he or she holds membership or by the District Advisory Board, and has been carefully considered and favorably reported by the Ministerial Credentials Board of the district assembly, may be elected to the order of elder by two-thirds vote of the district assembly. To be eligible for election, the candidate must have been an assigned minister for not less than two consecutive years either as a pastor or as a registered evangelist (spending the major portion of that time actively in the field), or the candidate must have served three consecutive years as associate or assistant pastor; or one year as pastor and two consecutive years as an assigned associate or assistant pastor; or have served four years as an assigned teacher in the religion department of one of our Nazarene institutions of higher education, or in a Christian ministry in such other institutions and assigned roles approved by the Board of General Superintendents. Further, any disqualification that may have been imposed by a district assembly must be removed in writing by the district superintendent and the District Advisory Board of the district where the disqualification was imposed before the minister is eligible for election to elder's orders. In addition, the candidate's marriage relationship must be such as not to render him or her ineligible for ordination. (35.1-35.3, 203.4, 320, 424)

E. The Recognition of Credentials

430. Ordained ministers from other evangelical denominations, desiring to unite with the Church of the Nazarene and presenting their ordination papers, may have their ordination recognized by the district assembly, after satisfactory examination by the District Ministerial Credentials Board as to their conduct, personal experience, and doctrine, provided that: (1) they complete satisfactorily an examination on the *Manual* and history of the Church of the Nazarene; (2) they file with the district assembly the Questionnaire for Candidates for Ordination and Elders Requesting Recognition of Credentials, carefully filled in; and (3) they meet all requirements for ordination as outlined in 429-29.3. (203.5, 225, 424)

430.1. The general superintendent having jurisdiction shall issue to the elder so recognized a certificate of recognition, bearing the signature of the general superintendent in jurisdiction, the district superintendent, and the district secretary. (433.6)

430.2. When the credential of a minister from another church has been duly recognized, the credential issued by said church shall be returned to him or her inscribed in writing or stamped across the face as follows:

Accredited by the ________________ District Assembly of the Church of the Nazarene this _____ day of _____, ______ (year), as the basis of the new credentials.

____________________, General Superintendent
____________________, District Superintendent
____________________, District Secretary

F. The Retired Minister

431. A retired minister is one who has been placed in the retired relation by the district assembly in which he or she holds ministerial membership, upon recommendation by the District Ministerial Credentials Board. Any change in status must be approved by the district assembly, upon recommendation by the District Ministerial Credentials Board. (203.26, 228.7)

431.1. Retirement shall not compel cessation from ministerial labors or in itself deprive of membership in the district assembly. A minister who was serving in an "assigned" role may be in a "retired assigned" relation. However, a minister in an "unassigned" status at retirement will be in a "retired unassigned" relation. (201, 433.9)

G. The Transfer of Ministers

432. When a member of the clergy desires to transfer to another district, transfer of ministerial membership may be issued by vote of the district assembly, or by the District Advisory Board in the interim of assemblies, in which his or her ministerial membership is held. Such transfer may be received by the District Advisory Board in the interim before the district assembly meets, granting to said minister full rights and privileges of membership on the district on which it is received, subject to final approval of the Ministerial Credentials Board and the district assembly. (203.6-3.7, 223)

432.1. The transfer of a licensed minister shall be valid only when a detailed record of the licensee's grades in the course of study for licensed ministers, properly certified by the secretary of the District Ministerial Studies Board of the issuing district assembly, has been sent to the secretary of the District Ministerial Studies Board of the receiving district. The secretary of the District Ministerial Studies Board of the receiving district shall notify his or her district secretary that the licensee's record of grades has been received. The minister being transferred shall actively pursue the matter of the reporting of his or her grades in the course of study to the receiving district. (230.1-30.2)

432.2. The district assembly receiving a transfer shall notify the district assembly issuing said transfer of the reception of the transferred person's membership. Until the transfer is received by vote of the district assembly to which addressed, the person thus transferred shall be a member of the issuing district assembly. Such transfer is valid only until the close of the next session following the date of issue of the district assembly to which addressed. (203.6, 223, 228.9-28.10)

H. General Regulations

433. The following **definitions** are of terms relating to general regulations for ministers of the Church of the Nazarene:

Clergy—Elders, deacons, and licensed ministers.

Laity—members of the Church of the Nazarene who are not clergy.

Active—Fulfilling an assigned role.

Assigned—The status of a member of the clergy who is active in one of the roles listed in Chapter II, Part V.

Unassigned—The status of clergy who are in good standing but not presently active in one of the roles listed in Chapter II, Part V.

Retired Assigned—The status of retired clergy who were assigned at the time retirement was requested.

Retired Unassigned—The status of retired clergy who were not assigned at the time retirement was requested.

Disciplined—The status of clergy who have been deprived of the rights, privileges, and responsibilities of the clergy by disciplinary action.

Filed Credential—The status of the credential of a member of the clergy in good standing who, because of inactivity in the ministry, has voluntarily temporarily given up the rights, privileges, and responsibilities of being a member of the clergy by filing his or her credential with the general secretary. A person who files his or her credential remains a member of the clergy and may have the rights, privileges, and responsibilities of being a member of the clergy reinstated by requesting that his or her credential be returned, in accordance with 435.2. (434)

Surrendered Credential—The status of the credential of a member of the clergy who, because of misconduct, accusations, confessions, result of action by a board of discipline, or voluntary action for any reason other than inactivity in the ministry has been deprived of the rights, privileges, and responsibilities of the clergy. The person who surrenders his or her credential is still a member of the clergy, under discipline. The rights, privileges, and responsibilities of the clergy may be restored.

Resigned—The status of the credential of clergy in good standing who, for personal reasons, have decided they no longer wish to be considered as ministers, and give up the rights, privileges, and responsibilities of being members of the clergy to become laypersons on a permanent basis. (434.1-34.2, 434.7) The person who resigns is no longer a member of the clergy. The rights, privileges, and responsibilities of being the clergy may be reinstated, in accordance with 435.3.

Removed—The status of the credential of clergy whose names have been removed from the roll of ministers in accordance with the provisions of 434.3.

Return of Credential—The reinstatement to the rights, privileges, and responsibilities of the clergy to one who has filed his or her credential.

Restoration of Credential—The reinstatement to the rights, privileges, and responsibilities of the clergy to one who has surrendered his or her credential.

Rehabilitation—The process of seeking to bring a minister who has been disciplined or has voluntarily surrendered the rights, privileges, and responsibilities of the clergy to a place of spiritual, emotional, mental, and physical health and to a place of usefulness and constructive activity. Rehabilitation does not necessarily include the restoration of the rights, privileges, and responsibilities of the clergy.

Accusation—A written document signed by at least two members of the Church of the Nazarene accusing a member of the Church of the Nazarene of conduct that if proven would cause the member to be subject to discipline under the terms of the *Manual*.

Knowledge—The awareness of facts learned by the exercise of one's own senses.

Information—Facts learned from others.

Belief—A conclusion reached in good faith based upon knowledge and information.

Investigating Committee—A committee appointed in accordance with the *Manual* to gather information with regard to alleged or suspected misconduct.

Charges—A written document describing specifically the conduct of a member of the Church of the Nazarene that if proven would be the basis of discipline under the terms of the *Manual.*

Suspension—A type of disciplinary action that temporarily denies a member of the clergy the rights, privileges, and responsibilities of the clergy.

Good Standing—The status of clergy who have no unresolved accusations pending, are not currently under discipline, and have neither surrendered nor resigned their credential.

433.1. In case a member of the clergy shall, without the written approval of the District Advisory Board of the assembly district in which he or she holds ministerial membership or the written approval of the Board of General Superintendents, regularly conduct independent church activities that are not under the direction of the Church of the Nazarene, or acts as a member of the staff of an independent church of another religious group, he or she shall be subject to discipline. (433.11, 505.1)

433.2. A member of the clergy shall always show due regard for the united advice of the district superintendent and the District Advisory Board. (416)

433.3. Any claim to participation by a member of the clergy, and/or his or her dependents in any plan or fund that the church may have now or hereafter for the assistance or support of its disabled or aged ministers shall be based only upon regular, full-time, active service rendered by the minister as an assigned pastor or evangelist or other recognized role, under the sanction of the district assembly. This rule shall exclude from such participation all those in part-time and occasional service.

433.4. A licensed minister assigned as pastor or full-time associate or assistant pastor of a Church of the Nazarene shall be a voting member of the district assembly. (201)

433.5. The candidate elected to the order of elder or order of deacon shall be ordained by the laying on of the hands of the general superintendent and ordained ministers with appropriate religious exercises, under the direction of the presiding general superintendent. (307.3)

433.6. The general superintendent having jurisdiction shall issue to the person so ordained a certificate of ordination, bearing the signature of the general superintendent in jurisdiction, the district superintendent, and the district secretary. (430.1)

433.7. In case the credentials of an elder or deacon have been misplaced, mutilated, or destroyed, a duplicate certificate may be issued upon the recommendation of the District Advisory Board. Such recommendation shall be made directly to the general superintendent in jurisdiction, and upon the authority of that approval the general secretary shall issue a duplicate certificate. On the back of the certificate, the original number should be identified along with the word DUPLICATE. If the general superintendent or the district secretary signing the original certificate is not available, the general superintendent having jurisdiction, the district superintendent, and the district secretary of the district requesting the duplicate certificate shall sign the certificate. On the reverse side thereof shall be the following statement inscribed in writing or printing, or both writing and printing, and signed by the general superintendent having jurisdiction, the district superintendent, and the district secretary.

> This certificate is given to take the place of former certificate of ordination given to (name), on the ____ day of (month), A.D. (year), by the (ordaining organization), at which date ___he was ordained and h___ former ordination certificate signed by ______________ and ______________.

The former certificate was (misplaced, mutilated, destroyed).

____________________, General Superintendent
____________________, District Superintendent
____________________, District Secretary

433.8. All elders and deacons shall hold church membership in some local church. (419)

433.9. All elders and deacons shall hold their ministerial membership in the district assembly of the district wherein their church membership is held, to which body they shall report annually. Any elder or deacon who for two consecutive years does not report to his or her district assembly either in person or by letter shall, if the district assembly so elect, cease to be a member thereof. (30, 201, 203.1, 418, 431.1)

433.10. In case an ordained minister has united with the church membership or ministry of another denomination, his or her church membership and ministerial membership in the Church of the Nazarene shall, because of that fact, immediately cease, and the district assembly shall cause to be entered into its minute record the following statement: "Removed from the membership and ministry of the Church of the Nazarene by uniting with another denomination." (107, 112)

433.11. No ordained minister shall regularly conduct independent church activities that are not under the direction of the Church of the Nazarene, or carry on independent missions or unauthorized church activities, or be connected with the operating staff of an independent church or other religious group or denomination, without the annual written approval of the District Advisory Board or the written approval of the Board of General Superintendents. When the said activities are to be conducted on more than one district, or a district other than the district on which said minister holds ministerial membership, the written approval of the Board of General Superintendents must be obtained prior to the participation in said activities. The Board of General Superintendents shall notify the respective District

Advisory Boards that a request for said approval is pending before their board.

Should an ordained minister fail to comply with these requirements, he or she may, on recommendation by a two-thirds vote of the entire membership of the Ministerial Credentials Board, and by action of the district assembly, be dropped from the membership of the Church of the Nazarene. The final determination as to whether any specific activity constitutes "an independent mission" or "an unauthorized church activity" shall rest with the Board of General Superintendents. (112-12.1)

433.12. An assigned minister may start a local church when authorized to do so by the district superintendent or the general superintendent having jurisdiction. Official organization reports are to be filed in the general Evangelism and Church Growth Division office by the district superintendent. (100, 208.1, 307.8)

433.13. Membership in the district assembly shall be by virtue of being a pastor or other assigned minister who is actively serving and maintains employment in such ministry as his or her primary vocation in one of the assigned ministerial roles defined in Chapter II.

433.14. It shall be the duty of every minister of the Church of the Nazarene to hold in trust and confidence any communication of a confidential nature given him or her by a counselee of the congregation while he or she is acting in his or her professional character as a licensed or ordained minister of the Church of the Nazarene. The public dissemination of such communication without the express written consent of the declarant is expressly condemned. Any Nazarene minister who violates the above regulation subjects himself or herself to the disciplinary sanctions set forth in Part VI, Subsection V of this *Manual*.

433.15. All elders and deacons are encouraged to be involved in lifelong learning by completing two continuing education credits or its equivalent per year to be administered by the District Ministerial Studies Board. (424.6)

I. The Resignation or Removal from the Ministry

434. The general secretary is authorized to receive and hold for safekeeping the credentials of clergy in good standing who, because of inactivity in the ministry for a period of time, wish to file them. At the time of filing the credential, the member of the clergy shall certify to the general secretary that the credential is not being filed for the purpose of avoiding discipline. The filing of the credential shall not prevent clergy from being subject to discipline as a member of the clergy. Members of the clergy who file their credentials with the general secretary may have them returned according to the provisions of 435.2.

434.1. When a member of the clergy in good standing ceases from an assigned ministry to pursue a calling or vocation other than the clergy in the Church of the Nazarene, he or she may resign the rights, privileges, and responsibilities of the clergy and return the credential to the district assembly in which he or she holds standing, to be placed in the care of the general secretary. The record in the district minutes will show that he or she was "removed from the Roll of Ministers, having resigned his or her order." Clergy who thus resign may have their credential returned according to the provisions of 435.3.

434.2. When a member of the clergy fails to fulfill the responsibilities of the clergy by remaining unassigned for a length of time which shall not be less than four years, that indicates that the person is no longer actively participating as clergy, the District Ministerial Credentials Board may determine that the individual has resigned by his or her own actions. In such instances, the District Ministerial Credentials Board shall report to the district assembly "the credential of (the elder or deacon in question) has been placed in the resigned status by the District Ministerial Credentials Board." This action should be considered nonprejudicial to character. The individual who resigns may have his or her credential reinstated according to the provisions of 435.3.

434.3. A member of the clergy may be removed from the Roll of Ministers if he or she receives a Letter of Commendation from his or her local church and does not use it in joining another Church of the Nazarene by the time of the next district assembly, or if he or she declares in writing that he or she has withdrawn from the Church of the Nazarene, or if he or she changes his or her residence from the address of record without providing the District Ministerial Credentials Board within one year with a new address of record, or if he or she joins another denomination either as a member or a minister, or if he or she fails to submit an annual report as required in 427.9 and 433.9; the District Ministerial Credentials Board may recommend and the district assembly may order that his or her name be removed from the membership roll of the local church and the Roll of Ministers of the Church of the Nazarene.

434.4. A member of the clergy may be expelled from the ministry of the Church of the Nazarene either through surrender of his or her credential or through disciplinary action according to paragraphs 505-8.

434.5. When an elder or deacon has been expelled, the credential of the member of the clergy shall be sent to the general secretary to be catalogued and preserved subject to the order of the district assembly of the district where the elder or deacon held membership at the time he or she was expelled. (324.5)

434.6. Pastors, local church boards, and others who determine assignments within the church shall not engage clergy who are not in good standing in any position of trust or authority such as supply minister, song director, Sunday School teacher, or other until the credential is restored. Exceptions to this prohibition require the written approval of both the district superintendent where such credential was lost and the general superintendent in jurisdiction of that district. (435.5-35.6)

434.7. When an unretired elder or deacon ceases from active service as a member of the clergy and takes full-time secular employment, after a period of four years he or she may be required by the District Ministerial Credentials Board to resign from the clergy order or file his or her credential and to return his or her credential to the general secretary. This four-year period shall begin at the district assembly immediately following the cessation of activity as a member of the clergy. The District Ministerial Credentials Board shall report its action to the district assembly. This action should be considered nonprejudicial to character.

434.8. Any member of the clergy within 48 hours of the filing of a request for divorce or legal termination of a marriage by the minister or within 48 hours of the physical separation of the minister and his or her spouse for the purpose of discontinuing the physical cohabitation shall *(a)* contact the district superintendent, notifying the superintendent of the action taken; *(b)* agree to meet with the district superintendent and a member of the District Advisory Board at a mutually agreeable time and place, or if no mutually agreeable time and place can be arranged, at a time and place designated by the district superintendent; *(c)* at the meeting designated in subsection *b* above, the member of the clergy shall explain the circumstances of the action taken and the marital conflict as well as the biblical basis for justification as to why the member of the clergy should be permitted to continue to serve as a member of the clergy in good standing. If a member of the clergy fails to comply with the subsections above, such noncompliance shall be cause for discipline.

J. The Restoration of Members of the Clergy to Church Membership and Good Standing

435. Any member of the clergy who is expelled or withdraws from local church membership when he or she is not in good standing may reunite with the Church of the Nazarene only with the consent of the district assembly of the assembly district from which he or she withdrew or was expelled. Should two appeals for restoration to either church membership or ministerial standing be denied, a request may be granted by the Board of General Superintendents to transfer responsibility for restoration to another district where placement may be considered. If all appeals for credential restoration are denied, an ordained minister may become a layperson, upon approval of the Board of General Superintendents.

435.1. If for any reason the name of an elder or deacon shall be removed from a district assembly roll, that elder or deacon shall not be recognized in any other district without having secured the written consent of the district assembly from whose roll his or her name was removed, except as provided for in paragraph 435.

435.2. When an elder or deacon in good standing has filed his or her credential, such credential may, at any subsequent time when the elder or deacon is in good standing, be returned to the elder or deacon upon order of the district assembly where it was filed, provided that the return of his or her credential shall have been recommended by the district superintendent and the District Advisory Board.

435.3. When an elder or deacon in good standing has resigned his or her order of ministry according to 434.1-34.2 and 434.7, he or she may be restored to said order by the district assembly, upon filling out the Ordination Questionnaire, reaffirming the vows of ministry, and after examination by and the favorable recommendation of the District Ministerial Credentials Board and upon approval by the general superintendent in jurisdiction.

435.4. When an ordained minister is deceased whose credential was filed and who was in good standing at the time of death, the minister's family may, upon written request to the general secretary, and approval by the district superintendent of the district where such filing is recorded, receive said minister's certificate of ordination.

435.5. Any time a member of the clergy ceases to be entitled to exercise the rights and privileges of the clergy, the Ministerial Credentials Board will prepare a written report concerning the facts and circumstances of the change in status. The report shall include the recommendations of the Ministerial Credentials Board concerning whether or not a plan of rehabilitation is appropriate. If a plan for rehabilitation is appropriate, the Ministerial Credentials Board shall, to the extent practical, work with the individual to design a plan for rehabilitation. The objective of the plan should be to return the individual to a place of spiritual, emotional, mental, and physical health. Primary responsibility for accomplishing the plan shall rest on the person being rehabilitated, but the facilitator(s) shall represent the church in providing support and assistance. The facilitator(s) or their designee shall report to the Ministerial Credentials Board once each quarter concerning the progress toward rehabilitation. The report shall be in the form established by the Ministerial Credentials Board. The Ministerial Credentials Board may revise the plan of rehabilitation from time to time as the circumstances warrant.

435.6. A member of the clergy who is not in good standing shall not preach, teach a Sunday School class, or hold any other position of trust or authority in the church or worship services, and shall not be given any ministerial role unless the District Advisory Board, the Ministerial Credentials Board, the district superintendent, and the general superintendent in jurisdiction determine that the individual has made sufficient progress toward rehabilitation to warrant once again allowing the individual to be of service in a position of trust or authority. Those considering approval shall carefully consider whether or not the individual who has lost good standing has appropriately repented of his or her misconduct. True repentance involves a deep sense of personal guilt coupled with a change of conduct that continues for a length of time sufficient to be evidence that the change is likely to be permanent. Approval to serve in a position of trust or authority may be granted with or without restrictions.

435.7. A member of the clergy who has lost good standing may be restored to good standing and have his or her credential restored only by the action of the Board of General Superintendents upon a recommendation for restoration from the district where good standing was lost. A recommendation for restoration shall require the approval of the district superintendent, the District Ministerial Credentials Board, and a two-thirds approval of the District Advisory Board. In considering whether or not to recommend that a credential be restored, progress on the plan of rehabilitation shall be the primary issue, but passage of time shall be an additional consideration.

However, in the event the member of the clergy has committed sexual misconduct, the member of the clergy shall not be eligible to apply for restoration until four years have passed.

435.8. Because some types of misconduct, such as sexual misconduct involving children or sexual misconduct of a homosexual nature, are rarely the result of a one-time moral lapse, individuals who are guilty of sexual misconduct that involves a high probability of repeated misconduct should not be restored to good standing.

PART VI

Judicial Administration

I. INVESTIGATION OF POSSIBLE WRONGFUL CONDUCT AND CHURCH DISCIPLINE

500. The objectives of church discipline are to sustain the integrity of the church, to protect the innocent from harm, to protect the effectiveness of the witness of the church, to warn and correct the careless, to bring the guilty to salvation, to rehabilitate the guilty, to restore to effective service those who are rehabilitated, and to protect the reputation and resources of the church. Members of the church who do violence to the General or Special Rules, or who willfully and continuously violate their membership vows, should be dealt with kindly yet faithfully, according to the grievousness of their offenses. Holiness of heart and life being the New Testament standard, the Church of the Nazarene insists upon a clean ministry and requires that those who bear its credentials as clergy be orthodox in doctrine and holy in life. Thus the purpose of the discipline is not punitive or retributive but is to accomplish these objectives. Determination of standing and continued relationship to the church is also a function of the disciplinary process.

II. RESPONSE TO POSSIBLE MISCONDUCT

501. A response is appropriate anytime a person with authority to respond becomes aware of information that a prudent person would believe to be credible and that would cause a prudent person to believe that harm is likely to come to the church, to potential victims of misconduct, or to any other person as a result of misconduct by a person in a position of trust or authority within the church.

501.1. When a person who does not have authority to respond for the church becomes aware of information that a prudent person would consider to be credible and that would cause a prudent person to believe that wrongful conduct by a person in a position of trust or authority may be occurring within the church, the person with the information shall make the representative of the church who has the authority to respond aware of the information.

501.2. The person who has authority to respond is determined by the position within the church of the individual or individuals who may be involved in misconduct as follows:

Person Implicated	*Person with Authority to Respond*
Nonmember	Pastor of local church where the conduct in question takes place.
Layperson	Pastor of church where layperson is a member.
Member of the clergy	District superintendent where the person implicated is a member or the pastor of the local church where the person is on staff.
District superintendent	General superintendent in jurisdiction
Not otherwise defined	General secretary/Headquarters Operations officer

The person with authority to respond may enlist the help of others in any fact-finding or response.

501.3. If no accusation has been made, the purpose of an investigation shall be to determine whether or not action is needed to prevent harm or to reduce the impact of harm that has previously been done. In circumstances in which a prudent person would believe that no further action was needed to prevent harm or to reduce the impact of harm, no investigation will continue unless an accusation has been filed. Facts learned during an investigation may become the basis of an accusation.

III. RESPONSE TO MISCONDUCT BY A PERSON IN A POSITION OF TRUST OR AUTHORITY

502. Whenever a person authorized to respond learns facts that indicate that innocent parties have been harmed by the misconduct of a person in a position of trust or authority, action shall be taken to cause the church to respond appropriately. An appropriate response will seek to prevent any additional harm to victims of the misconduct, seek to respond to the needs of the victims, the accused, and others who suffer as a result of the misconduct. Particular concern should be shown for the needs of the spouse and family of the accused. The response will also seek to address the needs of the local church, the district, and the general church concerning public relations, protection from liability, and protection of the integrity of the church.

Those who respond for the church must understand that what they say and do may have consequences under civil law. The duty of the church to respond is based on Christian concern. No one has the authority to accept financial responsibility for a local church without action by the church board, or for a district without action by the District Advisory Board. One who is uncertain about what action is appropriate should consider seeking counsel from an appropriate professional.

502.1. In each local church, it is appropriate for the church board to fashion a response to any crisis that may arise; however, it may be necessary to respond before a board meeting can take place. It is wise for each local church to have an emergency response plan.

502.2. On each district the primary responsibility for responding to a crisis rests with the District Advisory Board; however, it may be necessary to respond before a meeting of the board can take place. It is wise for a district to adopt an emergency response plan. The plan may include the appointment by the District Advisory Board of a response team composed of people with special qualifications such as counselors, social workers, those trained in communications, and those familiar with the applicable law.

503. Resolution of Disciplinary Matters by Agreement. The disciplinary process described in this *Manual* is intended to provide an appropriate process for resolving allegations of misconduct when the allegations are contested by the accused. In many situations, it is appropriate to resolve disciplinary matters by agreement. Efforts to resolve disciplinary matters by agreement are encouraged and should be pursued whenever practical.

503.1. Any matter that is within the jurisdiction of a Local Board of Discipline may be resolved by a written agreement between the person accused and the pastor if approved by the church board and the district superintendent. The terms of such an agreement shall have the same effect as an action by a Local Board of Discipline.

503.2. Any matter that is within the jurisdiction of a District Board of Discipline may be resolved by a written agreement between the person accused and the district superintendent if the agreement is approved by the District Advisory Board and the general superintendent in jurisdiction. The terms of such an agreement shall have the same effect as an action by a District Board of Discipline.

IV. CONTESTED DISCIPLINE OF A LAYPERSON

504. If a lay member is accused of unchristian conduct, such charges shall be placed in writing and signed by at least two members who have been in faithful attendance for at least six months. The pastor shall appoint an investigating committee of three members of the local church, subject to the approval of the district superintendent. The committee shall make a written report of its investigation. This report must be signed by a majority and filed with the church board.

After the investigation and pursuant thereto, any two members in good standing in the local church may sign charges against the accused and file same with the church board. Thereupon the church board shall appoint, subject to the approval of the district superintendent, a Local Board of Discipline of five members, who are unprejudiced and able to hear and dispose of the case in a fair and impartial manner. If in the opinion of the district superintendent, it is impractical to select five members from the local church due to the size of the church, the nature of the allegations, or the position of influence of the accused, the district superintendent shall, after consulting the pastor, appoint five laypersons from other churches on the same district to be the Board of Discipline. This board shall conduct a hearing as soon as practicable and determine the issues involved. After hearing the testimony of witnesses and considering the evidence, the Board of Discipline shall either absolve the accused or administer discipline as the facts shall establish to be proper. The decision must be unanimous. Discipline may take the form of reprimand, suspension, or expulsion from membership in the local church.

504.1. An appeal from the decision of a Local Board of Discipline may be taken to the District Court of Appeals within 30 days by either the accused or the church board.

504.2. When a layperson has been expelled from membership in the local church by a Local Board of Discipline, he or she may reunite with the Church of the Nazarene on the same district only with the approval of the District Advisory Board. If such consent is granted, he or she shall be received into the membership of that local church using the approved form for the reception of church members. (27, 33-39, 112.1-12.4, 801)

V. CONTESTED DISCIPLINE OF A MEMBER OF THE CLERGY

505. The perpetuity and effectiveness of the Church of the Nazarene depend largely upon the spiritual qualifications, the character, and the manner of life of its clergy. Members of the clergy aspire to a high calling and function as anointed individuals in whom is placed the church's trust. They accept their calling knowing that they will be held to high personal standards by those to whom they minister. Because of the high expectations placed upon them, the clergy and their ministry are peculiarly vulnerable to any accusation of misconduct. It is therefore incumbent upon members to use the following procedures with the biblical wisdom and maturity that befits the people of God.

505.1. If a member of the clergy is accused of misconduct, conduct unbecoming a minister, or of teaching doctrines out of harmony with the doctrinal statement of the Church of the Nazarene, or of serious laxity in the enforcement of the General or Special Rules of the church, such accusations shall be placed in writing and shall be signed by at least two members of the Church of the Nazarene who are at the time in good standing. Accusations of sexual misconduct cannot be signed by any person who consented to participate in the alleged misconduct. The written accusation must be filed with the District Advisory Board of the district where the accused has ministerial membership. This accusation shall become part of the record in the case.

The District Advisory Board shall give written notice to the accused that accusations have been filed, as soon as practical by any method that gives actual notice. When actual notice is not practical, notice may be provided in the manner that is customary for serving legal notices in that locality. The accused and his or her counsel shall have the right to examine the accusations and to receive a written copy of the same immediately upon request.

505.2. A person's signature on an accusation against a member of the clergy constitutes certification by the signer that, to the best of the signer's knowledge, information and belief formed after reasonable inquiry, the accusation is well-grounded in fact.

505.3. When a written accusation is filed, the District Advisory Board shall appoint a committee of three or more ordained ministers to investigate the facts and circumstances involved and report their finding in writing and signed by a majority of the committee. If after considering the committee's report, it shall appear that there are probable grounds for charges, such charges shall be drawn up and signed by any two ordained ministers. The District Advisory Board shall give the accused notice thereof, as soon as practical, by any method that gives actual notice. When actual notice is not practical, notice may be provided in the manner that is customary for serving legal notices in that locality. The accused and his or her counsel shall have the right to examine the charges and specifications and to receive a copy thereof immediately upon request. No accused shall be required to answer charges of which he or she has not been informed as specified herein. (222.3)

505.4. If, after investigation it appears that an accusation against a member of the clergy is without factual basis and has been filed in bad faith, the filing of the accusation may be grounds for disciplinary action against those who signed the accusation.

505.5. In case charges are filed, the District Advisory Board shall appoint five ordained ministers of the district to hear the case and determine the issues; these five ordained ministers so named shall constitute a District Board of Discipline to conduct the hearing and dispose of the case according to the laws of the church. No district superintendent shall serve as prosecutor or as assistant to the prosecutor in the trial of an ordained minister or licensed minister. This Board of Discipline shall have power to vindicate and absolve the accused in connection with said charges or to administer discipline commensurate with the offense. Such discipline may provide for discipline intended to lead to the salvation and rehabilitation of the guilty party. The discipline may include repentance, confession, restitution, suspension, recommendation for removal of credentials, expulsion from the ministry or membership of the church, or both, public or private reprimand, or any such other discipline that may be appropriate including suspension or deferment of discipline during a period of probation. (222.4, 505.11-5.12)

505.6. If either the accused or the District Advisory Board shall so request, the Board of Discipline shall be a Regional Board of Discipline. The regional board for each case shall be appointed by the general superintendent in jurisdiction of the district where the accused minister holds his or her membership.

505.7. It is provided that in no case shall disciplinary action be taken against a missionary by a Phase 1 district as such.

505.8. The decision of a Board of Discipline shall be unanimous, written and signed by all members, and shall include a finding of "guilty" or "not guilty" as to each charge and specification.

505.9. Any hearing by a Board of Discipline herein provided for shall always be conducted within the bounds of the district where the charges were filed at a place designated by the board that is to hear the charges.

505.10. The procedure at any hearing shall be according to Rules of Procedure hereinafter provided. (222.3-22.4, 427.10, 433.11, 508)

505.11. When a minister is charged with conduct unbecoming a minister and shall admit to guilt, or shall confess to guilt without being charged, the District Advisory Board may assess any of the disciplines provided for in 505.5.

505.12. When a minister is accused of conduct unbecoming a minister, and shall admit to guilt, or shall confess to guilt prior to being brought before a Board of Discipline, the District Advisory Board may assess any of the disciplines provided for in 505.5.

506. Following a decision by a Board of Discipline, the accused, the District Advisory Board, or those who sign the charges shall be entitled to appeal the decision to the General Court of Appeals for those in the United States and Canada, or to the Regional Court of Appeals in other world regions. The appeal shall be begun within 30 days after such decision, and the court shall review the entire record of the case and all steps that have been taken therein. If the court discovers any substantial error prejudicial to the right of any person, it shall correct such error by ordering a new hearing to be conducted in a manner capable of giving relief to that person affected adversely by previous proceedings or decision.

507. When the decision of a Board of Discipline is adverse to the accused minister and the decision provides for suspension from the ministry or cancellation of credentials, the minister shall thereupon immediately suspend all ministerial activity; and refusal to do so will result in the forfeiture of the right to appeal.

507.1. When the decision of a Board of Discipline provides for suspension or cancellation of credentials and the accused minister desires to appeal, he or she shall file with the secretary of the court to which the appeal is made, at the time the notice of appeal is filed, his or her written credentials as a minister, and his or her right of appeal shall be conditioned upon compliance with this provision. When such credentials are so filed, they shall be safely kept by the said secretary until the conclusion of the case, and thereupon the same shall either be forwarded to the general secretary or returned to the minister as the court may direct.

507.2. Appeals to the General Court of Appeals may be made by the accused or the Board of Discipline from decisions of a Regional Court of Appeals. Such appeals shall be by the same rules and procedures as other appeals to the General Court of Appeals.

VI. RULES OF PROCEDURE

508. The General Court of Appeals shall adopt uniform Rules of Procedure governing all proceedings before boards of discipline and courts of appeal. After such rules are adopted and published, they shall be the final authority in all judicial proceedings. Printed Rules of Procedure shall be supplied by the general secretary. Changes or amendments to such rules may be adopted by the General Court of Appeals at any time, and when these are adopted and published, they shall be effective and authoritative in all cases. Any steps that are thereafter taken in any proceeding shall be in accordance with such change or amendment. (505.1)

VII. DISTRICT COURT OF APPEALS

509. Each organized district shall have a District Court of Appeals composed of five ordained ministers elected by the district assembly according to 203.21. This court shall hear appeals of church members concerning any action of a local church or church board when they are aggrieved or adversely affected by such action. Notice of appeal must be given in writing within 30 days after such action or after appellant has knowledge thereof. Such notice shall be delivered to the District Court of Appeals or a member thereof, and a copy of such notice shall be delivered to the pastor of the local church and to the secretary of the church board concerned. (203.21)

509.1. The District Court of Appeals shall have jurisdiction to hear and decide all appeals of laypersons or churches from the action of a Board of Discipline appointed to discipline a layperson.

VIII. GENERAL COURT OF APPEALS

510. The General Assembly shall elect five ordained ministers to serve as members of the General Court of Appeals during each ensuing quadrennium, or until their successors are elected and qualified. This court shall have jurisdiction as follows:

510.1. To hear and determine all appeals from the action or decision of any District Board of Discipline.

510.2. To hear and determine appeals concerning the action of any district assembly affecting the interests of a minister amenable to that assembly.

510.3. To hear and determine appeals from the action of any district superintendent in matters affecting the interests of a minister. When such appeals are so determined by said court, such determination shall be authoritative and final. (214, 305.7)

511. Vacancies that may exist in the General Court of Appeals during the interim between sessions of the General Assembly shall be filled by appointment of the Board of General Superintendents. (317.6)

512. Per diem and expense allowances for members of the General Court of Appeals shall be the same as that of members of the General Board of the church, when the members of the court are engaged in official business of the court, and payment therefor shall be made by the general treasurer.

513. The general secretary shall be custodian of all permanent records and decisions of the General Court of Appeals. (324.4)

IX. REGIONAL COURT OF APPEALS

514. There shall be a Regional Court of Appeals for each region other than the United States and Canada. Each Regional Court of Appeals shall consist of five ordained ministers elected by the Board of General Superintendents following each General Assembly. Vacancies shall be filled by the Board of General Superintendents. The Rules of Procedure shall be the same for the Regional Courts of Appeals as for the General Court of Appeals, in both the church *Manual* and the *Judicial Manual.*

X. GUARANTY OF RIGHTS

515. The right to a fair and impartial hearing of charges pending against an accused minister or layperson shall not be denied or unduly postponed. Written charges shall be given an early hearing in order that the innocent may be absolved and the guilty brought to discipline. Every accused is entitled to the presumption of innocence until proven guilty. As to each charge and specification, the prosecution shall have the burden of proving guilt to a moral certainty and beyond a reasonable doubt.

515.1. The cost of preparing the record of a case, including a verbatim transcript of all testimony given at the trial, for the purpose of an appeal to the General Court of Appeals, shall be borne by the district where the hearing was held and disciplinary action taken. Every minister or layperson who appeals shall have the right to present oral as well as written argument upon his or her appeal, but this right may be waived in writing by the accused.

515.2. A minister or layperson who is accused of misconduct or any violation of the church *Manual* and against whom charges are pending shall have the right to meet his or her accusers face-to-face and to cross-examine the witnesses for the prosecution.

515.3. The testimony of any witness before a Board of Discipline shall not be received or considered in evidence unless such testimony be given under oath or solemn affirmation.

515.4. A minister or layperson who is brought before a Board of Discipline to answer charges shall always have the right to be represented by counsel of his or her own choosing, provided such counsel be a member in good standing in the Church of the Nazarene. Any full member of a regularly organized church against whom no written charges are pending will be considered in good standing.

515.5. A minister or layperson shall not be required to answer charges for any act that occurred more than five years before the filing of such charges, and no evidence will be considered at any hearing for any matter that occurred more than five years before the charges were filed. Provided, however, that if the person aggrieved by any such act was under the age of 18 or found to be mentally incompetent of making an accusation or filing a charge, such five-year limitation periods would not begin to run until the aggrieved person reached age 18 or became mentally competent. In the case of the sexual abuse of a child, no time limit shall apply.

If a minister is convicted of a felony by a court of competent jurisdiction, he or she shall surrender his or her credentials to the district superintendent. At the request of such minister, and if the Board of Discipline has not previously been involved, the District Advisory Board shall investigate the circumstances of the conviction and may restore the credentials if it deems appropriate.

515.6. A minister or layperson shall not be twice placed in jeopardy for the same offense. It shall not be considered, however, that such person was placed in jeopardy at any hearing or proceeding where the court of appeals discovers reversible error committed in the original proceeding before a Board of Discipline.

PART VII

Boundaries

ASSEMBLY DISTRICTS—UNITED STATES AND CANADA

ASSEMBLY DISTRICTS—WORLD MISSION

CHAPTER I

ASSEMBLY DISTRICTS UNITED STATES AND CANADA

600. The following are Phase 3 districts in the United States and Canada, whose boundaries have been established and recognized at the time of the 1997 General Assembly: (200-200.5)

601. Akron District shall include that portion of the state of Ohio in the counties of Belmont, Carroll, Columbiana, Guernsey, Harrison, Jefferson, Mahoning, Monroe, Noble, Portage, Stark, Summit, Trumbull, and Tuscarawas.

602. Alabama North District shall include that portion of the state of Alabama north of Pickens, Tuscaloosa, Bibb, Shelby, Talladega, Clay, and Randolph counties.

603. Alabama South District shall include that portion of the state of Alabama south of Lamar, Fayette, Walker, Jefferson, St. Clair, Calhoun, and Cleburne counties.

604. Alaska District shall include the state of Alaska.

605. Anaheim District shall include that part of the state of California in Orange County; that part of Los Angeles County lying south of a line beginning at the Pacific Ocean and Imperial Boulevard and continuing in a northeasterly direction along Imperial Boulevard, Alameda Street, Washington Boulevard, Rio Hondo River, the crest of Puente Hills, the San Dimas Canyon Road, and the southern boundary of the Angeles National Forest to the San Bernardino county line; and that part of Riverside and San Bernardino counties lying west of a line beginning at the junction of Highway 74 and the Orange county and Riverside county line, continuing along Highway 74 to Lake Elsinore, thence northward along Interstate 15 to Highway 138, thence northwesterly to the Los Angeles county line.

606. Arizona District shall include the state of Arizona and that portion of the state of Utah lying south of the northern boundary of Beaver, Piute, Wayne, and San Juan counties along with Clark and Lincoln counties in the state of Nevada.

607. CANADA ATLANTIC DISTRICT shall include the four Atlantic provinces of Nova Scotia, New Brunswick, Prince Edward Island, and Newfoundland.

608. CANADA CENTRAL DISTRICT shall include the province of Ontario.

609. CANADA PACIFIC DISTRICT shall include the province of British Columbia and the Yukon Territory.

610. CANADA WEST DISTRICT shall include the provinces of Alberta, Saskatchewan, Manitoba, and the Northwest Territories.

611. CENTRAL CALIFORNIA DISTRICT shall include that portion of the state of California beginning at the northern intersection of the Santa Clara-Stanislaus county lines, proceeding east along the northern boundary of the Stanislaus county line, and continuing to the intersection of Calaveras and Tuolumne county lines; then east along the northern boundary of the Tuolumne county line to the intersection with Alpine County; then south on a line along the western border of Alpine, Mono, and Inyo counties to the intersection with Kern County; then to include all of Kern County west and north of the Tehachapi Mountains, or west of Interstate 5 as the southern boundary of the district. The western boundary of the district shall be a line drawn along the western boundaries of Kern, Kings, Fresno, Merced, and Stanislaus county lines to the intersection with the San Joaquin county line.

612. CENTRAL FLORIDA DISTRICT shall include that portion of the state of Florida north of the northern county lines of Manatee, Hardee, Highlands, Okeechobee, and St. Lucie counties; and south of a line formed by the southern extent of Township 18, south, from the Atlantic Ocean north of Oak Hill to the east line of Lake County, then south to the north line of Orange County, then due west following the southern extent of Township 19, south, to the Gulf of Mexico near Homosassa.

613. Central Latin American District shall include the state of Texas, except that portion within the boundaries of the New Mexico District, and the states of Oklahoma and Kansas.

614. Central Ohio District shall include that portion of the state of Ohio in the counties of Athens, Fairfield, Franklin, Gallia, Hocking, Jackson, Lawrence, Licking, Meigs, Morgan, Muskingum, Perry, Pickaway, Pike, Ross, Scioto, Vinton, and Washington.

615. Chicago Central District shall include that portion of the state of Illinois that lies east of the west boundaries of McHenry, Kane, Kendall, Grundy, Kankakee, and Ford counties, and north of the north line of Champaign County and that part of Vermillion County that lies north of U.S. Highway 150, including the city of Danville but not including the town of Oakwood.

616. Colorado District shall include the state of Colorado.

617. Dakota District shall include the states of North and South Dakota.

618. Dallas District shall include that portion of the state of Texas east of the 97th meridian, but including that portion of Dallas County west of said meridian and excluding that portion of Denton County east of said meridian; and north of a line beginning at the east border of the north line of Sabine County and continuing west on the north boundary of San Augustine County to Grigsby, thence west through Alto and Teague to the 97th meridian, and including the towns and cities on this line.

619. East Tennessee District shall include that portion of the state of Tennessee that lies east of the west boundary line of Macon, Trousdale, Wilson, Rutherford, Bedford, and Lincoln counties.

620. Eastern Kentucky District shall be composed of that portion of the state of Kentucky east of the eastern boundaries of Gallatin, Owen, Scott, Fayette, Jessamine, Garrard, Lincoln, Pulaski, and Wayne counties.

621. Eastern Michigan District shall include that portion of the state of Michigan known as the Lower (Southern)

Peninsula that lies east of the west boundaries of Tuscola, Genessee, Livingston, Washtenaw, and Lenawee counties.

622. GEORGIA DISTRICT shall include the state of Georgia.

623. HAWAII PACIFIC DISTRICT shall include the state of Hawaii.

624. HOUSTON DISTRICT shall include that portion of the state of Texas lying east of the 97th meridian and south of a line beginning at the east border of the north line of Sabine County and continuing west along the north boundary of San Augustine County to Grigsby, thence west through Alto and Teague to the 97th meridian, with the exception of the towns and cities on this line.

625. ILLINOIS DISTRICT shall include that portion of the state of Illinois lying south of the north boundary of Adams, Brown, Cass, Menard, Logan, DeWitt, Piatt, and Champaign counties and that portion of Vermillion County south of U.S. Highway 150 and including the town of Oakwood, but excluding the city of Danville.

626. INDIANAPOLIS DISTRICT shall include that portion of the state of Indiana south of the 40th parallel east of a line formed by the west boundary of Boone, Hendricks, and Morgan counties; north of the south boundary of Morgan, Johnson, and Shelby counties; and east of the west boundary of Decatur, Jennings, and Jefferson counties.

627. INTERMOUNTAIN DISTRICT shall include that portion of the state of Idaho south of the Salmon River; that portion of the state of Oregon embracing the following counties, namely, Wallowa, Union, Baker, Grant, Harney, and Malheur; that portion of the state of Nevada embracing the following counties, namely, Humboldt, Pershing, Lander, Elko, Eureka, and White Pine; and that portion of the state of Utah lying north of the southern boundary of Millard, Sevier, Emery, and Grand counties.

628. IOWA DISTRICT shall include the state of Iowa.

629. JOPLIN DISTRICT shall include that portion of the state of Kansas lying east of the west boundaries of Coffey, Woodson, Wilson, and Montgomery counties and south of the north boundary of Coffey, Anderson, and Linn counties;

and that portion of the state of Missouri lying south of the north boundary of Bates, Henry, Benton, and Morgan counties and west of the east boundary of Morgan, Camden, Laclede, Wright, Douglas, and Ozark counties.

630. KANSAS DISTRICT shall include that portion of the state of Kansas lying west of the east boundaries of the following counties, namely, Marshall, Pottawatomie, Wabaunsee, Lyon, Greenwood, Elk, and Chautauqua.

631. KANSAS CITY DISTRICT shall include that portion of the state of Kansas lying east of the west boundary of Nemaha, Jackson, Shawnee, and Osage counties and north of the north boundary of Coffey, Anderson, and Linn counties; and that portion of the state of Missouri lying west of the east boundary of Mercer, Grundy, Livingston, Carroll, Saline, and Pettis counties and north of the north boundary of Bates, Henry, and Benton counties.

632. KENTUCKY DISTRICT shall be composed of that portion of the state of Kentucky west of the eastern boundaries of Gallatin, Owen, Scott, Fayette, Jessamine, Garrard, Lincoln, Pulaski, and Wayne counties, except for the city of Fulton, which is on the Tennessee District.

633. LOS ANGELES DISTRICT shall include that portion of the state of California lying south of the northern boundary of San Luis Obispo and Kern counties, with the exception of that portion of Kern County north of the Tehachapi Mountains or west of Interstate 5; and north of a line beginning at the Pacific Ocean and Imperial Boulevard and continuing in a northeasterly direction along Imperial Boulevard, Alameda Street, Washington Boulevard, Rio Hondo River, the crest of Puente Hills, and the San Dimas Canyon Road to the southern boundary of the Angeles National Forest and the San Bernardino county line; and the whole of Inyo County.

634. LOUISIANA DISTRICT shall include the state of Louisiana.

635. MAINE DISTRICT shall include the state of Maine.

636. METRO NEW YORK DISTRICT shall include that portion of the state of New York that lies south of the southern boundary of Delaware, Greene, and Columbia counties; that portion of the state of New Jersey lying north of a line drawn between Phillipsburg and Long Branch, including the city of Long Branch; that portion of the state of Connecticut west of a line running north from Bridgeport, Connecticut, including Bridgeport, to the Massachusetts line.

637. MICHIGAN DISTRICT shall include that portion of the state of Michigan known as the Lower (Southern) Peninsula that lies west of the west boundaries of Tuscola, Genessee, Livingston, Washtenaw, and Lenawee counties, and south of the north boundaries of Muskegon, Newaygo, Montcalm, Isabella, Midland, and Bay counties, except for the portion of Isabella County directly north of Montcalm County.

638. MINNESOTA DISTRICT shall include the state of Minnesota.

639. MISSISSIPPI DISTRICT shall include the state of Mississippi.

640. MISSOURI DISTRICT shall include that portion of the state of Missouri lying east of the western boundaries of the counties of Putnam, Sullivan, Linn, Chariton, Howard, Cooper, Moniteau, Miller, Pulaski, Texas, and Howell.

641. NEBRASKA DISTRICT shall include the state of Nebraska.

642. NEW ENGLAND DISTRICT shall include the states of New Hampshire, Vermont, Massachusetts, Rhode Island, and that portion of the state of Connecticut east of a line running north from Bridgeport, Connecticut, excluding Bridgeport, to the Massachusetts line; and the island of Bermuda.

643. NEW MEXICO DISTRICT shall include the state of New Mexico and that portion of the state of Texas west of the 103rd meridian, and south of the 32nd parallel.

644. NORTH ARKANSAS DISTRICT shall include that portion of the state of Arkansas that lies north of a line formed by Interstate 40 from the Tennessee state line to the city limits of North Little Rock at the Dark Hollow Interchange of Highways I-40, 67, and 167; thence due north to Jacksonville Boulevard at Bel-air and northeasterly along Jacksonville Boulevard to McCor Street, north to a point approximately four blocks beyond the intersection of Lansing and Hill Boulevard; then west to a point approximately one block north of the intersection of Lockridge with Crestwood, north to Riderwood Road and Greenhurst, west to Lowrance at a point approximately a block north of Tanglewood, north on Lowrance Drive to 63rd Street, west to High Street, south on High and Baucum to Crystal Street; thence westerly to the intersection of Hilliard with the west boundary of Burns Park, south along the park boundary to the Arkansas River; thence westerly along the Arkansas and Maumelle rivers to Pinnacle Valley Road, south on Pinnacle Valley Road to State Route 10, and west on Route 10 and the southerly line of Sebastian County to the Oklahoma state line. The towns and cities on Highway 10 and Sebastian county line are on the South Arkansas District.

645. North Carolina District shall include the state of North Carolina.

646. North Central Ohio District shall include that portion of the state of Ohio in the counties of Ashland, Ashtabula, Coshocton, Crawford, Cuyahoga, Delaware, Erie, Geauga, Holmes, Huron, Knox, Lake, Lorain, Marion, Medina, Morrow, Ottawa, Richland, Sandusky, Seneca, Wayne, and Wyandot.

647. North Florida District shall include that portion of the state of Florida lying north of a line formed by the southern extent of Township 18, south, from the Atlantic Ocean north of Oak Hill to the east line of Lake County, then south to the north line of Orange County, then due west following the southern extent of Township 19, south, to the Gulf of Mexico near Homosassa.

648. Northeast Oklahoma District shall include that portion of the state of Oklahoma east of the line formed by the Missouri, Kansas, and Texas Railway from Oklahoma City, in a northerly direction to the Arkansas River, including the towns and cities thereon except Oklahoma City; thence the Arkansas River to the Kansas state line; and north of U.S. Highway 62 from Oklahoma City to Henryetta; thence U.S. Highway 266 to Warner; thence U.S. Highway 64 to the Arkansas state line, excluding the towns and cities on highways 62, 266, and 64.

649. NORTHEASTERN INDIANA DISTRICT shall include that portion of the state of Indiana lying north of the 40th parallel and south and east of a line starting at the 40th parallel on the Hamilton and Madison county lines, running due north to the Miami county line, west to the Cass county line, north to the northwest corner of Miami County, thence east to the Wabash county line, following the Fulton and Kosciusko county lines to Marshall County, thence north along the eastern border of Marshall at St. Joseph counties to the Michigan state line.

650. NORTHERN CALIFORNIA DISTRICT shall include the following counties of the state of California: Del Norte, Humboldt, Mendocino, Lake, Sonoma, Marin, Napa, Contra Costa, Alameda, San Francisco, San Mateo, Santa Clara, Santa Cruz, San Benito, Monterey, and that portion of Solano County lying west of a line beginning where Napa, Solano, and Yolo counties meet, and running southward on the Napa-Solano county line to where the line turns sharply west, from that point due south to the Suisun Bay.

651. NORTHWEST DISTRICT shall include that portion of the state of Washington east of the Cascade Mountains; that portion of the state of Idaho north of the Salmon River; and Sherman, Gilliam, Morrow, and Umatilla counties in the state of Oregon.

652. NORTHWEST INDIANA DISTRICT shall include that portion of the state of Indiana lying north of the 40th parallel and west of a line starting at the 40th parallel on the Hamilton and Madison county lines, running due north to the Miami county line, west to the Cass county line, north to the northwest corner of Miami County, thence east to the Wabash county line, following the Fulton and Kosciusko county lines to Marshall County, thence north along the eastern border of Marshall and St. Joseph counties to the Michigan state line.

653. NORTHWEST OKLAHOMA DISTRICT shall include that portion of the state of Oklahoma that lies north of U.S.

Highway 66, not including the towns and cities thereon with the exception of that portion of Oklahoma County north of a line from the North Canadian River to MacArthur Avenue on 36th Street, west of MacArthur from 36th to 39th Street, north of 39th Street from MacArthur to May Avenue, west of May Avenue from 39th to 50th streets, and north of 50th Street from May Avenue to the Missouri, Kansas, and Texas Railway, and west of a line formed by the Missouri, Kansas, and Texas Railway running northeasterly from Oklahoma City to the Arkansas River, not including the towns and cities thereon, except for Oklahoma City, and thence northwesterly up the Arkansas River to the Kansas state line.

654. NORTHWESTERN ILLINOIS DISTRICT shall include that portion of the state of Illinois north of the south boundary of Hancock, Schuyler, Mason, Tazewell, and McLean counties and west of the east boundary of McLean, Livingston, LaSalle, DeKalb, and Boone counties.

655. NORTHWESTERN OHIO DISTRICT shall include that portion of the state of Ohio west of the west boundary of Pickaway, Franklin, Delaware, Marion, Wyandot, Seneca, Sandusky, and Ottawa counties and north of the north boundary of Preble, Montgomery, Greene, and Fayette counties.

656. OREGON PACIFIC DISTRICT shall include that portion of the state of Oregon west of the east boundary of Wasco County, south of the north boundary of Wheeler County, and west of the east boundary of Wheeler, Crook, Deschutes, and Lake counties.

657. PHILADELPHIA DISTRICT shall be composed of Clinton County and that part of the state of Pennsylvania lying east of the boundary line between Potter and Tioga counties and east of a line drawn from a point at the northern crest of the Allegheny Mountains to Duncannon, thence following the Susquehanna River to the Maryland state line; and that portion of the state of New Jersey that lies south of a line drawn between Long Branch and Phillipsburg, including the city of Phillipsburg.

658. PITTSBURGH DISTRICT, with the exception of Clinton County, which belongs to the Philadelphia District, shall include that portion of the state of Pennsylvania west of the boundary line of Potter and Tioga counties, thence following a line due south through Clinton County, to the crest of the Allegheny Mountains, and south along this crest to the Maryland state line.

659. Rocky Mountain District shall include the states of Montana and Wyoming.

660. Sacramento District shall include that portion of the state of California embracing the following counties, namely, Modoc, Siskiyou, Trinity, Shasta, Tehama, Butte, Glenn, Colusa, Sutter, Yuba, Nevada, Yolo, Sacramento, Placer, El Dorado, Alpine, Calaveras, Amador, San Joaquin, Mono, Lassen, Plumas, Sierra, and that portion of Solano County lying east of a line beginning at the point where Napa, Solano, and Yolo counties meet, and running southward on the Napa-Solano county line to where the line turns sharply west; from that point due south to the Suisun Bay; then due east along the Bay Channel to the westernmost tip of the Sacramento county line; and that portion of the state of Nevada embracing the following counties, namely, Washoe, Storey, Lyon, Douglas, Churchill, Mineral, Esmeralda, and Nye; and the independent city of Carson City.

661. San Antonio District shall include that portion of the state of Texas lying between the 97th meridian and the 103rd meridian, south of the 32nd parallel, except that all the incorporated city of Midland and none of the incorporated city of Hillsboro shall be included in the San Antonio District.

662. South Arkansas District shall include that portion of the state of Arkansas that lies south of a line formed by Interstate 40 from the Tennessee state line to the city limits of North Little Rock at the Dark Hollow Interchange of Highways I-40, 67, and 167; thence due north to Jacksonville Boulevard at Bel-air and northeasterly along Jacksonville Boulevard to McCor Street, north to a point approximately four blocks beyond the intersection of Lansing and Hill Boulevard; then west to a point approximately one block north of the intersection of Lockridge with Crestwood, north to Riderwood Road and Greenhurst, west to Lowrance at a point approximately a block north of Tanglewood, north on Lowrance Drive to 63rd Street, west to High Street, south on High and Baucum to Crystal Street; thence westerly to the intersection of Hilliard with the west boundary of Burns Park, south along the park boundary to the Arkansas River; thence westerly along the Arkansas and Maumelle rivers to Pinnacle Valley Road, south on Pinnacle Valley Road to State Route 10, and west on Route 10 and the southerly line of Sebastian County to the Oklahoma state line. The towns and cities on U.S. Highway 10 and Sebastian county line are on the South Arkansas District.

663. SOUTH CAROLINA DISTRICT shall include the state of South Carolina.

664. SOUTHEAST OKLAHOMA DISTRICT shall include that portion of the state of Oklahoma east of a line formed by the Santa Fe Railway from the Red River in a northerly direction to Oklahoma City, excluding the towns and cities thereon, but including that portion of Norman and Oklahoma City lying east of a line from the southern city limits of Norman along U.S. Highway 77 northerly to State Highway 9, east to 24th Street, northerly to Robinson Drive, west to 18th Street, north to Rock Creek Road, east to Air Depot Avenue, then northerly on Air Depot Avenue to the Oklahoma county line, west on Oklahoma county line to Eastern Avenue, north on Eastern Avenue to I-35 to U.S. Highway 62; and south of U.S. 62 from Oklahoma City to Henryetta; thence U.S. Highway 266 to Warner; thence U.S. Highway 64 to the Arkansas state line, including the towns and cities thereon.

665. SOUTHERN CALIFORNIA DISTRICT shall include that portion of the state of California in San Diego and Imperial counties; and that part of Riverside and San Bernardino counties lying east of a line beginning at the junction of Highway 74 and the Orange county and Riverside county line, continuing along Highway 74 to Lake Elsinore, thence northward along Interstate 15 to Highway 138, thence northwesterly to the Los Angeles county line.

666. Southern Florida District shall include that portion of the state of Florida lying south of and including the counties of Manatee, Hardee, Highlands, Okeechobee, and St. Lucie.

667. Southwest Indiana District shall include that portion of the state of Indiana that lies south of the 40th parallel west of a line formed by the east boundary of Montgomery, Putnam, and Owen counties; south of the north boundary of Monroe, Brown, and Bartholomew counties; and west of the east boundary of Bartholomew, Jackson, Scott, and Clark counties.

668. Southwest Oklahoma District shall include that portion of the state of Oklahoma that lies west of a line formed by the Santa Fe Railway running northerly from the Red River to Oklahoma City, including the towns and cities thereon, except the portion of Oklahoma City and Norman included in the Southeast Oklahoma District north of the intersection of U.S. Highway 77 and the southern city limits of Norman; also excepting that portion of Oklahoma County above specified; and south of U.S. Highway 66, including the towns and cities thereon with the exception of that portion of Oklahoma City north of a line from the North Canadian River to MacArthur Avenue on 36th Street, west of MacArthur from 36th to 39th Street, north of 39th Street from MacArthur to May Avenue, west of May Avenue from 39th to 50th Streets, and north of 50th Street from May Avenue to the Missouri, Kansas, and Texas Railway, and west of the Missouri, Kansas, and Texas Railway to the eastern Oklahoma County line.

669. Southwestern Ohio District shall include that portion of the state of Ohio west of the west boundary of Scioto, Pike, Ross, and Pickaway counties and south of the north boundary of Preble, Montgomery, Greene, and Fayette counties.

670. Tennessee District shall include that portion of the state of Tennessee that lies west of the east boundary of Sumner, Davidson, Williamson, Marshall, and Giles counties, and the city of Fulton, Kentucky.

671. UPSTATE NEW YORK DISTRICT shall include all the portion of the state of New York north of and including Delaware, Greene, and Columbia counties.

672. VIRGINIA DISTRICT shall include the state of Virginia.

673. WASHINGTON DISTRICT, with the exception of Clinton County, which belongs to the Philadelphia District, shall include that portion of the state of Pennsylvania lying west of a line drawn from a point at the northern crest of the Allegheny Mountains to Duncannon, including the town of Duncannon and west of the Susquehanna River and east of the crest of the Allegheny Mountains; all of the states of Delaware and Maryland; that portion of the state of West Virginia composed of the counties of Berkeley, Jefferson, and Morgan; and the District of Columbia.

674. WASHINGTON PACIFIC DISTRICT shall include that portion of the state of Washington west of the Cascade Mountains.

675. WEST TEXAS DISTRICT shall include that portion of the state of Texas north of the 32nd parallel and west of the 97th meridian, excepting the portion in Dallas County west of said meridian, with the addition of that portion of Denton County east of said 97th meridian.

676. WEST VIRGINIA NORTH DISTRICT shall include that portion of the state of West Virginia north of and excluding Cabell, Putnam, Kanawha, Fayette, Nicholas, Greenbrier, and Pocahontas counties, excluding Berkeley, Jefferson, and Morgan counties.

677. WEST VIRGINIA SOUTH DISTRICT shall include that portion of the state of West Virginia south of and excluding Mason, Jackson, Roane, Clay, Braxton, Webster, Randolph, and Pendleton counties.

678. WESTERN LATIN AMERICAN DISTRICT shall include the state of California.

679. WISCONSIN DISTRICT shall include the state of Wisconsin.

CHAPTER II

ASSEMBLY DISTRICTS WORLD MISSION

700. The following are Phase 3 districts outside the United States and Canada, whose boundaries have been established and recognized at the time of the 1997 General Assembly: (200-200.5)

701. ARGENTINA CENTRAL DISTRICT shall include that portion of the country of Argentina that is bordered on the north by the provinces of Santa Fe and Entre Rios; on the south by the city of Dolores; on the east by the Sea of Argentina and the Atlantic Ocean; and on the west by the Province of La Pampa.

702. ARGENTINA LITORAL DISTRICT shall include the province of Santa Fe in the country of Argentina.

703. AUSTRALIA NORTHERN PACIFIC DISTRICT shall include within Australia all of Queensland State and Northern Territory, as well as Tweed Heads City and Tweed Shire in New South Wales State.

704. BARBADOS DISTRICT shall include the country of Barbados.

705. BELIZE DISTRICT shall include the country of Belize.

706. BOLIVIA LA PAZ DISTRICT shall include the following provinces in the Department of La Paz: Ingavi, Pacajes, Aroma, Loayza, and Gualberto Villarroel; those sections of the provinces of Los Andes, Murillo, and Inquisivi that are not included in the Bolivia Titicaca District and the Bolivia Los Yungas District; Canton Lambate of Sud Yungas Province and Canton Totora of the province of Sajama in the Department of Oruro.

707. BRAZIL MINAS GERAIS DISTRICT shall include the state of Minas Gerais in the country of Brazil.

708. BRAZIL NORTHEAST CENTRAL DISTRICT shall be comprised of the states of Rio Grande do Norte, Paraiba, and Pernambuco in the country of Brazil.

709. Brazil Rio de Janeiro Baixada District comprises the western part of the state of Rio de Janeiro with its eastern boundary being formed by a straight line north from Recreio dos Bandeirantes to the headwaters of the Sarapui River and following the same river to the Guanabara Bay in the country of Brazil.

710. Brazil Rio de Janeiro Grande Rio District comprises the eastern part of the state of Rio de Janeiro with its western boundary being formed by a straight line north from Recreio dos Bandeirantes to the headwaters of the Sarapui River and following the same river to the Guanabara Bay in the country of Brazil.

711. Brazil Southeast Paulista District shall be comprised of the governmental region of Campinas, which includes the subregions of Casa Branca, Sïo Joïo da Boa vista, Rio Claro, Limeira, Piracicaba, Jundiaí, and Braganca Paulista in the country of Brazil.

712. British Isles North District shall include Scotland, Northern Ireland, and the English counties of Cumbria, Northumberland, Tyne and Wear, Durham, and Cleveland.

713. British Isles South District shall include Wales and all of England except the counties of Cumbria, Northumberland, Tyne and Wear, Durham, and Cleveland.

714. Cape Verde District shall include the country of Cape Verde and Senegal.

715. Dominican Republic Central District shall include that part of the country of the Dominican Republic comprised of the national district of Santo Domingo and the following provinces: San Cristóbal, Peravia, Azua, San Juan, Baoruco, Independencia, Elías Piña, Barahona, y Pedernales.

716. Ecuador Costa District shall include the provinces of Manabi, Guayas, El Oro, and the part of the province of Los Rios that lies to the south of the city of Quevedo.

717. El Salvador Central District shall include the following departments of the country of El Salvador: San Salvador, Cuzcatlán, La Paz, Chalatenango, San Vicente, and Cabañas.

718. GERMAN DISTRICT shall include the Federal Republic of Germany.

719. GUATEMALA CENTRAL DISTRICT shall include in the Republic of Guatemala the following departments: Guatemala, Sacatepequez, Chimaltenango, and Escuintla.

720. GUATEMALA NORTH FRANJA TRANSVERSAL DISTRICT shall include the municipalities of the following departments of the country of Guatemala: Alta Verapaz: Fray Bartolomé de las Casas, Chahal, and Chisec; Petén: San Luis and Sayaxché; and Quiché: Ixcán.

721. GUATEMALA NORTH VERAPAZ DISTRICT shall include the following departments in the country of Guatemala: Alta Verapaz, with the exception of the municipalities of Fray Bartolomé de las Casas, Chahal, and Chisec; and the northwest part of Izabal.

722. GUYANA BERBICE DISTRICT shall include that part of the country of Guyana comprised of the Berbice county.

723. GUYANA DEMERARA-ESSEQUIBO DISTRICT shall include that part of the country of Guyana comprised of the Demerara and Essequibo counties.

724. HAITI CENTRAL DISTRICT shall include that portion of the West Department of Haiti as follows: the western border being the La Gonave Gulf and the Bay of Port-au-Prince, to the National Route 200 to Jacmel, with the exception of L'Acul de Leogane, which remains on the Haiti Central District; the eastern border being the national border of the Dominican Republic; the northern border shall be the town of Montrouis within the West Department of Haiti and the southern portion of the Central Department of Haiti starting from the intersecting point of the West, the Central and Artibonite Departments and continuing east through the town of Mirebalais to the national border; the southern border shall be the La Selle mountain chain, which follows the border between the West and Southeast Departments of Haiti to the National Route 200 to Jacmel.

725. HAITI LA GONAVE DISTRICT shall include the island of La Gonave in the West Department of Haiti.

726. HAITI SOUTH DISTRICT shall include the Grand Anse

and South Departments of Haiti and the southwestern portion of the West Department of Haiti beginning from the national highway from National Route 200 to Jacmel, with the exception of L'Acul de Leogane.

727. HONDURAS DISTRICT shall include the nation of Honduras.

728. JAMAICA WEST DISTRICT shall include that part of the country of Jamaica comprised of the following parishes: Hanover, Manchester, St. Ann (west of Rio Cobre), St. Elizabeth, St. James, Trelawny, and Westmoreland.

729. JAPAN DISTRICT shall include the nation of Japan.

730. KOREA CENTRAL DISTRICT shall include within the Republic of Korea all of the special city of Seoul, Inchon City under the direct control of the government, and Kyŏnggi Province south of the DMZ, excluding Ich'ŏn City and the Yŏju district.

731. KOREA EAST DISTRICT shall include within the Republic of Korea all of the Kangwon Province south of the DMZ, as well as Ich'ŏn City and the Yŏju district of Kyŏnggi Province.

732. KOREA HONAM DISTRICT shall include within the Republic of Korea, all of North and South Chŏlla provinces and Cheju Island.

733. KOREA SOUTH DISTRICT shall include in the Republic of Korea all of North and South Ch'unch'ŏn provinces.

734. KOREA YONGNAM DISTRICT shall include within the Republic of Korea all of North and South Kyŏngsan provinces.

735. LEEWARD/VIRGIN ISLANDS DISTRICT shall include all English-speaking districts of the Caribbean Leeward Islands and the U.S. Virgin Islands.

736. MALAWI CENTRAL DISTRICT shall conform to the borders of the Malawi Central Region, and extend to the limits thereof as far as the Northern Region boundary in the North, to the border of Zambia in the West, to the Southern Region boundary in the South. The Eastern boundary shall follow the western boundaries of the Malawi Government's Nkhotakota district and Salima district.

737. MALAWI SOUTH DISTRICT shall encompass the whole of the Malawi Southern Region with the exception of the Malawi Government's Salima District.

738. MÉXICO CENTRAL DISTRICT shall include in the Republic of México the states of Guerrero, México, Morelos, Querétaro, the southern half of Hadalgo, the Federal District, and in Oaxaca the county of Cozoltepec.

739. MÉXICO EAST DISTRICT shall include in the Republic of México the states of Campeche, Quintana Roo, Yucatán, and that part of Veracruz from the Papaloapan River to the east.

740. MÉXICO GULF DISTRICT shall include in the Republic of México the states of Puebla, Tlaxcala, and that part of Veracruz from the Papaloapan River north, except for Congregacion Anáhuac.

741. MÉXICO NORTHEAST DISTRICT shall include in the Republic of México the states of Nuevo León, Tamaulipas, Coahuila, and the city of El Salvador, Zacatecas, and the city of Congregacion Anáhuac, Veracruz.

742. MÉXICO NORTHWEST DISTRICT shall include in the Republic of México the states of Baja California, Baja California Sur, and Sonora.

743. MÉXICO OAXACA DISTRICT shall include in the Republic of México the state of Oaxaca (except for Cozoltepec, Oax.).

744. MÉXICO SOUTH DISTRICT shall include in the Republic of México, the part of 92 counties in the state of Chiapas, north of and including the counties of Cintalapa de Figueeroa, Villa Corzo, Angel Albino Corzo, Siltepec, El Porvenir, and Mazapa de Madero.

745. MÉXICO SOUTH BORDER DISTRICT shall include in the Republic of México that part of the state of Chiapas with the counties of Motozintla de Madero, Huixtla, Tuzantán, Huehuetán, Mazatán, Tapachula, Cacahoatán, Tuxtla Chico, Metapa, Frontera Hidalgo, Suchiate, Unión Juarez, and Ejido Lázaro Cárdenas de Villa Comatitlán.

746. MÉXICO SOUTH PACIFIC DISTRICT shall include in the Republic of México that part of the state of Chiapas with the counties of Arriaga, Tonalá, Pijijiapan, Mapastepec, Acapetahua, Acacoyagua, Escuintla, and Villa Comatitlán.

747. MÉXICO WEST DISTRICT shall include in the Republic of México the states of Aguascalientes, Colima, Guanajuato, Jalisco, Michoacán, Nayarit, San Luis Potosí, except for the zone known as Huasteca (composed of 18 municipalities), Sinaloa, and Zacatecas, except for El Salvador, Zacatecas.

748. MOZAMBIQUE MAPUTO DISTRICT shall include, in the country of Mozambique, the whole of the Maputo Province.

749. NETHERLANDS DISTRICT shall include all of the Kingdom of the Netherlands.

750. NICARAGUA NORTH-CENTRAL DISTRICT shall include in the nation of Nicaragua all the provinces, with the exception of Carazo, Jinotepe, Rivas, Chontales, and Rio San Juan.

751. PAPUA NEW GUINEA WESTERN HIGHLANDS DISTRICT shall include within Papua New Guinea that part of the Western Highlands Province that is south and west of the Wagi Sepik Divide, inclusive of the Baiyer River drainage area.

752. PERU ALTO MARAÑON DISTRICT shall include the provinces of San Ignacio and Jaén in the department of Cajamarca, and the department of Amazonas with the exception of the province of Condorcanqui.

753. PERU CENTRAL DISTRICT shall include the departments of Lima, Ica, Pasco, Junín, and Huancavelica.

754. PERU NORTH DISTRICT shall include the departments of Lambayeque, La Libertad, and Ancash and the district of Llama in the province of Chota in the department of Cajamarca.

755. PERU NORTH PACIFIC DISTRICT shall include the departments of Piura and Tumbes.

756. PERU NORTHEAST DISTRICT shall include the department of San Martin with the exception of the province of Tocache.

757. PHILIPPINES LUZON DISTRICT shall include in the Republic of the Philippines the Philippine Government Regions 1 and 2, as well as the Cordillera Administrative Region.

758. PHILIPPINES METRO MANILA DISTRICT shall include within the Republic of the Philippines the National Capital Region and the Rizal Province.

759. PHILIPPINES WESTERN VISAYAS DISTRICT shall include within the Republic of the Philippines the Aklan, Antique, Capiz, Guimaras, Iloilo, and Negros Occidental provinces of the Philippine Government Region 6.

760. PUERTO RICO EAST DISTRICT shall include that part of the commonwealth of Puerto Rico east of the following municipalities: Vega Baja, Corozal, Naranjito, Comerío, Barranquitas, Aibonito, Coamo, and Santa Isabel.

761. PUERTO RICO WEST DISTRICT shall include that part of the commonwealth of Puerto Rico west of the following municipalities: Barceloneta, Manati, Ciales, Morovis, Orocovis, Villalba, Juana Diaz, and Ponce.

762. REPUBLIC OF SOUTH AFRICA DRAKENSBURG DISTRICT shall include that portion of the Republic of South Africa with eastern boundary west of farms: Madras in south to Lulekani in the north; east of Kruger National Park; west to a line from Lydenburg in the south to Phalabora in the north; with the southern boundary along Highway 536 from Hazyview to Highway 37 to Lydenburg.

763. REPUBLIC OF SOUTH AFRICA EASTERN DISTRICT shall include that portion of the Republic of South Africa with northern boundary from the east side of the Lulekani farm following the border of the Kruger National Park southward to the Sabie River; the southern boundary shall be the Sabie River; the western boundary shall be east of farms: Madras in the south to Lulekani in the north.

764. REPUBLIC OF SOUTH AFRICA GAUTENG DISTRICT shall include that portion of the Republic of South Africa within the Gauteng Province, or may contain local churches attached to said district.

765. REPUBLIC OF SOUTH AFRICA KWAZULU NATAL DISTRICT shall include the Republic of South Africa within the KwaZulu/Natal Province, or may contain local churches attached to said district.

766. REPUBLIC OF SOUTH AFRICA NORTHEAST DISTRICT shall

include that portion of the Republic of South Africa with eastern boundary from Dingaponga along Highway 530 to Kruger National Park; the northern boundary from Punda Maria along the Venda border to Soekmekaar; with the western boundary to The Downs.

767. REPUBLIC OF SOUTH AFRICA NORTHWEST DISTRICT shall include that portion of the Republic of South Africa with the eastern boundary on a line Mmafafe to Dandron to Pontdrif; the western boundary from Pontdrif to Rooibokkraal along the Botswana border; and the southern boundary on a line from Rooibokkraal to Nylstroom, Naboomspruit to Mmafafe.

768. REPUBLIC OF SOUTH AFRICA WESTERN CAPE DISTRICT shall include that portion of the Cape Province of the Republic of South Africa as follows: the eastern border shall be the 22nd meridian from the Indian Ocean to the 29th parallel; the northern border shall be the 29th parallel; the western and southern borders shall be the Atlantic and Indian oceans, respectively.

769. SWAZILAND CENTRAL DISTRICT shall include that portion of the Kingdom of Swaziland south of the Komati River excepting the Madlangampisi and Nkambeni area, and is bounded on the west by the boundary of Swaziland and on the south by the Great Usutu River to Bunya, thereafter directly west to the Swaziland boundary, and on the east by the Lubombo district boundary.

770. SWAZILAND EAST DISTRICT shall include that portion of the Lubombo District north of the Great Usutu River bounded on the north by South Africa and Mozambique, and on the east by Mozambique, on the south by the Great Usutu River and on the west by the Lubombo district boundary from Mananga Border Gate north to the Usutu in the south (two miles northwest of the Holomi station).

771. SWAZILAND NORTH DISTRICT shall include that portion of the Kingdom of Swaziland north of the Komati River with the exception of the Madlangampisi and Nkambeni areas, which are south of the Komati River, and also embracing Mavula and Sihhoye communities.

772. SWAZILAND SOUTH DISTRICT shall include that portion of the Kingdom of Swaziland south of the Great Usutu River to the borders of the Republic of South Africa and Mozambique.

773. TAIWAN DISTRICT shall include the Republic of China (Taiwan).

774. TRINIDAD AND TOBAGO DISTRICT shall include the country of Trinidad and Tobago.

775. URUGUAY SOUTH DISTRICT shall include all of the territory south of the Rio Negro River in the country of Uruguay.

776. ZIMBABWE EAST DISTRICT shall include greater Harare, which is in Mashonaland province, Masvingo province and Manicaland province.

PART VIII

Ritual

THE SACRAMENT OF BAPTISM

THE RECEPTION OF CHURCH MEMBERS

THE SACRAMENT OF THE LORD'S SUPPER

MATRIMONY

THE FUNERAL SERVICE

INSTALLATION OF OFFICERS

CHURCH DEDICATIONS

800. THE SACRAMENT OF BAPTISM

800.1. The Baptism of Believers

DEARLY BELOVED: Baptism is the sign and seal of the new covenant of grace, the significance of which is attested by the apostle Paul in his letter to the Romans as follows:

"Or don't you know that all of us who were baptized into Christ Jesus were baptized into his death? We were therefore buried with him through baptism into death in order that, just as Christ was raised from the dead through the glory of the Father, we too may live a new life. If we have been united with him like this in his death, we will certainly also be united with him in his resurrection" (Romans 6:3-5).

The earliest and simplest statement of Christian belief, into which you now come to be baptized, is the Apostles' Creed, which reads as follows:

"I believe in God the Father Almighty, Maker of heaven and earth;

"And in Jesus Christ, His only Son, our Lord; who was conceived by the Holy Ghost, born of the Virgin Mary, suffered under Pontius Pilate, was crucified, dead, and buried; He descended into hell; the third day He rose again from the dead;

He ascended into heaven, and sitteth at the right hand of God the Father Almighty; from thence He shall come to judge the quick and the dead.

"I believe in the Holy Ghost, the holy Church of Jesus Christ, the communion of saints, the forgiveness of sins, the resurrection of the body, and the life everlasting."

Will you be baptized into this faith? If so, answer, "I will."

Response: I will.

Do you acknowledge Jesus Christ as your personal Savior, and do you realize that He saves you now?

Response: I do.

Will you obey God's holy will and keep His commandments, walking in them all the days of your life?

Response: I will.

The minister, giving the full name of the person and using the preferred form of baptism—sprinkling, pouring, or immersion—shall say:

________________ , I baptize thee in the name of the Father, and of the Son, and of the Holy Spirit. Amen.

800.2. The Baptism of Infants or Young Children

When the sponsors shall have presented themselves with the child (or children) the minister shall say:

DEARLY BELOVED: While we do not hold that baptism imparts the regenerating grace of God, we do believe that Christ gave this holy sacrament as a sign and seal of the new covenant. Christian baptism signifies for this young child God's gracious acceptance on the basis of His prevenient grace in Christ, and points forward to his (her) personal appropriation of the benefits of the Atonement when he (she) reaches the age of moral accountability and exercises conscious saving faith in Jesus Christ.

In presenting this child for baptism you are hereby witnessing to your own personal Christian faith and to your purpose to guide him (her) early in life to a knowledge of Christ as Savior. To this end it is your duty to teach him (her), as soon as he (she) shall be able to learn, the nature and end of this holy sacrament; to watch over his (her) education, that he (she) may not be led astray; to direct his (her) feet to the sanctuary; to restrain him (her) from evil associates and habits; and as much as in you lies, to bring him (her) up in the nurture and admonition of the Lord.

Will you endeavor to do so by the help of God? If so, answer, "I will."

The minister may then ask the parents or guardians to name the child, and shall then baptize the child, repeating his (her) full name and saying:

_______________, I baptize thee in the name of the Father, and of the Son, and of the Holy Spirit. Amen.

The minister may then offer the following prayer or may use an extemporary prayer.

Heavenly Father, we humbly pray that Thou wilt take this child into Thy loving care. Abundantly enrich him (her) with Thy heavenly grace; bring him (her) safely through the perils of childhood; deliver him (her) from the temptations of youth; lead him (her) to a personal knowledge of Christ as Savior; help him (her) to grow in wisdom, and in stature, and in favor with God and man, and to persevere therein to the end. Uphold the parents with loving care, that with wise counsel and holy example they may faithfully discharge their responsibilities to both this child and to Thee. In the name of Jesus Christ our Lord. Amen.

800.3. The Dedication of Infants or Young Children

When the parents or guardians have presented themselves with the child (or children) the minister shall say:

"Then little children were brought to Jesus for him to place his hands on them and pray for them. But the disciples rebuked those who brought them. Jesus said, 'Let the little children come to me, and do not hinder them, for the kingdom of heaven belongs to such as these'" (Matthew 19:13-14).

In presenting this child for dedication you signify not only your faith in the Christian religion but also your desire that he (she) may early know and follow the will of God, may live and die a Christian, and come unto everlasting blessedness.

In order to attain this holy end, it will be your duty, as parents (guardians), to teach him (her) early the fear of the Lord, to watch over his (her) education, that he (she) be not led astray; to direct his (her) youthful mind to the Holy Scriptures, and his (her) feet to the sanctuary; to restrain him (her) from evil associates and habits; and, as much as in you lies, to bring him (her) up in the nurture and admonition of the Lord.

Will you endeavor to do so by the help of God? If so, answer, "I will."

Pastor: I now ask you, the congregation; will you commit yourself as the Body of Christ to support and encourage these parents as they endeavor to fulfill their responsibilities to this child and to assist ____________ by nurturing his (her) growth toward spiritual maturity?

Response: We will.

Pastor: Our loving Heavenly Father, we do here and now dedicate ____________ in the name of the Father, and of the Son, and of the Holy Spirit. Amen.

Then the minister may offer the following prayer, or may use an extemporary prayer.

Heavenly Father, we humbly pray that Thou wilt take this child into Thy loving care. Abundantly enrich him (her) with Thy heavenly grace; bring him (her) safely through the perils of childhood; deliver him (her) from the temptations of youth; lead him (her) to a personal knowledge of Christ as Savior; help him (her) to grow in wisdom, and in stature, and in favor with God and man, and to persevere therein to the end. Uphold the parents with loving care, that with wise counsel and holy example they may faithfully discharge their responsibilities both to this child and to Thee. In the name of Jesus Christ our Lord. Amen.

800.4. The Dedication of Infants or Young Children

(Ritual for Single Parent or Guardian)

When the parent or guardian has presented himself (herself) with the child (or children) the minister shall say:

"Then little children were brought to Jesus for him to place his hands on them and pray for them. But the disciples rebuked those who brought them. Jesus said, 'Let the little children come to me, and do not hinder them, for the kingdom of heaven belongs to such as these'" (Matthew 19:13-14).

In presenting this child for dedication you signify not only your faith in the Christian religion but also your desire that he (she) may early know and follow the will of God, may live and die a Christian, and come unto everlasting blessedness.

In order to attain this holy end, it will be your duty, as a parent (guardian), to teach him (her) early the fear of the Lord, to watch over his (her) education, that he (she) be not led astray; to direct his (her) youthful mind to the Holy Scriptures, and his (her) feet to the sanctuary; to restrain him (her) from evil associates and habits; and, as much as in you lies, to bring him (her) up in the nurture and admonition of the Lord.

Will you endeavor to do so by the help of God? If so, answer, "I will."

Pastor: I now ask you, the congregation; will you commit yourself as the Body of Christ to support and encourage this parent as he (she) endeavors to fulfill his (her) responsibilities to this child and to assist ________________ by nurturing his (her) growth toward spiritual maturity?

Response: We will.

Pastor: Our loving Heavenly Father, we do here and now dedicate ________________ in the name of the Father, and of the Son, and of the Holy Spirit. Amen.

Then the minister may offer the following prayer, or may use an extemporary prayer.

Heavenly Father, we humbly pray that Thou wilt take this child into Thy loving care. Abundantly enrich him (her) with Thy heavenly grace; bring him (her) safely through the perils of childhood; deliver him (her) from the temptations of youth; lead him (her) to a personal knowledge of Christ as Savior; help him (her) to grow in wisdom, and in stature, and in favor with God and man, and to persevere therein to the end. Uphold the parent with loving care, that with wise counsel and holy example he (she) may faithfully discharge his (her) responsibilities both to this child and to Thee. In the name of Jesus Christ our Lord. Amen.

801. THE RECEPTION OF CHURCH MEMBERS

The prospective members having come forward to stand before the altar of the church, the pastor shall address them as follows:

DEARLY BELOVED: The privileges and blessings that we have in association together in the Church of Jesus Christ are very sacred and precious. There is in it such hallowed fellowship as cannot otherwise be known.

There is such helpfulness with brotherly watch care and counsel as can be found only in the Church.

There is the godly care of pastors, with the teachings of the Word; and the helpful inspiration of social worship. And there is cooperation in service, accomplishing that which cannot otherwise be done. The doctrines upon which the church rests as essential to Christian experience are brief.

We believe in God the Father, Son, and Holy Spirit. We especially emphasize the deity of Jesus Christ and the personality of the Holy Spirit.

We believe that human beings are born in sin; that they need the work of forgiveness through Christ and the new birth by the Holy Spirit; that subsequent to this there is the deeper work of heart cleansing or entire sanctification through the infilling of the Holy Spirit, and that to each of these works of grace the Holy Spirit gives witness.

We believe that our Lord will return, the dead shall be raised, and that all shall come to final judgment with its rewards and punishments.

Do you heartily believe these truths? If so, answer, "I do."

Do you acknowledge Jesus Christ as your personal Savior, and do you realize that He saves you now?

Response: I do.

Desiring to unite with the Church of the Nazarene, do you covenant to give yourself to the fellowship and work of God in connection with it, as set forth in the General Rules and Special Rules of the Church of the Nazarene? Will you endeavor in every way to glorify God, by a humble walk, godly conversation, and holy service; by devotedly giving of your means; by faithful attendance upon the means of grace; and, abstaining from all evil, will you seek earnestly to perfect holiness of heart and life in the fear of the Lord?

Response: I will.

The minister shall then say to the person or persons:

I welcome you into this church, to its sacred fellowship, responsibilities, and privileges. May the great Head of the Church bless and keep you, and enable you to be faithful in all good works, that your life and witness may be effective in leading others to Christ.

The minister shall then take each one by the hand, and with appropriate words of personal greeting welcome each into the church.

(Alternate form for members joining by letter of transfer:)

________________________, formerly a member (members) of the Church of the Nazarene at ________________________, comes (come) to join the fellowship of this local congregation.

Taking each by the hand, or speaking to the group, the minister shall say:

It gives me pleasure on behalf of this church to welcome you into our membership. We trust that we will be a source of encouragement and strength to you and that you, in turn, will be a source of blessing and help to us. May the Lord richly bless you in the salvation of souls and in the advancement of His kingdom.

802. THE SACRAMENT OF THE LORD'S SUPPER

The administration of the Lord's Supper may be introduced by an appropriate sermon and the reading of 1 Corinthians 11:23-29, Luke 22:14-20, or some other suitable passage. Let the minister then give the following invitation:

The Lord himself ordained this holy sacrament. He commanded His disciples to partake of the bread and wine, emblems of His broken body and shed blood. This is His table. The feast is for His disciples. Let all those who have with true repentance forsaken their sins, and have believed in Christ unto salvation, draw near and take these emblems, and, by faith, partake of the life of Jesus Christ, to your soul's comfort and joy. Let us remember that it is the memorial of the death and passion of our Lord; also a token of His coming again. Let us not forget that we are one, at one table with the Lord.

The minister may offer a prayer of confession and supplication, concluding with the following prayer of consecration:

Almighty God, our Heavenly Father, who of Thy tender mercy didst give Thine only Son, Jesus Christ, to suffer death upon the Cross for our redemption: hear us, we most humbly beseech Thee. Grant that, as we receive these Thy creatures of bread and wine according to the holy institution of Thy Son, our Savior Jesus Christ, in remembrance of His passion and death, we may be made partakers of the benefits of His atoning sacrifice.

We are reminded that in the same night that our Lord was betrayed, He took bread and, when He had given thanks, He broke it and gave it to His disciples, saying, "This is my body given for you; do this in remembrance of me." Likewise, after supper, He took the cup, and when He had given thanks, He gave it to them, saying, "This cup is the new covenant in my blood, which is poured out for you; do this, whenever you drink it, in remembrance of me."

May we come before Thee in true humility and faith as we partake of this holy sacrament. Through Jesus Christ our Lord. Amen.

Then may the minister, partaking first, with the assistance of any other ministers present, and when necessary, of the stewards, administer the Communion to the people.

While the bread is being distributed, let the minister say:

The body of our Lord Jesus Christ, which was broken for you, preserve you blameless, unto everlasting life. Take and eat this, in remembrance that Christ died for you.

As the cup is being passed, let the minister say:

The blood of our Lord Jesus Christ, which was shed for you, preserve you blameless unto everlasting life. Drink this, in remembrance that Christ's blood was shed for you, and be thankful.

After all have partaken, the minister may then offer a concluding prayer of thanksgiving and commitment. (33.5, 413.3, 413.10, 427.7, 429.1)

NOTE: Only unfermented wine and unleavened bread should be used in the sacrament of the Lord's Supper. In world areas where this may cause special intrafaith difficulties, a district assembly may request the Board of General Superintendents for permission to use common bread.

803. MATRIMONY

At the day and time appointed for the solemnization of matrimony, the persons to be married—having been qualified according to law and by careful counsel and guidance by the minister—standing together, facing the minister, the man to the minister's left and the woman to the right, the minister shall address the congregation as follows:

DEARLY BELOVED: We are gathered together here in the sight of God, and in the presence of these witnesses, to join together this man and this woman in holy matrimony, which is an honorable estate, instituted of God in the time of man's innocency, signifying unto us the mystical union that exists between Christ and His Church. This holy estate Christ adorned and beautified with His presence and first miracle that He wrought, in Cana of Galilee, and St. Paul commended as being honorable among all men. It is, therefore, not to be entered into unadvisedly, but reverently, discreetly, and in the fear of God.

Into this holy estate these persons present now come to be joined.

Addressing the couple to be married, the minister shall say:

_______________ and _______________, I require and charge you both as you stand in the presence of God, to remember that the commitment to marriage is a commitment to permanence. It is the intent of God that your marriage will be for life, and that only death will separate you.

If the vows you exchange today be kept without violation, and if you seek always to know and do the will of God, your lives will be blessed with His presence, and your home will abide in peace.

Following the charge the minister shall say unto the man:

________________, will you have this woman to be your wedded wife, to live together after God's ordinance in the holy estate of matrimony? Will you love her, comfort her, honor and keep her in sickness and in health; and forsaking all others, keep yourself only unto her, so long as you both shall live?

Response: I will.

Then shall the minister say unto the woman:

________________, will you have this man to be your wedded husband, to live together after God's ordinance in the holy estate of matrimony? Will you love, honor, and keep him, in sickness and in health; and, forsaking all others, keep yourself only unto him, so long as you both shall live?

Response: I will.

Then the minister shall ask:

Who gives this woman to be married to this man?

Response (by the father, or whoever gives the bride in marriage): I do.

Facing each other and joining right hands, the couple shall then exchange the following vows:

The man shall repeat after the minister:

I, ____________, take you, ____________, to be my wedded wife, to have and to hold from this day forward, for better—for worse, for richer—for poorer, in sickness and in health, to love and to cherish, till death us do part, according to God's holy ordinance; and thereto I pledge you my faith.

The woman shall repeat after the minister:

I, ____________, take you, ____________, to be my wedded husband, to have and to hold from this day forward, for better—for worse, for richer—for poorer, in sickness and in health, to love and to cherish, till death us do part, according to God's holy ordinance; and thereto I pledge you my faith.

If desired, a ring ceremony may be inserted at this point. The minister receives the ring from the groomsman and, in turn, passes it to the groom. As he then places it upon the bride's finger, he shall repeat, after the minister:

This ring I give you as a token of my love and as a pledge of my constant fidelity.

Repeat for double ring ceremony.

The couple then shall kneel as the minister offers the following, or an extemporaneous prayer:

O Eternal God, Creator and Preserver of all mankind, Giver of all spiritual grace, the Author of everlasting life, send Thy blessing upon these Thy servants, this man and this woman, whom we now bless in Thy name; that as Isaac and Rebekah lived faithfully together, so these persons may surely perform and keep the vow and covenant made between them this hour and may ever remain in love and peace together, through Jesus Christ our Lord. Amen.

Then shall the minister say:

Forasmuch as this man and woman have consented together in holy wedlock, and have witnessed the same before God and this company, and have declared the same by joining of hands, I pronounce that they are husband and wife together, in the name of the Father, and of the Son, and of the Holy Spirit. Those whom God has joined together let not man put asunder. Amen.

The minister shall then add this blessing:

God, the Father, the Son, and the Holy Spirit, bless, preserve, and keep you; the Lord mercifully with His favor look upon you, and fill you with all spiritual benediction and grace. May you so live together in this life that in the world to come you may have life everlasting.

The minister may then conclude with an extemporaneous prayer and/or benediction. (427.7)

804. THE FUNERAL SERVICE

DEARLY BELOVED: We are gathered today to pay our final tribute of respect to that which was mortal of our deceased loved one and friend. To you members of the family who mourn your loss, we especially offer our deep and sincere sympathy. May we share with you the comfort afforded by God's Word for such a time as this:

"Do not let your hearts be troubled. Trust in God; trust also in me. In my Father's house are many rooms; if it were not so, I would have told you. I am going there to prepare a place for you. And if I go and prepare a place for you, I will come back and take you to be with me that you also may be where I am" (John 14:1-3).

"I am the resurrection and the life. He who believes in me will live, even though he dies; and whoever lives and believes in me will never die" (John 11:25-26).

INVOCATION (in the minister's own words or the following):

Almighty God, our Heavenly Father, we come into this sanctuary of sorrow, realizing our utter dependence upon Thee. We know Thou dost love us and canst turn even the shadow of death into the light of morning. Help us now to wait before Thee with reverent and submissive hearts.

Thou art our Refuge and Strength, O God—a very present Help in time of trouble. Grant unto us Thy abundant mercy. May those who mourn today find comfort and healing balm in Thy sustaining grace. We humbly bring these petitions in the name of our Lord Jesus Christ. Amen.

A Hymn or Special Song

Selections of Scripture:

"Praise be to the God and Father of our Lord Jesus Christ! In his great mercy he has given us new birth into a living hope through the resurrection of Jesus Christ from the dead, and into an inheritance that can never perish, spoil or fade—kept in heaven for you, who through faith are shielded by God's power until the coming of the salvation that is ready to be revealed in the last time. In this you greatly rejoice, though now for a little while you may have had to suffer grief in all kinds of trials. These have come so that your faith—of greater worth than gold, which perishes even though refined by fire—may be proved genuine and may result in praise, glory and honor when Jesus Christ is revealed. Though you have not seen him, you love him; and even though you do not see him now, you believe in him and are filled with an inexpressible and glorious joy, for you are receiving the goal of your faith, the salvation of your souls" (1 Peter 1:3-9).

(Other passages that might be used are: Matthew 5:3-4, 6, 8; Psalms 27:3-5, 11, 13-14; 46:1-6, 10-11.)

MESSAGE
A HYMN OR SPECIAL SONG
CLOSING PRAYER

* * *

AT THE GRAVESIDE

When the people have assembled, the minister may read any or all of the following scriptures:

"I know that my Redeemer lives, and that in the end he will stand upon the earth. And after my skin has been destroyed, yet in my flesh I will see God; I myself will see him with my own eyes—I, and not another" (Job 19:25-27).

"Listen, I tell you a mystery: We will not all sleep, but we will all be changed—in a flash, in the twinkling of an eye, at the last trumpet. For the trumpet will sound, the dead will be raised imperishable, and we will be changed. . . . Then the saying that is written will come true: 'Death has been swallowed up in victory. Where, O death, is your victory? Where, O death, is your sting?' The sting of death is sin; and the power of sin is the law. But thanks be to God! He gives us the victory through our Lord Jesus Christ.

"Therefore, my dear brothers, stand firm. Let nothing move you. Always give yourselves fully to the work of the Lord, because you know that your labor in the Lord is not in vain" (1 Corinthians 15:51-52, 54-58).

"Then I heard a voice from heaven say, 'Write: Blessed are the dead who die in the Lord from now on. Yes,' says the Spirit, 'they will rest from their labor; for their deeds will follow them'" (Revelation 14:13).

The minister shall then read one of the following committal statements:

For a Believer:

Forasmuch as the spirit of our departed loved one has returned to God, who gave it, we therefore tenderly commit his (her) body to the grave in sure trust and certain hope of the resurrection of the dead and the life of the world to come, through our Lord Jesus Christ, who shall give to us new bodies like unto His glorious body. "Blessed are the dead who die in the Lord."

For a Nonbeliever:

We have come now to commit the body of our departed friend to its kindred dust. The spirit we leave with God, for we know the merciful Judge of all the earth will do right. Let us who remain dedicate ourselves anew to live in the fear and love of God, so that we may obtain an abundant entrance into the heavenly Kingdom.

For a Child:

In the sure and certain hope of the resurrection to eternal life through our Lord Jesus

Christ, we commit the body of this child to the grave. And as Jesus, during His earthly life, took the children into His arms and blessed them, may He receive this dear one unto himself, for, as He said, "the kingdom of heaven belongs to such as these."

PRAYER:

Our Heavenly Father, God of all mercy, we look to Thee in this moment of sorrow and bereavement. Comfort these dear ones whose hearts are heavy and sad. Wilt Thou be with them, sustain and guide them in the days to come. Grant, O Lord, that they may love and serve Thee and obtain the fullness of Thy promises in the world to come.

"May the God of peace, who through the blood of the eternal covenant brought back from the dead our Lord Jesus, that great Shepherd of the sheep, equip you with everything good for doing his will, and may he work in us what is pleasing to him, through Jesus Christ; to whom be glory for ever and ever. Amen" (Hebrews 13:20-21).

805. INSTALLATION OF OFFICERS

Following the singing of an appropriate hymn, let the secretary read the names and positions of the officers to be installed. These may come forward and stand at the altar of the church, facing the minister. A covenant card* should be provided for each. The minister shall then say:

Recognizing God's method of setting apart certain workers for specific areas of Christian service, we come to this moment of installation of these officers (and/or teachers) who have been duly chosen to serve in our church for the ensuing year. Let us consider God's instructions to us from His Holy Word.

"Therefore, I urge you, brothers, in view of God's mercy, to offer your bodies as living sacrifices, holy and pleasing to God—this is your spiritual act of worship. Do not conform any longer to the pattern of this world, but be transformed by the renewing of your mind. Then you will be able to test and approve what God's will is—his good, pleasing and perfect will" (Romans 12:1-2).

"Do your best to present yourself to God as one approved, a workman who does not need to be ashamed and who correctly handles the word of truth" (2 Timothy 2:15).

"Let the word of Christ dwell in you richly as you teach and admonish one another with all

---

*Available from Nazarene Publishing House.

wisdom, and as you sing psalms, hymns and spiritual songs with gratitude in your hearts to God" (Colossians 3:16).

"Anyone who receives instruction in the word must share all good things with his instructor" (Galatians 6:6).

We now come to this important moment when you who stand before the altar are to take upon yourselves the task of caring for the affairs of the church and its auxiliary organizations. May you look upon the assignments you now assume as special opportunities for service for our Lord, and may you find joy and spiritual blessing in the performance of your respective duties.

Yours is no light task, for the ongoing of the church and the destiny of souls are in your hands. The development of Christian character is your responsibility, and leading the unsaved to Jesus Christ is your highest objective. May God grant you wisdom and strength as you do His work for His glory.

You have been given a card on which is printed a covenant. We shall read it in unison, and as we do so, let us make it a personal commitment.

WORKER'S COVENANT

In consideration of the confidence placed in me by the church in being selected for the office I now assume, I hereby covenant:

To maintain a high standard of Christian living and example in harmony with the ideals and standards of the Church of the Nazarene.

To cultivate my personal Christian experience by setting aside each day definite time for prayer and Bible reading.

To be present at the regular Sunday School, the Sunday morning and Sunday evening preaching services, and the midweek prayer meeting of the church, unless providentially hindered.

To attend faithfully all duly called meetings of the various boards, councils, or committees to which I have been, or will be, assigned.

To notify my superior officer if I am unable to be present at the stated time, or to carry out my responsibilities in this office.

To read widely the denominational publications, and other books and literature that will be helpful to me in discharging the duties of my office.

To improve myself and my skills by participating in Continuing Lay Training courses as opportunity is afforded.

To endeavor to lead people to Jesus Christ by manifesting an active interest in the spiritual welfare of others and by attending and supporting all evangelistic meetings in the church.

The minister shall then offer an appropriate prayer, and a special song of dedication may be sung, after which the minister shall say:

Having pledged together your hearts and hands to the task of carrying forward the work of this church in your particular assignments, I herewith install you in the respective positions to which you have been elected or appointed. You are now a vital part of the organizational structure and leadership of this church. May you, by example, by precept, and by diligent service, be effective workers in the vineyard of the Lord.

The minister shall ask the congregation to rise, and shall address them as follows:

You have heard the pledge and covenant entered into by your church leaders for the coming year. I now charge you, as a congregation, to be loyal in your support of them. The burdens that we have laid upon them are heavy, and they will need your assistance and prayers. May you always be understanding of their problems and tolerant of their seeming failures. May you lend assistance joyfully when called upon, so that, as we work together, our church may be an effective instrument in winning the lost to Christ.

The minister may then lead in a concluding prayer or have the congregation repeat the Lord's Prayer in unison.

806. CHURCH DEDICATIONS

Minister: Having been prospered by the hand of the Lord and enabled by His grace and strength to complete this building to the glory of His name, we now stand in God's presence to dedicate this structure to the service of His kingdom.

To the glory of God our Father, from whom cometh every good and perfect gift; to the honor of Jesus Christ, our Lord and Savior; and to the praise of the Holy Spirit, Source of light, and life, and power—our Sanctifier,

Congregation: We do now, with joy and gratitude, humbly dedicate this building.

Minister: In remembrance of all who have loved and served this church, establishing the heritage we now enjoy, and who are now part of the Church Triumphant,

Congregation: We gratefully dedicate this edifice (sanctuary, education building, fellowship hall, etc.).

Minister: For worship in prayer and song, for the preaching of the Word, for the teaching of the Scriptures, and for the fellowship of the saints,

Congregation: We solemnly dedicate this house of God.

Minister: For the comfort of those who mourn, for the strengthening of the weak, for the help of those who are tempted, and for the giving of hope and courage to all who come within these walls,

Congregation: We dedicate this place of fellowship and prayer.

Minister: For the sharing of the good news of salvation from sin, for the spreading of scriptural holiness, for the giving of instruction in righteousness, and for the service of our fellowmen,

Congregation: We reverently dedicate this building.

Unison: We, as laborers together with God, now join hands and hearts and dedicate ourselves anew to the high and holy purposes to which this building has been set apart. We pledge our loyal devotion, faithful stewardship, and diligent service to the end that in this place the name of the Lord shall be glorified, and His kingdom shall be advanced; through Jesus Christ our Lord. Amen.

PART IX

Auxiliary Constitutions

NAZARENE YOUTH INTERNATIONAL

NAZARENE WORLD MISSION SOCIETIES

BYLAWS OF THE SUNDAY SCHOOL

CHAPTER I

810. CONSTITUTIONS FOR NAZARENE YOUTH INTERNATIONAL

PREAMBLE

The Church of the Nazarene is vitally interested in young people. Effective youth ministry is an essential part of the mission of every local church. Nazarene Youth International is intended to serve the church in that mission.

NYI is a distinct auxiliary of the Church of the Nazarene. As such, its officers are accountable to the membership that elects them, and the auxiliary itself to the appropriate church body at each level.

This NYI Constitution provides guidelines by which the organization may facilitate and support, by way of the creative genius of its young people, the church's ministry to and through youth.

ARTICLE I. *Name*

This organization shall be called NAZARENE YOUTH INTERNATIONAL (NYI) of the Church of the Nazarene.

ARTICLE II. *Purpose*

The purpose of NYI shall be to lead youth into a relationship with Jesus Christ as their Savior and Lord and to establish them as His disciples, characterized by a life of holiness expressed through devotion, worship, fellowship, stewardship, and witness (Matthew 28:19-20). This shall be achieved by:

- reaching youth for Jesus Christ
- instructing them in the Word of God and the doctrines of the church

- building them up in the Christian faith and in holy character
- incorporating them into the life and ministry of the church
- encouraging them to join in the fellowship of membership in the Church of the Nazarene
- equipping them to advance the mission of the church, and
- mobilizing them to reach their world for Christ

ARTICLE III. *Motto*

"Don't let anyone look down on you because you are young, but set an example for the believers in speech, in life, in love, in faith and in purity" (1 Timothy 4:12).

ARTICLE IV. *Membership*

SECTION 1—Local

1. Membership in NAZARENE YOUTH INTERNATIONAL shall be open to all persons between the ages of 12 and 40 inclusive and officers and youth workers over age 40.

2. Local membership shall consist of those who affiliate themselves with NYI ministry by joining the organization and participating in its ministries, within a local church or youth ministry within an approved Nazarene Compassionate Ministries Center.

3. Each local congregation shall maintain an accurate roster of all active members.

4. Persons may be added to the membership roster after reaching their 12th birthday, by consenting to participate in the ministry of NYI.

SECTION 2—District

All local organizations and members of NYI within the boundaries of a given district shall form the District Nazarene Youth International, which shall be directly accountable to the district superintendent and the District Advisory Board.

SECTION 3—General

All regional, district, and local NYI organizations and their members shall constitute the General Nazarene Youth International, which shall be directly accountable to the responsible general superintendent for NYI, and related to the General Board through the Sunday School Ministries and NYI Department. The NYI Ministries office shall function as the operational body of Nazarene Youth International at Nazarene Headquarters.

SECTION 4—Ministry Focus and Age Divisions

1. The ministry focus of NYI will be to youth ages 12 and older, college/university students, and young adults. The ministry focus may be modified as seen fit by regional, district, or local NYI Councils.

2. Three specific age divisions may function within the NYI, for the purposes of representation and ministry programming:

- Early Youth or Junior High (12-14)
- Senior Youth or Senior High (15-18)
- Young Adult or College/Career (postsecondary)

NYI Councils may expand or narrow the boundaries of each age division, according to needs.

ARTICLE V. *Officers*

SECTION 1—Local

1. The local NYI officers of this organization shall be a president, a vice president, a secretary, and a treasurer, or a president and at least three persons elected at-large by the annual meeting and assigned job descriptions according to local church needs. All officers shall be members of the local church whose organization they serve.

2. The local NYI officers shall be elected annually by the members of the organization and shall serve until their successors are elected and installed.

3. The NYI officers of the local organization shall be nominated by a Nominating Committee, consisting of not fewer than four nor more than seven members of the local NYI,

including the local NYI president and the pastor and appointed by the pastor.

4. The Local NYI Nominating Committee shall submit the names of at least two persons (who have reached their 15th birthday) for the office of a local NYI president providing, however, that a local NYI president may be reelected by a "yes" or "no" vote when such election is recommended by the Local NYI Nominating Committee and approved by the pastor. The local NYI president shall be elected by majority vote of the members present who are also members of the Church of the Nazarene, voting by ballot. His or her election shall be subject to the approval of the church board. The local church board may establish, prior to the annual election, the minimum age of 19 for the local NYI president to serve on the church board. He or she shall submit a report monthly to the church board and annually to the annual meeting of the local church. The local NYI president shall also recommend to the church board the asking budget for the local NYI as prepared by the local NYI Council.

5. The elected local NYI president shall chair the local NYI Council and shall serve ex officio on the church board, on the local Sunday School Ministries Board, and as a delegate to the district assembly. A paid staff person may not serve as local NYI president. (Paid staff may serve on the Sunday School Ministries Board to coordinate youth Sunday School.) Should the local NYI president be unable to serve or attend, alternate representation may be provided by the local NYI vice president or representative elected by the local NYI Council, with the approval of that board or council.

6. Should a vacancy occur in the office of local NYI president, the vacancy shall be filled by the local NYI Council by majority vote, in a meeting chaired by the local pastor or paid staff with youth responsibilities.

7. The local NYI Council may designate a Local NYI Executive Committee that shall consist of the pastor and/or paid staff with youth responsibilities (as determined by the pastor), and the local NYI officers.

8. In churches not having an organized NYI, the pastor, with church board approval, may appoint the local NYI president.

9. In churches not yet having organized its NYI, the church board may serve as the Local NYI Executive Committee, so the needs of the youth of the church may be served.

SECTION 2—District

1. The district NYI officers shall be a president, vice president, secretary, and treasurer. They shall be elected to serve for one year or at the recommendation of the District NYI Nominating Committee and the approval of the district superintendent for two years, until their successors are elected and installed.

2. The nomination and election of the district NYI president shall be by ballot by two-thirds vote of the District NYI Convention. An incumbent district NYI president may be reelected by a "yes" or "no" vote when such vote is recommended by the District NYI Council, with the approval of the district superintendent, and approved by ballot by two-thirds of the District NYI Convention. Otherwise, upon recommendation of the District NYI Council, with the District NYI Council being chaired by the district superintendent, a ballot consisting of the incumbent district NYI president and one or more qualified persons may be constructed for recommendation to the District NYI Convention. In the case where the incumbent district NYI president chooses not to serve another term of office, the nominating process will be by a nominating ballot.

3. Other district NYI officers shall be nominated by a Nominating Committee consisting of not fewer than four nor more than seven members of the district NYI, including the district superintendent and the district NYI president, and appointed by the District NYI Council. The district NYI officers shall be elected by ballot at the annual District NYI Convention. The annual District NYI Convention may instruct the District NYI Council to appoint the district NYI treasurer. The District NYI Council may designate the dis-

trict NYI officers to serve as a District NYI Executive Committee.

4. All district NYI officers shall reside on and be members of the Church of the Nazarene within the bounds of the district.

5. The district NYI president shall chair the District NYI Council, shall be an ex officio member of the District Sunday School Ministries Board to coordinate youth Sunday School on the district, and shall serve as a delegate to the General NYI Convention. Should the district NYI president be unable to serve or attend, alternate representation may be provided by the district NYI vice president or representative elected by the council, with the approval of that board or council.

6. Should a vacancy occur in the office of district NYI president, a nominating committee of three to five members of the District NYI Council shall be appointed by the district superintendent, who shall serve as chairman. The committee shall submit at least two nominees for election by majority vote of the District NYI Council, in a meeting chaired by the district superintendent.

Section 3—Regional

1. The regional NYI officers shall be the regional NYI president, who shall be the chairperson, chosen in the regional caucus and elected by the General NYI Convention, and such other officers as vice president, secretary, treasurer, as determined and elected by the Regional NYI Council, following the election of the regional NYI president. The Regional NYI Council may designate the regional NYI officers to serve as a Regional NYI Executive Committee (see also Regional NYI Bylaws, Article I, paragraph 4).

2. When a Regional NYI Council is a functioning body, each District NYI Council shall submit one nomination for the office of regional NYI president to a meeting of the Regional NYI Council (or to the general NYI secretary for transmission to the members of the Regional NYI Council), for consideration by the Regional NYI Council, serving as a

Nominating Committee. In addition, any member of the Regional NYI Council may also nominate qualified and suitable persons. The Nominating Committee shall submit to the regional caucus at the General NYI Convention two to six names, from which the regional NYI president shall be elected by two-thirds majority vote by ballot. Other regional NYI officers as determined by the Regional NYI Council may be nominated by District NYI Councils or Regional NYI Council members, and elected by two-thirds majority vote of the Regional NYI Council.

Where there is no functioning Regional NYI Council, or where it does not prove feasible to convene the Regional NYI Council, the Executive Committee of the Regional NYI Council shall serve as the Nominating Committee.

3. All regional NYI officers shall reside on and be members of the Church of the Nazarene within the bounds of the region.

4. The regional NYI president shall chair the Regional NYI Council, shall be an ex officio member of the General NYI Council, and shall serve as a delegate to the General NYI Convention. Should the regional NYI president be unable to serve or attend, alternate representation may be provided by the regional NYI vice president or representative elected by the council, with the approval of that board or council.

5. Regional NYI presidents shall hold office until the conclusion of the subsequent General Assembly when their successors are elected and qualified. No person may serve in the office of regional NYI president for more than two full terms. An incumbent regional NYI president who is eligible to be elected for a second term may be reelected by a "yes" or "no" vote, when such election is recommended by the Regional NYI Council, and approved by two-thirds ballot of the regional caucus and elected by the General NYI Convention.

6. In the case of a vacancy in the office of regional NYI president between General NYI Conventions, the region shall elect a new regional NYI president as follows:

a. Each District NYI Council shall submit a nominee

to the general NYI secretary, who shall order a special Regional NYI Council meeting to hold an election from the nominations received.

b. The election shall be by majority vote by the Regional NYI Council. Should the general NYI secretary so order, balloting may be conducted by mail.

c. In regions without a functioning Regional NYI Council or where it does not prove feasible to convene the Regional NYI Council, the district NYI presidents of the region shall elect from the nominations submitted.

SECTION 4—General

1. The general NYI officers shall be a president and a secretary, who shall be nominated by ballot and elected by the General NYI Convention by a two-thirds majority vote by ballot. They shall serve without salary. A general NYI president or general NYI secretary shall serve in their position no more than one full quadrennium.

2. The general NYI president shall be a member of the General Assembly at the close of his or her quadrennium.

3. The general NYI president may not also serve as general NYI Ministries director. (See the General Board Bylaws for the method of election and responsibilities of the general NYI Ministries director.)

4. In the case of a vacancy in the office of the general NYI president or general NYI secretary between General NYI Conventions, such vacancies shall be filled by nomination of the Executive Committee of the General NYI Council, in consultation with the NYI Ministries director and the responsible general superintendent, and with the approval of the Board of General Superintendents, and election by two-thirds vote of the members of the General NYI Council.

SECTION 5—Use of Terms Across Cultures

Should the terms used to describe various officer titles not communicate or are offensive to a particular culture, more appropriate titles may be used, by vote of the NYI Council on that level.

Article VI. *Councils*

Section 1—Local

1. The local NYI Council shall be responsible for planning the ministry for youth in the local church. It may elect or appoint NYI program personnel as needed. (In the case of a local church designating that paid staff be given youth ministry responsibility, it shall be understood that the staff member shall oversee, in cooperation with the elected local NYI officers, all aspects of the NYI programming and ministry.)

2. The local NYI Council shall consist of the local NYI officers, at least one elected representative from each functioning age division, and other council roles (which can be designated as elected officer positions) as deemed necessary by the local church, and all youth leaders with designated responsibilities for youth ministry, that is, Sunday School, weekly NYI meeting, quizzing, mission education, etc. (The programming area of mission education will be represented by a youth mission director. This person will be appointed jointly by the local NWMS Executive Committee and the local NYI president and will become a member of both the NWMS Council and the local NYI Council. Nominees for this position shall be approved by the pastor.) Age division representatives shall be nominated by the Local NYI Nominating Committee (Article V, Section 1, paragraph 3).

3. The local NYI Council shall fill any vacancies that occur during the year, by majority vote.

4. Three specific age divisions may function within the local NYI, for the purposes of local NYI Council representation and ministry/programming (see Article IV, Section 4, Paragraph 2). Local churches may expand or narrow the boundaries of each age division, according to local church needs.

5. Local churches with large NYI membership may wish to develop age-division committees within the local NYI. Directors for each division/committee may be appointed by the local NYI Council, to maximize ministry to that age

level. Representation for each age division on the local NYI Council may be increased accordingly. The church may also choose to function with a combination or variation of these age divisions.

6. Local churches with multiple paid staff who minister to specific age divisions within the local NYI may develop councils or committees for each of these age divisions. If so, only one local NYI president or representative may serve on the local church board, unless the board structure allows for expanded representation. The church may decide whether or not a coordinating body is used for the various age divisions.

7. In local churches with less than seven NYI members, the pastor may appoint the members of the local NYI Council, so that the needs of the youth of the church may be served.

SECTION 2—District

1. The District NYI Council shall be responsible for planning the total ministry for youth within the district.

2. The District NYI Council shall be composed of the officers of the District Nazarene Youth International, the district superintendent, the full-time district paid youth staff person (if there be such), six members-at-large elected by ballot by the annual District NYI Convention, two of whom shall be elected from each age division (see Article IV, Section 4, paragraph 2), and age-division ministry directors as deemed necessary by the District NYI Convention, who shall be elected by majority vote by ballot from nominees submitted by the District NYI Nominating Committee (Article V, Section 2, paragraph 3).

3. The District NYI Convention may elect the necessary number of persons from nominations submitted by the District NYI Nominating Committee to fill council positions to serve with the officers and members-at-large, as district age division directors and ministry directors (camps, Bible quizzing, talent, etc.) on the District NYI Council. These elected members, along with the district NYI officers and

members-at-large, shall organize for district ministry needs as determined by the District NYI Convention.

4. The District NYI Convention may authorize the District NYI Council to appoint the district NYI ministry directors.

5. Only those NYI members who are members of the Church of the Nazarene on that district may serve as District NYI Council members.

6. The District NYI Council shall fill any vacancies that occur in the council between District NYI Conventions, by majority vote.

7. The District NYI Council, in cooperation with the district superintendent and within the existing structure of the district, may organize the district NYI into zones and provide for leadership in order to maximize NYI ministry (see District NYI Bylaws, Article IV).

Section 3—Regional

1. The Regional NYI Council shall be composed of:
   a. The regional NYI president and other officers of the regional NYI, as determined by the Regional NYI Council.
   b. The district NYI presidents of the districts within the region.
   c. Student body presidents of the regional or subregional Nazarene colleges/universities.
   d. The regional director where appropriate (ex officio), or a member of the regional director's staff who has been assigned particular coordinating responsibility for NYI.
   e. Other ministry directors as necessary, elected by the Regional NYI Council.
   f. Where deemed appropriate by the Regional NYI Council, a multicultural minority representative(s) nominated and elected by the Regional NYI Council.
   g. One representative from the regional college/university may be appointed by the college/university president.

h. All Regional NYI Councils that do not have a youth minister serving in the capacity of district NYI president or regional NYI president may elect a youth pastor at-large to the Regional NYI Council.

2. A treasury shall be established with each district contributing to the needs of the agreed-upon ministries. The Regional NYI Council is accountable to the General NYI Council for these funds.

3. In regions having not yet organized a functioning Regional NYI Council, the General NYI Council may appoint three to five persons recommended by the regional NYI president, to serve with the regional NYI president as a Regional NYI Executive Committee, so that the needs of young people on that region may be met (see also Regional NYI Bylaws, Article I, paragraph 4).

Section 4—General

1. The duties of the General NYI Council shall be defined by the General NYI Bylaws adopted by the General NYI Convention.

2. The General NYI Council shall be composed of the general NYI officers, the regional NYI presidents, three members-at-large, one of whom shall be between the ages of 12 and 14 inclusive at the time of election, one of whom shall be between the ages of 15 and 18 inclusive at the time of election, and one of whom shall be between the ages of 19 and 23 inclusive at the time of election. The general NYI Ministries director shall be an ex officio member of the General NYI Council. The current student cochairperson of Nazarene Student Leadership Conference shall be a member of the General NYI Council. This General NYI Council shall serve until the close of the following General Assembly when their successors are elected and installed.

3. All elected General NYI Council members shall be members of Nazarene Youth International and the Church of the Nazarene.

4. Members-at-large shall be nominated by ballot by the regional caucuses for the purpose of election by majority

vote of the General NYI Convention. Each caucus may present up to two nominees.

5. A vacancy occurs when a General NYI Council member resigns from office, or in the case of a regional NYI president, moves his or her residence or church membership from the region during the quadrennium.

6. In the case of a vacancy among the General NYI Council members-at-large in the interim between General NYI Conventions, such vacancies shall be filled by nomination of the Executive Committee of the General NYI Council in consultation with the general NYI Ministries director, and election by two-thirds vote of the members of the General NYI Council.

7. The General NYI Council shall authorize the regional NYI president to chair the Regional NYI Council. Where feasible each region shall organize itself for coordination and mutual support.

8. The General NYI Council may order the formation of a General NYI Executive Committee as may be deemed necessary for advancing its work (see General NYI Bylaws, Article IV, Section 2).

SECTION 5—Paid Staff

NYI Councils at all levels shall work in cooperation with paid staff persons, who are accountable to their operational supervisors and ultimately to the board that hired them.

ARTICLE VII. *Legislative Meetings*

SECTION 1—Local

1. An annual meeting of local Nazarene Youth International shall be held in harmony with the *Manual,* paragraph 113.6, within 90 days of the district assembly. Other business meetings may be held during the year on call of the Local NYI Executive Committee, with the approval of the pastor.

2. The local officers of the organization shall be elected by majority ballot at the annual meeting in harmony with Article V, Section 1. Delegates to the District NYI Con-

vention shall also be elected by majority ballot at the annual meeting in harmony with Article VII, Section 2. An equal number of alternate delegates shall be elected by plurality vote. These delegates shall be nominated by the Local NYI Nominating Committee (Article V, Section 1, paragraph 3).

3. Only those whose names appear on the local NYI membership roster may vote in the business meetings of the NYI. Only those NYI members who are also members of the Church of the Nazarene may vote in the election of the local NYI president.

SECTION 2—District

1. There shall be an annual District NYI Convention, at which reports shall be received from the district NYI officers, District NYI Council coordinators, and district NYI zone presidents. Any business pertaining to the work of the district NYI may be transacted. The District NYI Council shall arrange for and oversee the annual District NYI Convention in cooperation with the district superintendent. The District NYI Convention shall convene at a time and place designated by the District NYI Council with the approval of the district superintendent.

2. The District NYI Convention shall be composed of the members of the District NYI Council, the district superintendent, the district NYI zone presidents, pastors of local churches, full-time salaried associates, newly elected NYI presidents or vice presidents, assigned ordained ministers of the district, lay members of the District Advisory Board, and three elected delegates who are actively involved in the local NYI for each local NYI organization with 30 or fewer members, and one additional delegate for each successive 30 members or final major part of 30 members (i.e., 16-29 members). Where practical at least half of the delegation shall be 12 through 23, and each of the three age divisions shall be represented in the election delegation. Delegates to the District NYI Convention shall be members of the Church of the Nazarene and of Nazarene Youth International on that district.

3. One delegate between the ages of 12 and 40 may be appointed by the pastor of each local church not having an organized NYI.

4. One delegate between the ages of 12 and 40 may be appointed by the director of an approved Nazarene Compassionate Ministries Center, provided that delegate is a member of the Church of the Nazarene.

5. The District NYI Convention shall elect delegates to the General NYI Convention as specified in Article VII, Section 3, paragraph 2, of the Constitution. It shall also elect alternate delegates (by plurality vote) not exceeding the number of its delegates. Nomination shall be by the District NYI Nominating Committee (Article V, Section 2, paragraph 3).

SECTION 3—Regional

1. There may be a quadrennial convention of the regional Nazarene Youth International, which may convene at a time and place approved by the General NYI Council at the recommendation of the Regional NYI Council, during which reports may be received from the regional NYI officers, ministry NYI coordinators, and subregional or field NYI coordinators. Any business pertaining to the work of the regional NYI may be transacted at the Regional NYI Convention. When a Regional NYI Convention does not convene, the regional caucus at the General NYI Convention shall function as the Regional NYI Convention.

2. If convened, the Regional NYI Convention shall be composed of the regional NYI officers, members of the Regional NYI Council, the regional director (if applicable), subregional or field NYI coordinators, any paid staff with responsibility for NYI at the regional level, district NYI presidents on the region serving at the time of the Regional NYI Convention, and the student body president of each Nazarene college, university, or seminary (or a representative elected by the student body) on the region.

In addition, district representation shall consist of one ministerial delegate who is an assigned elder, deacon, or district-licensed minister who is active in NYI at the local or district levels, and an elected delegate who is actively involved in NYI at the local or district levels representing each of the age divisions, for the first 500 or fewer members; and one additional ministerial and age division delegate for each successive 500 members or final major part of 500 members (i.e., 251-499 members), based on the membership report of the district assembly prior to the Regional NYI Convention, provided that the district assembly report used precedes the Regional NYI Convention by at least 180 days. Each age-group delegate shall be elected by majority vote by a meeting of the District NYI Convention held within two years of the Regional NYI Convention. Any vacancies in the elected delegation shall be filled by vote of the District NYI Council. All delegates shall be members of the NYI and Church of the Nazarene on the district they represent.

3. On districts not having a functioning NYI, one delegate from each age division may be nominated by the district superintendent and appointed by the District Advisory Board.

SECTION 4—General

1. There shall be a quadrennial General NYI Convention of Nazarene Youth International. The General NYI Convention shall provide for distinct legislative, programming, and inspirational sessions. The length of the General NYI Convention and the time it shall convene shall be approved by the Board of General Superintendents at the recommendation of the General NYI Council. The general NYI Ministries director and staff shall oversee the quadrennial General NYI Convention in cooperation with the planning and administration of the General NYI Council.

2. The General NYI Convention shall be composed of the general NYI president and general NYI secretary, the general NYI Ministries director, and members of the General NYI Council, district NYI presidents serving at the time of General NYI Convention, the student body president-elect of each college/university with membership in the Nazarene Student Leadership Conference (NSLC), and the student

body president-elect of each church college or theological school in world areas and the NSLC student cochairperson serving at the time of the General NYI Convention.

In addition, district representation shall consist of one ministerial delegate who is an assigned elder, deacon, or district-licensed minister active in the local or district NYI at the time of the General NYI Convention, one lay delegate active in the local or district NYI at the time of his or her election, and one delegate between the ages of 12 and 23 at the time of the General NYI Convention who is active in the local or district NYI, for the first 1,000 or fewer members; and one ministerial delegate, one lay delegate, and one delegate between the ages of 12 and 23 at the time of the General NYI Convention, for each successive 1,500 members and the final major part of 1,500 members (i.e., 751-1,499 members), based on the membership report of the district assembly prior to the General NYI Convention, provided that the district assembly report used precedes the General NYI Convention by at least 180 days.

All members of the General NYI Convention shall be members of the Church of the Nazarene and Nazarene Youth International and 12 years of age or older at the time of the General NYI Convention. All delegates shall be elected by ballot by majority vote at a session of the District NYI Convention within 18 months of the General NYI Convention, or within 24 months in areas where travel visas or extensive preparations are necessary. An equal number of alternate delegates may be elected by plurality vote. Delegates and alternates must be elected by December 31 of the year prior to the General NYI Convention.

3. Each delegate to the General NYI Convention shall at the time of the General NYI Convention be a member of the Church of the Nazarene on the district and reside on the district he or she represents. (This is not intended to apply to those living near district boundaries where home residence may be across the district line from the place of regular church participation.)

4. In the case of districts without an organized NYI,

General NYI Convention representation shall be comprised of one member of NYI membership age, who shall be chosen by the district assembly.

ARTICLE VIII. *Amendments*

1. This Constitution may be amended by a two-thirds vote of all members present and voting at the General NYI Convention, with the approval of the General Assembly. All resolutions concerning such amendments must be in the hands of the general NYI secretary and the NYI Ministries office at least 120 days prior to the opening of the General NYI Convention.

2. Resolutions for amendment of the Constitution of Nazarene Youth International may be submitted to the general NYI secretary and general NYI Ministries director by the District NYI Convention of any Phase 3 district of the Church of the Nazarene or their elected Resolutions Committee, and the General NYI Council, or when sponsored by at least six delegates, and shall be considered by the General NYI Convention provided they are in proper resolution form and received by the 120-day deadline. The resolutions shall be considered by the General NYI Council, and by a Resolutions Committee of the General NYI Convention (consisting of up to two delegates from each region) prior to the General NYI Convention, and presented to the General NYI Convention for vote.

3. Culturally conditioned adaptations of this Constitution shall be referred to the Executive Committee of the General NYI Council for approval (or rejection).

CHAPTER II

811. CONSTITUTIONS FOR NAZARENE WORLD MISSION SOCIETIES

811.1. Local Nazarene World Mission Society

ARTICLE I. *Name*

This society shall be called the Nazarene World Mission Society of the ________________ Church of the Nazarene.

ARTICLE II. *Object*

The object of this society shall be to enlist the entire church in active mission involvement, in united prayer, and in the study of the salvation needs of the world; to promote a wider knowledge of the mission fields of the Church of the Nazarene; to inspire and challenge the youth to open minds and willing hearts for God-called missionary service on the mission fields of the church; and to raise funds, as elsewhere provided for in this Constitution, for extending the kingdom of Jesus Christ around the world. This society shall be a constituent part of the local church and subject to the supervision of the pastor and the church board.

ARTICLE III. *Membership*

The membership of the local NWMS shall be divided into two classes: member and associate.

SECTION 1. Members

Any person who is a member of the Church of the Nazarene may become a member of the society in that local church. Voting and holding office shall be limited to members who are 15 years old or older, except in children's and youth groups.

(Unless otherwise stated, when reference is to MEMBERS, these are NWMS members who are members of the church.)

SECTION 2. Associate Members

Any person who is not a member of the Church of the Nazarene may become an associate member of the society.

ARTICLE IV. *Officers*

SECTION 1. Election of Council

The local council shall be nominated by a committee of not less than three and not more than seven members of the NWMS. The committee shall be appointed by the pastor who will serve as chairman. If possible, the number of nominees on the ballot should be twice the number to be elected.

The officers of the society shall be: president, vice president, secretary, treasurer, and secretaries for mission education, LINKS, membership, Prayer and Fasting, and any other officer duly elected. An officer may serve in more than one position if desired.

The vice president, secretary, and treasurer shall be elected by ballot for a term of one or two full assembly years by plurality vote, by members of the society.

All other secretaries may be elected by the society or appointed by the Executive Committee. The local society may choose to elect four to six council members, in addition to the president and treasurer. These elected persons shall organize and assign the council members' responsibilities in accordance with paragraph two.

The Executive Committee shall be composed of the president, vice president, secretary, treasurer, and two other council members elected by the council. If the members of the society are electing only the president, vice president, secretary, and treasurer, the two additional Executive Committee members shall be elected by ballot by plurality vote by members of the society.

In consultation with the pastor, a local council may add other officers, namely, a Work and Witness coordinator, an

Alabaster secretary, a World Mission Radio secretary, a Publicity secretary, and a Compassionate Ministries coordinator, and any other officer deemed necessary. The nomination and election of these officers shall follow the same procedure specified for officers other than the local president.

These officers, together with chapter chairpersons, children's and youth mission directors, and pastor, shall constitute the local NWMS Council.

Any duly elected District NWMS Council member shall be a member ex officio of the local NWMS Council of the church of which he or she is a member with the approval of the local NWMS Council.

SECTION 2. Election of President

The president shall be nominated by a committee of not less than three nor more than seven members of the Nazarene World Mission Society appointed by the pastor, who shall serve as chairperson. This committee shall submit one or more names for the office of president, providing, however, that any incumbent president may be reelected by a "yes" or "no" vote when such election is recommended by the Nominating Committee and approved by the pastor. The president shall be elected by a majority vote by ballot of the members present and voting for a term of one or two full assembly years, upon recommendation of the local NWMS Council and with the approval of the pastor. This election shall be subject to the approval of the church board. The president shall be a member of the local church whose society is served, a member ex officio of the church board, a member of the Sunday School Ministries Board, and a member of the district assembly. In the case where the pastor's spouse serves as local president, if he or she so desires not to serve on the church board, the vice president is authorized to serve on the church board in his or her place.

NOTE: Where there are two or more chapters in the local society, follow the plan provided for in Article VIII.

See local bylaws for duties of officers, appointment of directors, assistants, and committees.

SECTION 3. Vacancies

Any vacancy in the office of the president shall be filled by ballot by majority vote by the members of the society at any regular meeting. Vacancies occurring in any other elected office shall be filled by a plurality vote of NWMS members present at any regular monthly meeting of the society.

In the case of a vacancy in the office of the local president, the Executive Committee shall nominate one or more names for the office of president.

ARTICLE V. *Representation at District Convention*

Local representation at the District NWMS Convention shall be composed of:

1. The pastor of the local church, full-time salaried associate ministers of local churches, the local NWMS president of year ending, and the president-elect (if there is a change) by virtue of office are members of the District NWMS Convention. In the event the local president is unable to attend or serve, the local vice president of year ending is seated in his or her place. In the event the local vice president of year ending is unable to attend or serve, the newly elected vice president may be seated in his or her place.

2. Two elected delegates for the first 25 NWMS members or less, and one additional delegate for each additional 25 members or major portion thereof.

NOTE: See District Constitution, Article II, District Convention; Section 2, Membership.

ARTICLE VI. *Meetings*

SECTION 1. Monthly

There shall be one or more meetings for mission information, inspiration, and prayer held each calendar month. These meetings may take the form of regular mission services or special services with missionary speakers, lesson presentations, events, or emphases.

SECTION 2. Annual

The annual meeting of the society shall be held no later than 30 days prior to the district assembly, at which time officers for the ensuing year shall be elected.

Chapter officers shall be elected and/or appointed before the District Convention.

Officers shall assume their duties at the beginning of the new church year.

ARTICLE VII. *Funds*

SECTION 1. World Evangelism Fund

All funds raised by this society for the World Evangelism Fund shall be sent directly to the general treasurer.

Funds for the support of World Evangelism Fund shall be raised in the following manner: (1) from the regular mission society World Evangelism Fund offerings; (2) from Prayer and Fasting offerings; (3) from other World Evangelism Fund offerings, such as Easter and Thanksgiving offerings, and Faith Promise.

SECTION 2. Specials

Opportunity shall be given to contribute to world mission specials over and above the World Evangelism Fund apportionment, such as Alabaster and World Mission Radio. Additional world mission specials may be approved and authorized by appropriate personnel at International Headquarters.

SECTION 3. Medical Plan Fund

The Medical Plan Fund shall be held in trust by the general treasurer for the General Nazarene World Mission Society and shall be used for medical assistance for active and retired missionaries, such assistance to be granted by the World Mission Department according to their established policy. Funds shall be raised by (1) placing names on the Memorial Roll by the payment of $50.00 for that purpose ($25.00 for duplicates); (2) presenting a Distinguished Service Award to a chosen recipient to be honored for service to the Kingdom by the payment of $100 for that purpose; (3) receiving one or more special offerings a year for Medical Plan.

SECTION 4. General Funds Exclusive

No part of the above general funds shall be used for local or district expense or charitable purposes.

SECTION 5. Local Expense

A local expense fund shall be provided either by assessment or freewill offerings (the amount to be determined by local needs). A percentage of the local expense fund may be set aside to help defray the expenses of the delegates to the District Convention.

ARTICLE VIII. *Chapters*

SECTION 1. Chapters

This society may have one or more chapters as may be authorized by the Executive Committee and approved by the pastor and local church board. These together shall constitute the local society. A chapter is an integral part of the local society, the provision being made for the matter of convenience.

A local society may request the organization of women's chapters, men's chapters, chapters including both men and women, youth chapters, and children's chapters. Age groupings should correspond with NYI and Sunday School Ministries.

SECTION 2. Election

These chapters meeting in joint session shall elect the officers authorized in Article IV. The Executive Committee of the local society shall have general oversight of the work of the various chapters, receiving all literature for distribution to the various chapters, and keeping records and sending reports for the combined chapters.

SECTION 3. Chapter Officers

The officers of each chapter shall be chairperson, vice-chairperson, secretary, treasurer, and secretaries for mission education, LINKS, membership, and Prayer and Fasting.

These officers shall be elected by ballot annually by the members of the chapter prior to the District Convention. (Officers of the local society may hold office in any chapter.) The chapter chairperson, vice-chairperson, secretary, treasurer, and two other members elected by the chapter shall constitute the chapter Executive Committee.

SECTION 4. Nomination of Chapter Officers

Chapter officers shall be nominated by a nominating committee appointed by the pastor.

A chapter chairperson is a member of the local NWMS Council.

ARTICLE IX. *Amendments*

This Constitution may be amended by a two-thirds vote of all members present and voting at the General Convention of the Nazarene World Mission Society, and by the approval of the World Mission Department.

811.2. District Nazarene World Mission Society

ARTICLE I. *Membership*

All local Nazarene World Mission Societies within the boundaries of ________________ District shall be members of the District Nazarene World Mission Society. The activities of this society shall be under the supervision of the district superintendent, the District Advisory Board, the district assembly, and the District NWMS Council.

ARTICLE II. *District Convention*

SECTION 1. Purpose

There shall be an annual District Convention of the Nazarene World Mission Society for the purpose of hearing reports, uniting in prayer for the work, making aggressive plans for propagating missionary information and inspiration in the local societies, and conducting business pertaining to the district organization.

The time and place of the annual NWMS Convention shall be decided by the District NWMS Council in consultation with the district superintendent.

SECTION 2. Membership

The District Convention shall be composed of the District NWMS Council, the district superintendent, lay members of the District Advisory Board, all assigned ministers and full-time salaried associate ministers of the local churches, NWMS zone directors, the presidents (of year ending) of local societies, two delegates from each local society having an NWMS membership (excluding associate) of 25 or less, and one additional delegate for each additional 25 members (or major portion thereof); and General NWMS Council members, retired missionaries, retired assigned ministers, missionaries on furlough, and missionary appointees who hold their church membership on the district, and any former district presidents who reside on the district that they served. The membership of the District Convention shall also include the newly elected NWMS presidents, or newly elected vice presidents if the newly elected presidents cannot attend.

ARTICLE III. *Officers*

SECTION 1. District Council

The officers of this society shall be president, vice president, secretary, treasurer, and secretaries for mission education, LINKS, membership, and Prayer and Fasting. The eight named officers shall constitute the District NWMS Council. The district superintendent shall be ex officio member of the District NWMS Council.

The District Executive Committee shall be composed of the president, vice president, secretary, treasurer, and two other council members (elected by ballot, by the District Council). The district superintendent shall be an ex officio member of the Executive Committee.

When a District Council in consultation with the district superintendent shall desire, other officers may be added to the District Council, namely, a Work and Witness coordinator, an Alabaster secretary, a World Mission Radio secretary, a Compassionate Ministries coordinator, a Publicity secretary, a Deputation secretary, and children and youth mission directors. The nomination and election of these officers shall be by the District Council or shall follow the same procedure specified in Article III, Section 2, for officers other than district presidents. The determination of election method of the additional officers shall be the decision of the District Council, in consultation with the district superintendent.

SECTION 2. Election of Officers

The District President

The District Convention shall elect a district president who shall be: *(a)* elected by two-thirds favorable vote by ballot from two or more nominees presented by a nominating committee, appointed by the District Executive Committee, and chaired by the district superintendent; *(b)* or the district president may be reelected by a "yes" or "no" vote for a term of one or two full assembly years when such vote is recommended by the District NWMS Council with the approval of the district superintendent. The district president shall serve without salary.

Other Officers

The other district officers shall be elected by ballot by the convention from two nominees presented for each office by a nominating committee appointed by the District Executive Committee.

Or the District Convention may elect a district treasurer, a district secretary, and five others to serve on the District NWMS Council. Or the district treasurer and district secretary may be elected by a "yes" or "no" vote when such vote is recommended by the District NWMS Council, with the approval of the district superintendent. They shall be elected by ballot from nominees submitted by a nominating committee appointed by the District Executive Committee.

In any district where there is a desire to do so, delegates at the District Convention may elect or reelect council members (these other officers) to serve for terms of up to two years.

Where deemed advisable, these nominees may be selected and presented in such a way that each zone is represented on the District Council on the basis of proportionate representation in relation to its NWMS membership.

Example:	Zone A	6 nominees	Vote for 3
	Zone B	4 nominees	Vote for 2
	Zone C	4 nominees	Vote for 2
	Zone D	2 nominees	Vote for 1

The five council members thus elected, along with the district president, district NWMS treasurer, and district NWMS secretary shall organize, assigning each council member responsibilities in accordance with Section 1.

SECTION 3. Election of Youth Representatives

The District Convention may elect by ballot one, and not more than two, youth members to the District NWMS Council.

The Nominating Committee appointed by the District Executive Committee shall nominate twice the number to be elected.

SECTION 4. Vacancies

A vacancy in the district presidency shall be filled by a majority vote of the District NWMS Council, two nominees having been submitted by the District NWMS Executive Committee in consultation with the district superintendent.

All other vacancies occurring in the District Council between annual conventions shall be filled by majority vote of the District NWMS Council.

ARTICLE IV. *Amendments*

This Constitution may be amended by a two-thirds vote of all members present and voting at the General Convention of the General Nazarene World Mission Society, and by the approval of the World Mission Department.

811.3. General Nazarene World Mission Society

ARTICLE I. *Membership*

All district and local Nazarene World Mission Societies shall constitute the General Nazarene World Mission Society. It shall be auxiliary to the World Mission Division.

ARTICLE II. *General Convention*

SECTION 1. Time and Place

There shall be a General Convention of the Nazarene World Mission Society preceding the General Assembly. The time and place shall be decided upon by the General Council in consultation with the responsible general superintendent and the World Mission Department.

SECTION 2. Members of the General Convention

1. This convention shall be composed of the following members: members of the General Council; the regional NWMS program coordinators of World Mission regions; district NWMS presidents; two delegates from each Phase 3 or Phase 2 district of 1,000 or fewer NWMS members (excluding associate), and one additional delegate for each additional 700 members (or final major part thereof), delegates to be elected by ballot by the District Convention within 16 months of the General Convention or within 24 months in areas where travel visas or other unusual preparations are necessary. It is suggested that the number to be nominated on the ballot be three times the number of delegates to be elected.

There shall also be one delegate from each Phase 1 district, this delegate to be the district NWMS president; one career missionary delegate for every region of 50 or fewer missionaries and two career missionary delegates for each region with 51 or more missionaries. The missionaries are to be nominated by their respective Field Council and elected by the Regional Advisory Council of each region.

2. Any elected General Convention delegate must be at

the time of the General NWMS Convention residing on the district where he or she held membership at the time of his or her election. If any elected delegate moves off the district, the privilege of representing the former district is forfeited. (Not intended to apply to those living near district boundaries where their home residence may be across the line from the place of regular church participation.)

3. In the event the district president cannot attend the General Convention, the district vice president (ex officio) shall be allowed to represent the district.

4. In the case of world mission districts, General Convention representation shall be governed by the divisions of the general church and their respective policies. However, when district presidents of Phase 1 districts cannot attend, the district president, with the approval of the district superintendent, may designate an alternate to be seated.

Section 3. Election of General Convention Alternates

Alternates to the General Convention may be elected on a separate ballot by plurality vote; or at the recommendation of the District NWMS Council, alternates may be elected by plurality vote on the same ballot as the delegates.

Article III. *General Council*

Section 1. Nomination and Election of the General President

The general president shall be elected from nominees selected by a nominating committee composed of the general director, 3 regional representatives from the General Council, and 9 non-General Council members. The 12 committee members shall be appointed by the Executive Committee of the General Council. No two members of the Nominating Committee may be from the same region. The general director shall serve as chairperson of the Nominating Committee.

The committee shall submit the names of two and not more

than three persons for general president. The nominations shall be approved by the Board of General Superintendents.

From these nominees the General Convention shall elect a general president by two-thirds favorable vote by ballot.

The term of general president shall be limited to two full terms of service.

The general president shall be an ex officio member of the General Council and shall serve without salary.

SECTION 2. Nomination of General Council Members

Regional representatives on the General Council shall be nominated by regional caucuses, held at the General Convention. Each District NWMS Council on the region has the privilege of submitting one or two names from the region to the caucus.

The region in caucus shall elect by ballot two nominees from the region (twice the number to be elected). Of the nominees submitted to the regional caucus for election, no two shall be from the same district.

SECTION 3. Election of the General NWMS Council

The members of the General NWMS Council shall consist of one representative per region.

A member of the General Council shall be a member of and resident in the region, except in the case where the council member moves from that region within 12 months prior to the General Convention.

All council members (except general president and general director, otherwise provided for) shall be elected by regional caucuses held at the General Convention, by majority vote by ballot. The two from different districts receiving the highest number of votes on the nominating ballot in the regional caucus elections shall be declared General Council nominees.

The term of service of a General Council member shall be limited to two full consecutive terms.

The director of the World Mission Division shall be an ex officio member of the General Council.

Section 4. Council Organization

The general director shall be nominated by the director of the World Mission Division, in consultation with the responsible general superintendent for the World Mission Division, and shall be approved by a majority vote of the General Council before being submitted to the World Mission Department of the General Board for approval by a majority vote with the recommendation submitted for election by the Board of General Superintendents. The general director shall be an ex officio member of the General NWMS Council and a member of the staff of the World Mission Division.

The council shall also elect from its own number a vice president and two other members, who with the general president and general director shall constitute the Executive Committee, three of whom shall constitute a quorum.

The General Council shall be authorized to elect a man to serve as a voting member of the council whose responsibility is to encourage the continued involvement of men in the mission program of the church.

Council members shall hold office until the final adjournment of the next General Convention, except as provided for in Section 3, and until their successors are elected and qualified. The council shall assign to its members responsibility for the various emphases and projects.

Section 5. The Executive Committee

The Executive Committee shall:

1. In case of vacancy in the general presidency in the interim between sessions of the General Convention, submit the names of two nominees for general president in accordance with Article IV, Section 1, of the General Constitution.

2. Transact any business deemed necessary between sessions of the General Council.

Section 6. Responsible General Superintendent

One general superintendent shall be appointed by the Board of General Superintendents as adviser to the General Council.

SECTION 7. General Board Representative

The General Council shall nominate to the General Assembly two members of the council, one of whom shall be elected by the General Assembly as a member of the General Board of the Church of the Nazarene as a representative of the General Nazarene World Mission Society.

Should a vacancy occur in the General Board representative during the quadrennium, two nominees shall be submitted from the Executive Committee of the General NWMS Council in consultation with the responsible general superintendent and with the approval of the Board of General Superintendents. The General NWMS Council shall elect the General Board representative by a majority vote.

SECTION 8. Council Meeting

The council shall meet a minimum of three times during the quadrennium. A majority shall constitute a quorum. A condensed report of the business transacted in each meeting of the council shall be referred to the World Mission Department for approval.

ARTICLE IV. *Vacancies*

SECTION 1. General President

Should a vacancy occur in the office of general president in the interim between sessions of the General Convention, a general president shall be elected from nominees selected by the Executive Committee of the General Council in consultation with the responsible general superintendent by two-thirds vote of the General NWMS Council to fill the vacancy and to perform the duties of general president until adjournment of the next General Convention; provided the question of calling for an election to fill the vacancy shall be decided by the General Council in consultation with the responsible general superintendent.

SECTION 2. Council

Should a vacancy occur in the council during the quadrennium, each District Executive Committee on the region concerned shall be requested to present one nominee from the region to the General Executive Committee for consideration. From these names, the General Executive Committee shall present two names as nominees approved by the director of the World Mission Division and the responsible general superintendent. The vacancy shall then be filled by majority vote by mail ballot by the district NWMS presidents on the region, provided that the question of calling for an election to fill the vacancy is approved by the General NWMS Executive Committee, the director of the World Mission Division, and the responsible general superintendent of NWMS.

SECTION 3. Executive Committee

Should a vacancy occur in the Executive Committee during the quadrennium, two names as nominees from the council shall be presented. The vacancy shall then be filled by a majority vote by ballot of the General NWMS Council.

ARTICLE V. *Amendments*

This Constitution may be amended by a two-thirds vote of members present and voting at a General Convention of the General Nazarene World Mission Society, and by the approval of the World Mission Department.

CHAPTER III

812. BYLAWS OF THE SUNDAY SCHOOL

Mission Statement

The mission of Sunday School Ministries (SSM) is to carry out the Great Commission to children, youth, and adults in preparation for a lifetime of Christian holiness.

Purpose

The purpose of the Sunday School is threefold:

A. To teach the Word of God effectively until pupils are saved, sanctified wholly, and maturing in Christian experience.

B. To help Christians grow spiritually by involving them in a reaching, teaching, and soul-winning ministry.

C. To locate and visit unchurched people until they become enrolled and regular in attendance.

Article I. Membership

Responsibility List (Enrollment)

Each local church should assume responsibility for reaching all persons in the community who are not actively involved in another local church. To assist in this mission, maintaining three lists will be helpful:

A. **Active Responsibility List (Line 25, Pastor's Annual Report {PAR}).** This is the traditional enrollment list and shall include all persons who declare their willingness to attend with some degree of regularity. Each teacher is expected to be responsible for the spiritual welfare of those on his or her class Responsibility List.

B. **Prospect List.** This list includes the names of all who have not agreed to attend with any degree of regularity, but who have the possibility of becoming regular attenders. Each Sunday School class should consistently strive to bring them into regular attendance. This list should include persons who only attend morning worship.

C. **Extended (Outreach) Ministry List (Line 27, PAR).** This list shall include all persons who are regularly involved in an outreach Sunday School ministry, but not in a regular Sunday School session each week (Article II, Section 1).

SECTION 1. The local Sunday School Ministries Board shall determine whether the following shall be included on the Sunday School active responsibility list (enrollment), the prospect list, or the extended ministry (outreach) list:

a. **CRADLE ROLL PARENTS (Line 16, PAR):** Children under four years of age who, along with their parents, do not attend Sunday School may be enrolled on the prospect list as Cradle Roll Parents.

- The children are considered as prospects for the Sunday School preschool classes, and the parents as prospects in the corresponding adult classes.
- When the supervisor has been appointed, he or she is responsible for regular visits and program materials to be taken to these families.
- When they begin attending Sunday School with some degree of regularity, they should be transferred to the Sunday School active responsibility list (enrollment) of the corresponding age-group class.
- If they have not started attending by the child's fourth birthday, they should be transferred to the prospect list of the Preschool and Adult departments and dropped from the Cradle Roll Parents list.
- Until they begin attending with some degree of regularity they shall continue to be listed on the prospect list.

b. **HOME DEPARTMENT:** Any person physically or vocationally unable to attend a regular Sunday School class may be enrolled in the Home Department.

- The Sunday School superintendent and adult ministries director, in consultation with the pastor, shall appoint a Home Department supervisor each church year whose responsibility is to visit and teach the Sunday School lesson each week.

- Those persons visited weekly and taught the Sunday School lesson shall be listed on the active responsibility list, and included in the weekly regular Sunday School attendance (**Line 26, PAR**).
- If there is no regular weekly visit or Sunday School lesson taught, these persons should be listed on the extended (outreach) ministry list (**Line 27, PAR**).

c. **NURSING HOME/CONVALESCENT CENTER/ HEALTH CARE FACILITY:** Any residents confined to one of these centers who attend a weekly session sponsored by the local church may be listed on the active responsibility list (enrollment) or the extended (outreach) ministry list according to the following guidelines:

1. If the resident actively participates in a weekly study of the Nazarene Sunday School curriculum he or she shall be included on the active responsibility list (enrollment) (**Line 25, PAR**), and counted in the average weekly attendance (**Line 26, PAR**).

2. If the resident attends a weekly service but is unable to actively participate or if the Nazarene Sunday School curriculum is not taught, he or she shall be added to the extended (outreach) ministry list (**Line 27, PAR**) and counted in the extended ministries average weekly attendance (**Line 28, PAR**).

3. If there is any question, list all names on the extended (outreach) ministry list.

d. **EXTENSION SUNDAY SCHOOL AND/OR CHURCH-TYPE MISSION:** Any group sponsored by the local church who meets weekly in another location to study the Sunday School lesson with the goal of becoming an organized Church of the Nazarene shall be added to the active responsibility list (enrollment) (**Line 25, PAR**) and average weekly regular Sunday School attendance (**Line 26, PAR**) of the sponsoring church by designating name/location of the new work.

e. **NAZARENE DAYCARE/K-12 SCHOOLS:** Any group

of students in a Nazarene daycare/K-12 school under the sponsorship of the local church shall be listed according to the following guidelines:

1. If students, not currently enrolled in a Nazarene Sunday School, actively participate in a regular weekly study of the Nazarene Sunday School curriculum, they shall be included on the active responsibility list (enrollment) (**Line 25, PAR**), and counted in the average weekly attendance (**Line 26, PAR**).

2. If students attend a weekly class but the Nazarene Sunday School curriculum is not taught, they shall be added to the extended (outreach) ministry list (**Line 27, PAR**) and counted in the extended ministries average weekly attendance (**Line 28, PAR**).

f. **BIBLE STUDY/CELL GROUPS:** Any group assembled under the sponsorship of the local church for the purpose of studying the Bible, which would include some persons who are on the Sunday School active responsibility list (enrollment) and some who are not. These persons who are not, shall be added to the extended (outreach) ministry list and extended (outreach) ministry average weekly attendance (**Lines 27 and 28, PAR**).

SECTION 2. Once a person is listed on any responsibility list, the local church should actively seek to minister to that person until he or she is brought into the fellowship of that church. Dropping names should be done only with the approval of the pastor when:

a. they die
b. they move out of town
c. they join another Sunday School
d. they specifically ask to have their names removed

Article II. Attendance

Counting Sunday School Attendance

The purpose of counting Sunday School attendance in the local church is to measure the effectiveness of that church's effort to reach people with the biblical message. All Sunday School ministry efforts should lead to bringing people into fellowship with Christ, by experiencing the new birth and identification with the local church.

Sunday School attendance represents the number of different persons being ministered to by the local church through a study of approved curriculum materials each week. This ministry can include a regular Sunday School, extension Sunday School and/or church-type mission, and other extended (outreach) ministries.

It is important to remember that even though some people may be involved in more than one Sunday School ministry, they shall be counted only once in the regular Sunday School attendance. If people are involved in a regular Sunday School ministry other than Sunday morning (excluding outreach), they shall be counted in the following Sunday morning's attendance.

These categories of Sunday School ministries shall be counted and reported separately each week by each local church, according to the criteria listed below.

SECTION 1. Regular Sunday School Session. A regular Sunday School session shall be defined as an organized group of people who meet each week at a specified time and place. The purpose of this meeting must be to study the Bible, using Sunday School curriculum approved by the Sunday School Ministries Board, for at least a half hour. This will constitute the regular Sunday School weekly attendance (**Line 26, PAR**).

a. Attendance counts shall be closed no later than the halfway point of the regular Sunday School session. This shall also apply to unified or special services.

b. An enrollee in a local Sunday School shall be considered present in his or her local Sunday School when attending on that Sunday, a local, zone, district, region, or general church-sponsored function such as a retreat, assembly, camp meeting, etc., as long as he or she is not counted in another local Sunday School where he or she is attending. Such functions shall include at least a half hour of Bible study.

c. All regular Sunday School sessions shall be used in determining the average attendance for the year and that attendance shall be reported monthly to the district. For most churches, the number of Sunday School sessions held will be 52. In some geographical areas weather will occasionally prohibit regular Sunday School sessions. The District Sunday School Ministries Board, in consultation with the district superintendent, shall determine any valid exceptions.

SECTION 2. Extension Sunday School and/or Church-Type Missions. Extension Sunday Schools and/or church-type missions are defined as a group of people meeting under the sponsorship of a local church or a district with the purpose of someday becoming a fully organized church. This meeting must be held at least a half hour weekly to study the Bible, using an approved Sunday School curriculum. The attendance figures of any extension Sunday School or church-type mission shall be listed separately from the regular Sunday School session of the sponsoring church when reporting to the district each month, but included in the monthly Sunday School attendance total for the district.

a. If a local church sponsors an extension Sunday School or church-type mission in close geographical proximity to the church, this attendance should be listed and reported separately by name and location under the sponsoring church's attendance. If a local church sponsors more than one new work, each new work should be listed by name and location.

b. If a district or local church is promoting a large group of church planting situations, these extension Sunday Schools and/or church-type missions may be listed separately with their own name and location, if desired by the district.

c. Extended (Outreach) Ministry. The attendance of all extended ministries shall be counted as the extended ministry attendance for the local church (**Line 28, PAR**). Extended ministry attendance shall be defined as persons involved in a study of the Bible for at least one-half hour, but not otherwise meeting the criteria of a regular Sunday School session or extension Sunday School and/or church-type mission (Article II, Section 1). A local church having more than one type of extended (outreach) ministry, should combine responsibility lists figures and report a single figure each month. The same is true for extended (outreach) ministry weekly attendance. Annual totals for extended (outreach) ministry responsibility lists are to be entered on **Line 27 of the PAR** and extended (outreach) ministries attendance reported on **Line 28 of the PAR.**

d. Since extended (outreach) ministries and new works can begin or end anytime during the church year, the yearly average should be determined by dividing accumulative figures by the number of weeks the ministries were conducted.

e. Attendance totals for the week, month, and year should be recorded as follows:

Regular Sunday School Attendance	125
Extension Sunday School (Corporate Hills)	30
Church-Type Mission (Blue Valley)	15
Total Extended (Outreach) Ministries	25

SUMMARY: The General Sunday School Ministries Division needs to have correct enrollment and attendance figures from each district in order to compile an accurate report of Sunday School growth within the denomination each year.

SECTION 3. Nazarene Daycare/K-12 Schools (see Article I, Section 1e).

Article III. Classes and Departments

SECTION 1. The Sunday School shall be divided into classes for children and youth on the basis of age or school grade. For adults the classes should be determined by common interests.

SECTION 2. When the number of classes within the children's, youth, or adult age-groups increase, attention should be given to departmentalization with a supervisor appointed by the Sunday School Ministries Board.

SECTION 3. The duties of the department supervisor shall be to: *(a)* coordinate the work of the teachers within the department; *(b)* conduct departmental meetings when necessary; *(c)* insure that each teacher within the department has the necessary curriculum, additional resources, and equipment available when needed; *(d)* be responsible for ordering all necessary curriculum and materials for the department (give order to ordering secretary); *(e)* work with the corresponding age-group director of the Sunday School Ministries Board to promote Sunday School enrollment and attendance and implement any special campaigns; *(f)* present training needs of the department's teachers to the corresponding age-group director for presentation to the Sunday School Ministries Board; *(g)* keep accurate enrollment and attendance records for the department and see that all absentees and prospects are contacted regularly; *(h)* work with the teachers in the department to see that the entire area is attractive and conducive to learning; and *(i)* be responsible for the securing of substitute teachers within the department.

Article IV. Teachers

SECTION 1. The department supervisors and teachers shall be appointed annually according to *Manual* 146.8.

SECTION 2. While the ideal is for each teacher to serve for the entire year, in certain circumstances it may be advisable to appoint teachers for a shorter term.

SECTION 3. In cases of proven unsoundness of doctrine, imprudent conduct, or neglect of duty, the Sunday School Ministries Board shall have the right to declare the office of any officer or teacher vacant according to *Manual* 146.8.

SECTION 4. All Sunday School teachers and substitutes should: *(a)* attend workers' meetings regularly; *(b)* contact each student, absentee, and prospect on a regular basis; *(c)* avail themselves of all training opportunities provided; *(d)* provide fellowship opportunities for the class periodically;

(e) be responsible for seeing that the teaching area is attractive and conducive to learning; *(f)* prepare an effective lesson each week; and *(g)* be alert to salvation opportunities for each student.

Article V. Officers and Their Duties

SECTION 1. The local Sunday School superintendent shall be elected each year according to *Manual* 113.8-13.9. The duties of the Sunday School superintendent shall be to: *(a)* be superintendent of the Sunday School under the direction of the pastor; *(b)* plan regular teachers' and workers' meetings; *(c)* provide training opportunities for teachers, substitute teachers, and prospective teachers; *(d)* communicate Sunday School enrollment and attendance growth campaign plans to all workers; *(e)* report the statistics of the Sunday School to the zone chairman each month; and *(f)* encourage attendance at district and general Sunday School Ministries functions.

SECTION 2. The duties of the age-group directors are outlined in *Manual* 148.1-48.9.

SECTION 3. The Sunday School Ministries Board shall elect a person to keep the Sunday School records. He or she shall keep an accurate record for the entire Sunday School, of the responsibility list (enrollment), prospect list, extended (outreach) ministry list, attendance, visitors, and other statistics as may be required.

SECTION 4. The Sunday School Ministries Board shall elect a treasurer to keep an accurate account of all moneys raised by the Sunday School each week and authorize the disbursement according to the direction of the board. A monthly report shall be given to the Sunday School superintendent.

SECTION 5. The Sunday School Ministries Board shall appoint a person to be responsible for ordering the Sunday School curriculum and other resources requested by the age-group directors and/or department supervisors. The appointee shall distribute to the appropriate age-group director all information received from Nazarene Publishing House and prepare the order after approval of the superintendent and pastor.

Article VI. Administration and Supervision

SECTION 1. The Sunday School is under the care of the pastor, amenable to the local church board, under the general supervision of the Sunday School Ministries Board and the immediate leadership of the superintendent and age-group directors.

SECTION 2. If a church who has employed a full-time director of Christian education wishes to elect that person as Sunday School superintendent, the procedure is as follows: *(a)* the local church Nominating Committee would recommend to the annual church meeting that no superintendent be elected for the coming church year, and that the full-time associate will serve as superintendent; *(b)* the congregation should affirm the decision by majority vote; *(c)* the full-time associate will become the Sunday School superintendent and will attend church board meetings to discuss Christian education interests but will not be a voting member, *Manual* 161.4.

The same procedure should be followed for full-time paid associates who are requested to serve as the Children's or Adult Ministry directors.

It shall be understood that these are temporary arrangements, and that all possible effort should be made to train and resource local lay leaders for these positions as soon as possible.

Article VII. Conventions

SECTION 1. District Sunday School Ministries Convention. It is important that each district plan a District Sunday School Ministries Convention annually in order to provide inspiration, motivation, and training for all

Sunday School Ministries workers. The promotion of Sunday School should be a highlight of each convention.

a. Ex officio members of the District Sunday School Ministries Convention shall be: the district superintendent; all pastors, district licensed ministers, retired assigned ministers, full-time associates; district Sunday School Ministries chairperson, and local Sunday School superintendents newly elected prior to and holding office at the time of the District Convention; the district and all local children's and adult directors; the district NYI president and all local NYI presidents; elected members of the District Sunday School Ministries Board; lay members of the District Advisory Board; and any Nazarene full-time professors of Christian education with membership on that district.

b. In the annual church meeting, each local Sunday School shall elect additional representatives to the Convention, equal to 25 percent of the officers and teachers of the Sunday School (**Line 24, PAR**).

c. The Sunday School Ministries Board shall serve as a nominating committee to select twice the number of nominees to be elected by plurality vote. These nominees should be members of the Church of the Nazarene, actively involved in one of the ministries of Sunday School Ministries, and should be selected from the various age-groups (children, youth, adult workers). In case elected representatives cannot attend, alternate representatives shall be designated in the order of the votes received.

d. The representatives to the District Sunday School Ministries Convention may elect the District Sunday School Ministries chairperson and the elected members of the District Sunday School Ministries Board according to *Manual* 239, and representatives to the General Sunday School Ministries Convention each quadrennium.

SECTION 2. General Sunday School Ministries Convention.

a. Ex officio representatives to the General SSM Convention shall be: district superintendents, district SSM chairpersons, district directors of Children's and Adult Ministries, professors of Christian education at Nazarene colleges/universities and the seminary, and directors and staff of the General Sunday School Ministries Division.

b. Each district should elect four additional representatives, which is the number equal to the district ex officio members or a number equal to 1 percent of the Sunday School officers on the district, whichever number is larger.

c. The following guidelines should be adhered to in elections for General SSM Convention representatives:

1. The Nominating Committee shall be comprised of the district superintendent, District SSM Board chairperson, and at least three others appointed by the District SSM Board. They shall select three times the number of nominees to be elected.

2. The District SSM Convention shall elect an equal number of representatives and alternates from all Sunday School Ministries (including youth Sunday School teachers/workers). Those elected should be persons who are presently and actively involved in the respective area to which they are elected. The number of alternates elected should include alternates for ex officio members.

Persons should not be elected who will serve as delegates to the General Nazarene World Mission Society Convention or the General Nazarene Youth International Convention, because the three conventions run concurrently.

3. Representatives shall be elected by ballot in the District Sunday School Ministries Convention within 16 months of the meeting of the General Assembly, or within 24 months in areas where travel visas or other unusual preparations are necessary.

4. As nearly as possible, elect an equal number of laypersons and clergy—50 percent laypersons and 50 percent full-time active ministers, elders, or licensed ministers. When the total number is uneven, the extra representative shall be a layperson.

5. Incumbent district Sunday School Ministries leaders newly elected prior to and holding office at the time of the

General Convention shall be the ex officio members of the convention.

6. All elected and ex officio representatives present in the District SSM Convention shall be eligible to vote for General SSM Convention representatives.

7. A plurality vote shall be sufficient for election.

8. In case elected representatives cannot attend, alternate representatives shall be designated in the order of the votes they received.

9. At the convening of the General SSM Convention, each representative shall reside on and be a member of a Church of the Nazarene on the district he or she was elected to represent. (This is not intended to apply to those living near district boundaries where home residence may be across the district line from the place of regular church participation.)

10. If a district cannot finance the full number of representatives to the General Sunday School Ministries Convention as recommended, the District Sunday School Ministries Board may elect as many persons as the district can afford to send.

11. Representatives who attend the convention should have financial assistance from the district comparable to expenses provided from the district for Nazarene Youth International and Nazarene World Mission Society convention delegates.

12. If election of representatives for the General SSM Convention does not take place at the District SSM Convention, representatives shall be elected at the District Assembly.

Article VIII. Amendments

These bylaws may be amended by a majority vote of the General Board members present and voting.

PART X

Forms

THE LOCAL CHURCH

THE DISTRICT ASSEMBLY

BILLS OF CHARGES

CHAPTER I

813. THE LOCAL CHURCH

813.1. Recommendation to the District Assembly

(Check the appropriate board.)

_____ The Church Board of the ______________________

_____ The District Advisory Board (*Manual* 222.10) _____

recommends ______________________________ to the

______________________ (Ministerial Credential Board)

District Assembly for*

_____ District minister's license

_____ Renewal of district minister's license

_____ Renewal of Deaconess' license

_____ Renewal of Director of Christian Education license

Ministry Role Certifications

_____ Registered Evangelist (*district licensed only*)

_____ Song evangelist

_____ Minister of Music

_____ Minister of Christian Education

_____ Other (See *Manual* 402-23)

____

____

(*NOTE: This form may be used for different recommendations. Mark the title you need.)

We certify that ______________________ has fulfilled all the requirements for such request.

By vote of the Board this ______ day of ____________, ______ (year)

____
Chairman

____
Secretary

Referred _______ Reported _______ Disposition _______

813.2. Certificate of Commendation

This certifies that ________________________________
is a member of the Church of the Nazarene at ___________
and is hereby commended to the Christian confidence of those to whom this certificate may be presented.

____
Pastor

Date ______________________________, ________ (year)

NOTE: When a certificate of commendation is given, that person's membership immediately ceases in the local church issuing the certificate. (111.1)

813.3. Letter of Release

This certifies that ________________________________
has been until this date a member of the Church of the Nazarene at ______________________________ and, at h________ request, is granted this letter of release.

____
Pastor

Date ______________________________, ________ (year)

NOTE: Membership terminates immediately upon issuance of a letter of release. (112.2)

813.4. Transfer of Members

This certifies that ____________________________ is a member in the Church of the Nazarene at ______________
and, at h_______ request, is hereby transferred to the Church of the Nazarene at ______________________ in the ________________ District.

When the reception of this transfer is acknowledged by the receiving local church, membership in this local church will cease.

____
Pastor

____
Address

Date ____

NOTE: A transfer is valid for three months only. (111)

813.5. Transfer Acknowledged

This certifies that ______________________________
has been received into membership by the Church of the Nazarene at ________________ this _____ day of _______, _______(year).

____
Pastor

____
Address

NOTE: Forms 813.2, 813.3, 813.4, and 813.5 may simply be prepared on local church stationery as needed.

813.6. Local Minister's License

THIS IS TO CERTIFY that _______________ is licensed as a Local Minister in the Church of the Nazarene for one year, provided that _____ spirit and practice are such as become the gospel of Christ, and ____________ teachings correspond with the established doctrines of the Holy Scriptures as held by said church.

By Order of the Church Board of the ________ Church of the Nazarene.

Done at _______________, this _____ day of ____________, _______(year).

____
Chairman

____
Secretary

CHAPTER II

814. THE DISTRICT ASSEMBLY

Official district forms may be secured from the General Secretary, 6401 The Paseo, Kansas City, MO 64131-1213.

CHAPTER III

815. BILLS OF CHARGES

Section 1. In Trial of a Church Member

Section 2. In Trial of an Ordained Minister

Section 3. In Trial of a Licensed Minister

Bills of Charges may be secured from the General Secretary, 6401 The Paseo, Kansas City, MO 64131-1213.

PART XI

Appendix

GENERAL OFFICERS

ADMINISTRATIVE BOARDS, COUNCILS, AND EDUCATIONAL INSTITUTIONS

ADMINISTRATIVE POLICIES

INTERPRETATION OF CHURCH LAW

CURRENT MORAL AND SOCIAL ISSUES

CHAPTER I

900. GENERAL OFFICERS

900.1. General Superintendents

John A. Knight	Paul G. Cunningham
William J. Prince	Jerry D. Porter
James H. Diehl	Jim L. Bond

General Superintendents Emeriti and Retired

V. H. Lewis, Emeritus
Orville W. Jenkins, Emeritus
William M. Greathouse, Emeritus
Eugene L. Stowe, Emeritus
Raymond W. Hurn, Emeritus
Jerald D. Johnson, Emeritus
Donald D. Owens, Emeritus

900.2. General Secretary

Jack Stone

900.3. General Treasurer

Robert L. Foster

INTERNATIONAL HEADQUARTERS

6401 THE PASEO

KANSAS CITY, MO 64131-1213

CHAPTER II

901. ADMINISTRATIVE BOARDS, COUNCILS, AND EDUCATIONAL INSTITUTIONS

901.1. General Board

MEMBERS BY CHURCH REGIONS

Minister	*Layperson*
	Africa Region
Collin Elliott	Maria Teresa Amado
Wally Marais	Mordecai Gabriel Nhabanga
L. Daniel Mokebe	Charles R. Prinsloo
	Asia-Pacific Region
Dong-hyung Ryu	Jonathan Fulton
John W. Smith	Kyae-suk Lee
	Canada Region
Wes Campbell	Robert Collier
	Caribbean Region
Scoffield Eversley	Carmen Acosta
Anthony Quimby	William Woolford
	Central U.S.A. Region
James Mellish	John Q. Dickey Sr.
C. Neil Strait	Gene Snowden
	East Central U.S.A. Region
Jack R. Archer	Paul Gamertsfelder
Larry W. White	Glenn F. Thorne
	Eastern U.S.A. Region
Randall E. Davey	Jan Lanham
Dallas Mucci	Daniel C. West

Eurasia Region

Geoff Austin
David Barnes
Jacob Overduin
Paul Tarrant

Mexico-Central America Region

Abel Cruz
Blanca Garcia de Urizar
Felipe Ruvalcaba N.
Florencio Vargas F.

North Central U.S.A. Region

Jesse Middendorf
D. Ray Cook
Pal Wright
Leland King

Northwest U.S.A. Region

Dan Ketchum
Monte Chitwood
Gerald E. Manker
Richard Hagood

South America Region

Luciano Duarte S.
Haroldo Millet Neves
Lazaro Aguiar Valvassoura
Oswaldo Quispe Tarqui

South Central U.S.A. Region

Russell C. Human
Kenny Marchant
Melvin McCullough
David McClung

Southeast U.S.A. Region

D. Moody Gunter
Charles Davis
Gary Henecke
Mark Greathouse
J. Fred Huff
Dennis Moore

Southwest U.S.A. Region

Daniel R. Copp
Craig K. Furusho
Thomas L. Goble
Barbara Hornbeck

Education

John Bowling
Loren Gresham

Nazarene World Mission Society

Beverlee Borbe

Nazarene Youth International

Bruce Oldham

901.2. General Court of Appeals

Jerry Lambert
Melvin McCullough
Millard Reed
C. Neil Strait
Gordon Wetmore

901.3. General Council of Nazarene Youth International

Bruce Oldham, *President*
Deirdre Brower, *General Secretary*
Isaac Ndhlovu, Africa Region
Jacob Urri, Asia-Pacific Region
Bill Sunberg, Canada Region
Lealand Henry, Caribbean Region
Dean Pennington, Central U.S.A. Region
Steve Wheeler, East Central U.S.A. Region
Ken Stanford, Eastern U.S.A. Region
Deirdre Brower, Eurasia Region
Francisco Javier Anzueto Hilerio, Mexico-Central America Region
Kendall Franklin, North Central U.S.A. Region
Gary Ringhiser, Northwest U.S.A. Region
Abraham Lopez, South America Region
Keith Newman, South Central U.S.A. Region
Greg Kenerly, Southeast U.S.A. Region
Mike Archer, Southwest U.S.A. Region
Amber Hoskins, Early Youth Member-at-large
Manuel Marquez, Senior Youth Member-at-large
Neustander Espinosa Cuevas, Young Adult Member-at-large
Amy Lawyer, Nazarene Student Leadership Conference Representative
Fred Fullerton, Nazarene Youth International Director
Jerry D. Porter, Responsible General Superintendent

901.4. General Council of the Nazarene World Mission Society

Dr. Nina G. Gunter, *General Director*
Mrs. Beverlee Borbe, *President*
Mrs. Joan Benjamin, Africa Region
Mrs. Patricia Jolliff, Asia-Pacific Region
Mrs. Margaret Rossiter, Canada Region
Mrs. Margaret Eversley, Caribbean Region
Mrs. Doris J. Dickey, Central U.S.A. Region
Mrs. Sue Fox, East Central U.S.A. Region
Mr. Robert Prescott, Eastern U.S.A. Region
Mrs. Elaine C. Danker, Eurasia Region
Sra. Raquel de Hidalgo, Mexico-Central America Region
Rev. Eunice Brubaker, North Central U.S.A. Region
Mrs. Mary Winkle, Northwest U.S.A. Region
Rev. Nazir Celestino, South America Region
Mrs. Jane Bowers, South Central U.S.A. Region
Mr. Dennis L. Moore, Southeast U.S.A. Region
Rev. John Wilcox, Southwest U.S.A. Region
Dr. Louie E. Bustle, World Mission Division Director
Dr. William J. Prince, General Superintendent Adviser

901.5. Nazarene Institutions of Higher Education

INTERNATIONAL HIGHER EDUCATION COUNCIL

Africa Region

Africa Nazarene School of Extension
Nairobi, Kenya
Africa Nazarene University
Nairobi, Kenya
Institut Biblique Nazareen
Côte d'Ivoire, West Africa
Nazarene Nursing College
Manzini, Swaziland
Nazarene Teacher Training College
Manzini, Swaziland

Nazarene Theological College of Central Africa
Malawi, Central Africa
Nazarene Theological College, South Africa
Honeydew, Republic of South Africa
Nigeria Nazarene Theological College
Nigeria, West Africa
Seminario Nazareno de Mozambique
Maputo, Mozambique
Swaziland Nazarene Bible College
Siteki, Swaziland

Asia-Pacific Region

Asia-Pacific Nazarene Theological Seminary
Manila, Philippines
Japan Christian Junior College
Chiba Shi, Japan
Japan Nazarene Theological Seminary
Tokyo, Japan
Korean Nazarene University
Chonan, South Korea
Luzon Nazarene Bible College
Baguio City, Philippines
Nazarene Bible College
Mount Hagen, Papua New Guinea
Nazarene College of Nursing
Mount Hagen, Papua New Guinea
Nazarene Theological College
Queensland, Australia
Sekolah Tinggi Theologica Nazarene (Indonesia)
Yogyakarta, Indonesia
South Pacific Nazarene Theological College
Apia, Western Samoa
Southeast Asia Nazarene Bible College
Bangkok, Thailand
Taiwan Nazarene Theological College
Taiwan, Republic of China
Visayan Nazarene Bible College
Cebu City, Philippines

Caribbean Region

Caribbean Nazarene Theological College
Santa Cruz, Trinidad
Instituto Biblico Nazareno
Ciudad Habana, Cuba
Seminaire Theologique Nazareen
Haiti
Seminario Nazareno Dominicano
Dominican Republic

Eurasia Region

CIS Education Centers
Kyiv, Ukraine
Eastern Mediterranean Nazarene Bible College
Amman, Jordan
European Nazarene Bible College
Schaffhausen, Switzerland
India Nazarene Nurses Training College
Maharashtra, India
Nazarene Theological College-Manchester
Manchester, England
South Asia Nazarene Bible College
Maharashtra, India

Mexico-Central America Region

Instituto Biblico Nazareno
Coban, Guatemala
Escuela Biblica Nazarena de la Huesteca
Huasteca, Mexico
Instituto Biblico Nazareno del Noreste
Monterrey, Mexico
Instituto Biblico Nazareno del Noroeste
Ensenada, Mexico
Seminario Nazareno de las Americas
San Jose, Costa Rica
Seminario Nazareno Mexicano, A.C.
Mexico City D.F., Mexico

Seminario Teologico Nazareno de Guatemala
Guatemala City, Guatemala
Instituto Biblico Nazareno del Sureste
Tuxtla, Guiterrez

South America Region

Instituto Biblico Nazareno
Chiclayo, Peru
Seminario Biblico Nazareno
Chiclayo, Peru
Seminario Biblico Nazareno
Santiago, Chile
Seminario Nazareno Boliviano
La Paz, Bolivia
Seminario Nazareno Sudamericano (CRECE)
Buenos Aires, Argentina
Seminario Teologico Nazareno do Brasil
São Paulo, Brazil
Seminario Teologico Nazareno Sudamericano
Quito, Ecuador

U.S./CANADA Council of Education

Canadian Nazarene College
Alberta, Canada
Eastern Nazarene College
Quincy, Massachusetts, U.S.A.
MidAmerica Nazarene University
Olathe, Kansas, U.S.A.
Mount Vernon Nazarene College
Mount Vernon, Ohio, U.S.A.
Nazarene Bible College
Colorado Springs, Colorado, U.S.A.
Nazarene Theological Seminary
Kansas City, Missouri, U.S.A.
Northwest Nazarene College
Nampa, Idaho, U.S.A.

Olivet Nazarene University
Kankakee, Illinois, U.S.A.
Point Loma Nazarene College
San Diego, California, U.S.A.
Southern Nazarene University
Bethany, Oklahoma, U.S.A.
Trevecca Nazarene University
Nashville, Tennessee, U.S.A.

CHAPTER III

902. ADMINISTRATIVE POLICIES

902.1. Annuities

The General Board and institutions of the church are prohibited from using annuity gifts until such have become their valid property by the death of the annuitant. Such gifts are to be carefully invested in funds usually accepted as trust funds by the courts of the land. (1993)

902.2. Debt

No institution may incur any debt on the strength of pledges. Pledges are not to be counted as assets. (1993)

902.3. Bible Societies

(1) Approved Bible Societies

The Church of the Nazarene places special emphasis upon the Bible as the written revelation of God, and we believe that it is the only effective agency to win new followers to Jesus Christ, and because there is an increasing need for more copies of the Scripture; therefore be it Resolved,

First, That the General Assembly express its hearty approval of and sympathy with the work of the United Bible Societies around the world.

Second, That we endorse the observance of Universal Bible Sunday, directing attention on this day to the essential place the Scriptures should occupy in the lives of Christian people.

Third, That the General Assembly authorize its general secretary and director of Sunday School Ministries Division, or any alternates who may be appointed, to attend during the ensuing quadrennium each annual session of the Advisory Council of the American Bible Society held in December at Bible House in New York City.

(2) Offering for Bible Societies

Resolved, That the Church of the Nazarene designate the second Sunday of December of each year as a special time for the presentation of this important matter and the taking of an offering for each nation's Bible Society. The Bible Society chosen shall be members (associate or full) of the worldwide fellowship of the United Bible Societies or in the absence of a member society, such other Bible Society designated by the district; also that a special effort be made to have all of our churches take part in such an offering. (1993)

NOTE: It is understood that our churches in Scotland send their contributions to the National Bible Society in Scotland; the churches in England, to the British and Foreign Bible Society; and the churches in Canada, to the Canadian Bible Society. The churches of the United States forward contributions to our denominational Headquarters, 6401 The Paseo, Kansas City, MO 64131-1213, for the support of the American Bible Society.

902.4. Athletics

The schools, colleges, and universities of the Church of the Nazarene shall be bound by such regulations regarding intercollegiate activities as shall be recommended by the International Board of Education and adopted by the General Board. (1964, 1976, 1989)

902.5. Dramatics

WHEREAS, There is danger in the excessive use of dramatic productions in our schools and colleges; be it

Resolved, That this practice be carefully restricted and greater emphasis be placed on the spiritual exercise that leads to sound Christian experience. (1997)

902.6. *Manual* Editing Resolution

Be it *Resolved,* That the members of the *Manual* Editing Committee appointed by the Board of General Superintendents be and they are hereby constituted the *Manual* Editing Committee; and be it further

Resolved, That the *Manual* Editing Committee be and they are hereby authorized to harmonize conflicting statements that may appear in the record of the actions of the Twenty-fourth General Assembly in regard to changes in the *Manual;* and also to make such editorial changes in the text of the present *Manual* as will correct the language without altering the meaning; also to make such editorial changes in the copy of the newly adopted matter as may serve to correct the language without altering the meaning.

The *Manual* Editing Committee is hereby further authorized to substitute plainly understood words or expressions for confusing words or expressions, to revise the numbering of chapters, paragraphs, sections, and other divisions of the *Manual* in harmony with any actions adopted by the Twenty-fourth General Assembly, and also to prepare the index in harmony with any actions adopted by the Twenty-fourth General Assembly.

Further resolved that the supervision of all translations of the *Manual* shall be a duty of the *Manual* Editing Committee. (1997)

902.7. *Manual* Appendix Review

Any item remaining in Chapters III and V of the Appendix for three quadrennia without reconsideration shall be referred by the Committee on Reference to the proper committee of the General Assembly for the same consideration as a resolution to the General Assembly. (1964, 1976, 1989)

902.8. Tenure of Committees

Any special committee created for any purpose, unless specified otherwise, will cease to exist at the following General Assembly. (1993)

902.9. General Assembly Business

(From the 1997 *Delegate's Handbook*)

RESOLUTIONS AND PETITIONS

Rule 26. Presentation. District assemblies, a committee authorized by the district assembly, regional councils, the General Board or any of its recognized divisions, official boards or commissions of the general church, the General Nazarene World Mission Society Convention, the General Nazarene Youth International Convention, or five or more members of the General Assembly, may present resolutions and petitions for the consideration of the General Assembly in accordance with the following rules:

a. Resolutions and petitions shall be presented in duplicate and typewritten on the official form furnished by the general secretary.

b. Each resolution or petition presented will include the subject and the name of the delegates or group making the presentation.

c. Proposals for changes in the church *Manual* must be presented in writing and shall give paragraph and section of *Manual* to be affected and the text of the change, should it be adopted.

d. They shall be presented to the general secretary **no later than December 1** prior to the convening of the assembly to be numbered and sent to the Reference Committee for reference in accordance with Rule 37 and *Manual* 305.1, and in order that they may be printed in the *Delegate's Handbook.*

Rule 27. Resolutions and Petitions for Late Reference. With the consent of the assembly, resolutions, petitions, and other items for consideration by the assembly may be presented to the general secretary for reference to a legislative committee no later than **June 1** prior to the convening of the assembly, with the exception of the general conventions, which meet just prior to the General Assembly.

Rule 28. *Manual* Changes. Resolutions adopted by the General Assembly shall be submitted to the *Manual* Editing Committee to be harmonized with other *Manual* provisions.

902.10. Restrictions on Membership General Church Boards

No person shall serve on more than one of the following boards: General Board, Nazarene Theological Seminary

Trustees, Nazarene Bible College Trustees. (1964, 1976, 1989)

902.11. Historic Sites and Landmarks

District and regional assemblies may designate places of historic significance within their boundaries as Historic Sites. At least 50 years must elapse after a place achieves historic significance before it is recognized as a Historic Site. A Historic Site does not have to have original buildings or structures surviving in order to be designated. The assembly secretary shall report newly designated Historic Sites to the general secretary, reporting the action taken, information on the site, and the site's significance.

District and regional assemblies can ask the General Assembly to designate places of denomination-wide significance as Historic Landmarks. Nominations are restricted to previously designated Historic Sites. The general superintendents or a committee appointed for the purpose of screening nominations must concur with a nomination before it receives General Assembly consideration.

The general secretary shall keep a register of Historic Sites and Landmarks and publicize them appropriately (paragraph 325.2). (1997)

CHAPTER IV

903. INTERPRETATION OF CHURCH LAW

Judiciary Actions

903.1. Special Rule 34.5 relating to "using of tobacco in any of its forms, or trafficking therein."

Does this prohibit church membership in the Church of the Nazarene to a person who is employed in a store, either as clerk or manager, where among other things he or she is obliged to sell tobacco?

Ans. There is a distinction between trafficking as the owner of a business and selling as a clerk; and, therefore, we would not interpret the selling as a clerk as violating the letter of the *Manual.*

903.2. If a licensed minister meets all the requirements for the renewal of a minister's license according to 427.3, is the district assembly obliged to renew such license?

Ans. A district assembly is not under obligation according to 427.3 to renew said license.

903.3. A church has a debt on its property. It elects a finance committee of three who are members of the church board with instructions to receive and disburse all money that applies to the church debt. Has the church the right to make this committee custodian of that part of the church funds and to receive and disburse the same independent of the regularly elected church treasurer?

Ans. The church does have such a right.

903.4. Clarify the status of an ordained minister who may be dropped from the local membership roll on account of absence of over a six-month period, which is unsatisfactorily explained, and the nonsupport of the church during this period. If a local church drops his or her name from the roll, what is that person's assembly relationship?

Ans. It is the opinion of the Committee on Judiciary that

the dropping of an ordained minister from the church roll of which he or she is a member under the conditions mentioned cannot affect his or her status as a member of the assembly district but does place responsibility on such ordained minister to comply with 433.8. (1976)

CHAPTER V

904. CURRENT MORAL AND SOCIAL ISSUES

904.1. Sanctity of Human Life

The Church of the Nazarene believes in the sanctity of human life and strives to protect against abortion (36), euthanasia, and the withholding of reasonable medical care to handicapped or elderly.

Genetic Engineering and Gene Therapy. The Church of the Nazarene supports the use of genetic engineering to achieve gene therapy. We recognize that gene therapy can lead to preventing and curing disease, and preventing and curing anatomical and mental disorders. We oppose any use of genetic engineering that promotes social injustice, disregards the dignity of persons, or that attempts to achieve racial, intellectual, or social superiority over others (Eugenics). We oppose initiation of DNA studies whose results might encourage or support human abortion as an alternative to term live birth. In all cases, humility, a respect for the inviolable dignity of human life, human equality before God, and a commitment to mercy and justice should govern genetic engineering and gene therapy (Micah 6:8).

Euthanasia (Including Physician Assisted Suicide). We believe that euthanasia (intentionally ending the life of a terminally ill person, or one who has a debilitating and incurable disease that is not immediately life-threatening, for the purpose of ending suffering) is incompatible with the Christian faith. This applies when euthanasia is requested or consented to by the terminally ill person (voluntary euthanasia) and when the terminally ill person is not mentally competent to give consent (involuntary euthanasia). We believe that the historic rejection of euthanasia by the Christian church is confirmed by Christian convictions that derive from the Bible and that are central to the Church's confession of faith in Jesus Christ as Lord. Euthanasia violates Christian confidence in God as the sovereign Lord of life by claiming sovereignty for oneself; it violates our role as stewards before God; it contributes to an erosion of the value the Bible places on human life and community; it attaches too much importance to the cessation of suffering; and it reflects a human arrogance before a graciously sovereign God. We urge our people to oppose all efforts to legalize euthanasia.

Allowing to Die. When human death is imminent, we believe that either withdrawing or not originating artificial life-support systems is permissible within the range of Christian faith and practice. This position applies to persons who are in a persistent vegetative state and to those for whom the application of extraordinary means for prolonging life provide no reasonable hope for a return to health. We believe that when death is imminent, nothing in the Christian faith requires that the process of dying be artificially postponed. As Christians we trust in God's faithfulness and have the hope of eternal life. This makes it possible for Christians to accept death as an expression of faith in Christ who overcame death on our behalf and robbed it of its victory. (1997)

904.2. Organ Donation

The Church of the Nazarene encourages its members who do not object personally to support donor/recipient anatomical organs through living wills and trusts.

Further, we appeal for a morally and ethically fair distribution of organs to those qualified to receive them. (1989)

904.3. Discrimination

The Church of the Nazarene reiterates its historic position of Christian compassion for people of all races. We believe that God is the Creator of all people, and that of one blood are all people created.

We believe that each individual, regardless of race, color, gender, or creed, should have equality before law, including the right to vote, equal access to educational opportunities, to all public facilities, and to the equal opportunity, according to one's ability, to earn a living free from any job or economic discrimination.

We urge our churches everywhere to continue and strengthen programs of education to promote racial understanding and harmony. We also feel that the scriptural admonition of Hebrews 12:14 should guide the actions of our people. We urge that each member of the Church of the Nazarene humbly examine his or her personal attitudes and actions toward others, as a first step in achieving the Christian goal of full participation by all in the life of the church and the entire community.

We reemphasize our belief that holiness of heart and life is the basis for right living. We believe that Christian charity between racial groups or gender will come when the hearts of people have been changed by complete submission to Jesus Christ, and that the essence of true Christianity consists in loving God with one's heart, soul, mind, and strength, and one's neighbor as oneself. (1993)

904.4. Abuse of the Unempowered

The Church of the Nazarene abhors abuse of any person of any age or sex and calls for increased public awareness through its publications and by providing appropriate educational information.

The Church of the Nazarene reaffirms its historical policy that all those who act under the authority of the church are prohibited from sexual misconduct and other forms of abuse of the unempowered. When placing people in positions of trust or authority, the Church of the Nazarene will presume that past conduct is usually a reliable indicator of likely future behavior. The Church will withhold positions of authority from people who have previously used a position of trust or authority to engage in sexual misconduct or abuse of the unempowered, unless appropriate steps are taken to prevent future wrongful behavior. Expressions of remorse by a guilty person shall not be considered sufficient to overcome the presumption that future wrongful conduct is likely, unless the expressions of remorse are accompanied by an observable change of conduct for a sufficient length of time, to indicate that a repeat of the wrongful misconduct is unlikely. (1997)

904.5. Responsibility to the Poor

The Church of the Nazarene believes that Jesus commanded His disciples to have a special relationship to the poor of this world; that Christ's Church ought, first, to keep itself simple and free from an emphasis on wealth and extravagance and, second, to give itself to the care, feeding, clothing, and shelter of the poor. Throughout the Bible and in the life and example of Jesus, God identifies with and assists the poor, the oppressed, and those in society who cannot speak for themselves. In the same way, we, too, are called to identify with and to enter into solidarity with the poor and not simply to offer charity from positions of comfort. We hold that compassionate ministry to the poor includes acts of charity as well as a struggle to provide opportunity, equality, and justice for the poor. We further believe that the Christian responsibility to the poor is an essential aspect of the life of every believer who seeks a faith that works through love.

Finally, we understand Christian holiness to be inseparable from ministry to the poor in that it drives the Christian beyond his or her own individual perfection and toward the creation of a more just and equitable society and world. Holiness, far from distancing believers from the desperate economic needs of people in our world, motivates us to place our means in the service of alleviating such need and to adjust our wants in accordance with the needs of others. (1989)

(Exodus 23:11; Deuteronomy 15:7; Psalms 41:1; 82:3; Proverbs 19:17; 21:13; 22:9; Jeremiah 22:16; Matthew 19:21; Luke 12:33; Acts 20:35; 2 Corinthians 9:6; Galatians 2:10)

904.6. Women in Ministry

We support the right of women to use their God-given spiritual gifts within the church. We affirm the historic right of women to be elected and appointed to places of leadership within the Church of the Nazarene. (1993)

904.7. The Church and Human Freedom

Concerned that our great Protestant heritage be understood and safeguarded, we remind our people that both political and religious freedom rest upon biblical concepts of the dignity of man as God's creation and the sanctity of one's own individual conscience. We encourage our people to participate in political activity in support of these biblical concepts and to be ever vigilant against threats to this precious freedom.

These freedoms are constantly in danger, therefore we urge election of persons to public office at all levels of government who believe in these principles and who are answerable only to God and the constituency that elected them when carrying out a public trust. Further, we resist any invasion of these principles by religious groups seeking special favors.

We believe that the role of the Church is to be prophetic and constantly to remind the people that "righteousness exalts a nation" (Proverbs 14:34). (1993)

904.8. War and Military Service

The Church of the Nazarene believes that the ideal world condition is that of peace and that it is the full obligation of the Christian Church to use its influence to seek such means as will enable the nations of the earth to be at peace and to devote all of its agencies for the propagation of the message of peace. However, we realize that we are living in a world where evil forces and philosophies are actively in conflict with these Christian ideals and that there may arise such international emergencies as will require a nation to resort to war in defense of its ideals, its freedom, and its existence.

While thus committed to the cause of peace, the Church of the Nazarene recognizes that the supreme allegiance of the Christian is due to God, and therefore it does not endeavor to bind the conscience of its members relative to participation in military service in case of war, although it does believe that the individual Christian as a citizen is bound to give service to his or her own nation in all ways that are compatible with the Christian faith and the Christian way of life.

We also recognize that, as an outgrowth of the Christian teaching and of the Christian desire for peace on earth, there are among our membership individuals who have conscientious objection to certain forms of military service. Therefore the Church of the Nazarene claims for conscientious objectors within its membership the same exemptions and considerations regarding military service as are accorded members of recognized noncombatant religious organizations.

The Church of the Nazarene, through its general secretary, shall set up a register whereon those persons who supply evidence of being members of the Church of the Nazarene may record their convictions as conscientious objectors. (1993)

904.9. Creation

The Church of the Nazarene believes in the biblical account of creation ("In the beginning God created the heavens and the earth . . ."—Genesis 1:1). We oppose a godless interpretation of the evolutionary hypothesis. However, the church accepts as valid all scientifically verifiable discoveries in geology and other natural phenomena, for we firmly believe that God is the Creator. (Articles I. 1., V. 5.1, VII.) (1993)

904.10. Evidence of Baptism with the Holy Spirit

The Church of the Nazarene believes that the Holy Spirit bears witness to the new birth and to the subsequent work of heart cleansing, or entire sanctification, through the infilling of the Holy Spirit.

We affirm that the one biblical evidence of entire sanctification, or the infilling of the Holy Spirit, is the cleansing of the heart by faith from original sin as stated in Acts 15:8-9:

"God, who knows the heart, showed them that he accepted them by giving the Holy Spirit to them, just as he did to us. He made no distinction between us and them, for he purified their hearts by faith." And this cleansing is manifested by the fruit of the Spirit in a holy life. "But the fruit of the Spirit is love, joy, peace, patience, kindness, goodness, faithfulness, gentleness and self-control. Against such things there is no law. Those who belong to Christ Jesus have crucified the sinful nature with its passions and desires" (Galatians 5:22-24).

To affirm that even a special or any alleged physical evidence, or "prayer language," is evidence of the baptism with the Spirit is contrary to the biblical and historic position of the church. (1997)

904.11. Magazines, Literature, Radio, and Other Media

Since we are living in a day of great moral confusion in which we face the potential encroachment of the evils of the day into the sacred precincts of our homes through various avenues such as current literature, radio, television, and other media, it is essential that the most rigid safeguards be observed to keep our homes from becoming secularized and worldly.

While we recognize these agencies are of great value in the propagation of the gospel and the salvation of souls, we do deplore the low moral tone of much current literature, comic magazines, articles and pictures of some magazines, and the contents of many books.

We do likewise deplore the content of many radio and television programs and other media. Due to the rapid decline in quality of programming suitable for Christian viewing and the fact that television is one of the major factors in the communication breakdown in families, which in turn is a major cause in the rising divorce rates; and due to the fact that television stresses by implication the use of alcohol, the acceptance of the practice of homosexuality, the practice of promiscuity, and the philosophy of secular humanism; and due to the apparent lack of discrimination in home television, and due to the availability of uncensored movies in the home, we urge our people to avoid programs that glamorize the world's philosophy of secularism, sensualism, and materialism.

We especially recommend that reading, listening, and viewing on the Lord's Day be consistent with our high standards of holiness and that unless providentially hindered we do not allow anything (even religious radio and television programs) to become a substitute for church attendance.

We therefore call upon our leaders and pastors to give strong emphasis in our periodicals and from our pulpits to such fundamental truths as will develop the principle of discrimination between the evil and good to be found in these mediums.

We suggest that the standard given to John Wesley by his mother, namely, "Whatever weakens your reason, impairs the tenderness of your conscience, obscures your sense of God, or takes off the relish of spiritual things, whatever increases the authority of your body over mind, that thing for you is sin," form the basis for this teaching of discrimination. (1993)

904.12. Pornography

Pornography is an evil that is undermining the morals of society. Printed and visual materials that degrade the dignity of humankind and are contrary to the scriptural view of the sanctity of marriage and the wholesomeness of sex are to be abhorred.

We believe that we are created in the image of God and that pornography degrades, exploits, and abuses men, women, and children. The pornography industry is motivated by greed, is the enemy of family life, has led to crimes of violence, poisons minds, and defiles the body.

To honor God as Creator and Redeemer, we urge active opposition to pornography by every legitimate means and the making of positive efforts to reach for Christ those who are involved in this evil. (1997)

904.13. Public Swimming and Recreational Activities

Recognizing the increasing trend toward immodesty of dress in public places of recreation such as beaches and swimming places, we remind our people of our traditional concept of "modesty that becometh holiness" and urge that Christian judgment be exercised in the matter of swimming or sunbathing in public places. (1993)

904.14. Substance Abuse

The Church of the Nazarene continues to strongly object to substance abuse as a social malignancy. We encourage church members to take an active and highly visible role and to participate in education relative to substance abuse and the incompatibility of such use with a Christian experience and a holy life. (1989)

904.15. Alcohol Desocialization

The Church of the Nazarene publicly supports the desocialization of alcohol consumption. We encourage civic, labor, business, professional, social, voluntary, and private agencies and organizations to assist in such desocialization to counteract the advertising and media promotion of the social acceptability of the "alcohol culture." (1989)

904.16. Tobacco Use and Advertising

The Church of the Nazarene urges its people to continue to speak out against the use of tobacco, both as a health hazard and a social evil. Our historic stand is based on God's Word, where we are admonished to maintain our bodies as temples of the Holy Spirit (1 Corinthians 3:16-17; 6:19-20).

Our stand opposing the use of tobacco in all its forms is strongly supported by medical evidence, documented by numerous social, governmental, and health agencies around the world. They have demonstrated that it is a major health hazard, and have shown conclusively that its use may produce changes in normal bodily physiology, both serious and permanent.

We recognize that our young people are greatly influenced by the millions of dollars that are spent on tobacco advertising, and its twin evil, beverage alcohol. We endorse a ban on all advertising of tobacco and beverage alcohol in magazines, on billboards, and on radio and television. (1980, 1989)

SPECIAL REVISION INDEX

Changes authorized by the 1997 General Assembly are indexed here.
These changes are indexed in numerical order.

INDEX OF VACANT PARAGRAPHS

MANUAL INDEX

(Numbers refer to paragraphs.)